Praise for Deborah Fleming's *Resurrection of the Wild*, winner of the 2020 PEN/America Diamonstein-Spielvogel Award for the Art of the Essay

"A literary journey home that is well worth following."
—*Foreword Reviews*

"[One of] 9 Dazzling Small-Press Essay Collections You May Have Missed."—*Chicago Review of Books*

"In places, this is an elegy: 'The earth has made us what we are, sustains us, and will take us back again when we have seen our share of passing seasons.' Elsewhere, it is joyful and hopeful: 'We need only look around to see that nature is trying to show us the gate that will lead us back inside.' Fleming's work holds a key to that gate."
—**From the PEN/America judges' citation**

"Every place on Earth needs a writer as attentive as Deborah Fleming, to study it with a loving and clear-eyed gaze. In these essays, she explores the natural and human history of her home ground, the hill country of eastern Ohio, a landscape battered by strip mining, careless farming, and deforestation. Yet wildness persists, there as everywhere, an irrepressible creative force. With a wealth of examples, Fleming demonstrates how nature's resilience, aided by human care, can restore the land to health. May her book inspire readers to join such healing efforts in their own home places."
—**Scott Russell Sanders,** author of *Earth Works: Selected Essays*

"Fleming reenvisions how natural history is to be practiced in a rural Ohio landscape that is both wild and settled, both green fields and brown, both indigenous and colonized, both diminished and resilient. Rather than pining for wilderness that has been long lost, the author attends to the regenerative capacities of the land here and now. This book's chief virtue is its detailed fluency in the local coupled with a personal feel for the topics raised. The cyclical time of the landscape—expressed in its seasons and ecological processes—is brought into conjunction with the flow of the historical as framed by the author's personal interactions with the land."—**James Hatley**, coeditor of *Facing Nature: Levinas and Environmental Thought*

"Just as Aldo Leopold chronicles and celebrates the landscape around his 'shack' in Sauk County, Wisconsin, in *Resurrection of the Wild* Deborah Fleming conveys the history and character of her home on eastern Ohio's Allegheny Plateau. This region, like the cutover terrain Leopold calls 'Sand County,' is one in which a broad collapse of agriculture and depopulation of settlements have ushered in a resurgence of forests and wildlife. An elegiac story from one perspective thus becomes a tale of rewilding from another, as well as a field of new opportunities for independent-minded and scientifically oriented settlers. I loved the precise and energetic way Fleming interwove descriptions of her home landscape's geology, such notable figures from its past as Johnny Appleseed and Louis Bromfield of Malabar Farm, and her own special fascination with horses."
—**John Elder**, author of *Reading the Mountains of Home*

"Deborah Fleming's warm and wryly humorous persona pervades 'Waiting for the Foal' and other marvelous personal essays about her life in rural southeastern Ohio. Further, broader pieces address the area's history, the Amish community, and other unusual people, as well as material threats to the hill country's ecology. *Resurrection of the Wild* will sit on my bookshelf right next to David Kline's classic *Great Possessions: An Amish Farmer's Journal* for repeated reading."
—**Carolyn V. Platt**, author of *Ohio Hill Country: A Rewoven Landscape* and *Cuyahoga Valley National Park Handbook*

"Whether writing about her garden, or raising horses, or the impact of coal mining, Deborah Fleming offers an intimate natural history of her farm and her state. By book's end, Ohio is no longer dull, barren, flyover land but one beautiful, fragile web of ecological relationships to which Fleming belongs and is committed."
—**Tom Montgomery Fate**, author of *Cabin Fever: A Suburban Father's Search for the Wild*

Ghosts of an Old Forest

Ghosts of an Old Forest

Essays on Midwestern Rural Heritage

Deborah Fleming

The Kent State University Press
Kent, Ohio

© 2025 by The Kent State University Press, Kent, Ohio 44242
All rights reserved
ISBN 978-1-60635-493-3
Published in the United States of America

No part of this book may be used or reproduced, in any manner whatsoever, without written permission from the Publisher, except in the case of short quotations in critical reviews or articles.

Cataloging information for this title is available at the Library of Congress.

29 28 27 26 25   5 4 3 2 1

For the people of Ohio who still love the land

Contents

Acknowledgments ix
1 The Divide 1
2 Mohican 6
3 Heritage 15
4 Barn Burning 38
5 Time and the Stream 48
6 The Kreutzer Sonata 60
7 Walking the Trash Line 81
8 Dysart Woods 97
9 Into the Woods 106
10 Further Reflections on Louis Bromfield and Malabar Farm 121
11 Modern Pioneers 144
12 Sacrifice Zone 169
13 Home, or Where I'm From 182
14 Progress, Economy, and Preservation 195
Bibliography 202
Index 209

Acknowledgments

My sincere thanks go to the following people for their help in compiling or verifying information in these essays: Annette McCormick and Irv Oslin, for information on the Mohican Park and State Forest; Sara England and Tom Bachelder, for research on Malabar Farm State Park; Tom Kruse, for his history of Byers Woods Park of Ashland County; Brian McCarthy of Ohio University, for his expertise on Dysart Woods; Tom O'Grady of Friends of Ohio Barns; Guy Denney of the Ohio Department of Natural Resources Division of Natural Areas and Preserves; and Timothy McKee, for his film on the Mohican Park and State Forest.

The country where he lives
is haunted
by the ghost of an old forest.

—*Wendell Berry, "Window Poems"*

One

The Divide

OHIO'S RAREST WILDFLOWER, the endangered flame azalea (*Rhododendron calendulaceum*), is the only native azalea with petals of two colors, yellow to bright orange. It blossoms in the valley where a river once flowed, mostly in Jackson and Pike Counties, but which is now a ghost that geologists refer to as the Teays. Several species of magnolias, asters, and iris—including the dwarf iris, bigleaf magnolia, and golden-star lily—also thrive in the valley where deep gorges provide microclimates that allow for much biodiversity.

In the first annual geological survey of the Ohio country, in 1838, P. Hildreth hypothesized about the existence of this ghost watercourse. His contemporaries did not widely embrace his ideas, but in 1886 Gerard Fowke speculated that a steep ridge west of Chillicothe must have been cut by a mighty river that no longer existed. While at Denison University, geologist and botanist William Tight (1865–1910) advanced the theory of a great ghost river. In his estimate, a small stream running westward from Charleston, West Virginia, could not have formed the deep valley through which it flowed. Tight named this ghost river the Teays for a nearby mountain village.

Earlier than the Ice Ages, before Lake Erie and the Ohio River existed, other rivers carved their ways through what is now Ohio.

One, which geologists named the Erigan, flowed northeastward. Prior to the advance of Pleistocene glaciers into Ohio, beginning about 2 million years ago, a major river system surged from its headwaters in North Carolina across Virginia and West Virginia and entered Ohio near present-day Portsmouth. That river, the Teays, flowed northward to the vicinity of Chillicothe, where it swung westward across Ohio, Indiana, and Illinois, finally joining the course of the ancient Mississippi. The riverbed serves as a pathway for migration of many species of Appalachian plants. When an early glacier advanced into Ohio 790–880,000 years ago, it blocked the Teays River, forming an ice dam that created a large lake (now called Lake Tight, covering an estimated ten thousand square miles) in the former river valley in southern Ohio, inundating and eradicating most Appalachian species that had migrated along the riverine corridor. When Lake Tight eventually began to spill over a low divide, a new drainage system formed, obliterating the lake. Glacial sediments filled in the old

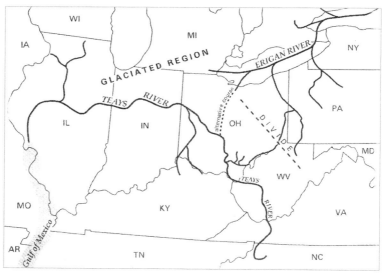

Teays River Valley, Ohio Department of Natural Resources, Division of Geological Survey (Used by permission)

river valley in western Ohio, but the presence of deep water-wells and geological data have outlined the course of this buried stratus, which is up to four hundred feet deep in some areas.

The preglacial Groveport River once joined the Teays at points where Butler and Fredericktown are now located in Richland and Knox Counties. Hemlock Falls descends a hundred feet over cliffs of Black Hand sandstone. A new river was formed 150,000 years ago—what we now call the Clear Fork—and in an ecosystem typical of the edge of a glacier, plants growing in the valley resemble the those of the mixed mesophytic forest land of the Appalachian range, the most biodiverse region in North America and one of the most diverse temperate zones in the world.

Between the city of Ontario, near Mansfield in Richland County, and the town of Crestline, a geological uplift demarcates two watersheds. Less famous and spectacular than the east–west Continental Divide through the Rocky Mountains, the north–south demarcation begins in Newfoundland, zigzags southward through the Ohio country, and turns northward again toward British Columbia and the Pacific Coast. North of this uplift, water flows to the Great Lakes, Saint Lawrence Seaway, and Atlantic Ocean. Southward, it flows to the Ohio River and Mississippi toward the Gulf of Mexico. Immigrants transformed the Saint Lawrence Seaway into a shipping route that supported industry and international trade, while the Ohio River, heading in the opposite direction, drew its fame from riverboats and rafts.

The geological uplift also identifies dialect variations created by human migration patterns—Germans along the northern route, Scots-Irish along the southern—and social differences formed in part by culture but also by the type of farming the land could support. Early on, the area was exploited because of mineral wealth and rich soil but also because of the availability of water—not only the lake and river but the abundance of springs, streams, and nearly universal groundwater.

In Richland County, rain that falls at the divide feeds two small lakes. One of them, Summit Lake, becomes the origin of the northward-running Black Fork and the southward-running Clear Fork. Streams empty into the Sandusky and Vermillion Rivers, which flow northward to Lake Erie, while the Walhonding and Mohican Rivers flow to the Ohio.

In that section of Richland County, a barn once stood where it was said that rainwater falling onto the northern side of the roof ran to the lake while rainwater reaching the southern side eventually found its way to the river. A famous black-and-white photograph, thought to have been taken in 1903, shows the barn and seven men of varying ages standing in a field. The image includes two barns: the larger watershed barn, a German-style bank barn with a sizable extension, and a smaller one of the New England type on flat ground. (See chapter 3 for a discussion of these structures.) The angle of the photo is toward the northwest, as is evident because large wind doors—which would have been placed on the structure's east side—are visible. A solid wooden fence encloses a paddock. The windows sport old-fashioned lattices.

The picture reveals the agricultural character of the county in the nineteenth century. Four of the men in the photo have taken off their hats, perhaps in some show of deference. One wears overalls; the others don suits. Only one appears to smile. Three of them are portly like successful nineteenth-century businessmen; one is lean like a pioneer. Trees in leaf behind the barn and grass reaching half way to the men's knees indicate that the season is summer. Publicity made much of the "divide" during those years, but its fame at last subsided. By the 1950s, the barn had been torn down, and a road later constructed across the land eventually became a paved highway. Where the barn stood, a modern church was built, once part of the Grace Brethren denomination; the rectangular structure now belongs to Hesed Agape Ministries of Mansfield. In front of it, a ramp stretches from North Fourth Street to busy, four-lane State Route 30.

Nothing remains of that farm, but a visit to the Cuyahoga Valley National Park to see the remnants of the Ohio & Erie Canal inspires meditation on what creations from our own time will one day be uprooted. The more famous Erie Canal, which connected Buffalo with the Hudson River, 360 miles away, represented the hard labor of fifty thousand workers from 1817 to 1825. Irish immigrants and settled German farmers attracted by high pay dug the Ohio & Erie Canal in the 1820s and 1830s, first connecting Akron with the Cuyahoga River and later Cleveland with Portsmouth. Railroads reduced the canal's importance for trade after 1861; the great flood of 1913 washed out aqueducts and levees, causing it to be abandoned.

The ruins of buildings only two centuries old make clear the transience of human culture; formed of things, events, and people we never heard of, we are brief travelers on one side or the other of the great watershed. The Teays River and Lake Tight, however, exist today in the wells and streams of the state. Flowers, such as the flame azalea, growing in the valleys of ghost rivers testify to the permanence of geological time and the resilience and diversity of the biosphere.

Two

Mohican

ON SATURDAY, MARCH 4, 1995, I attended a demonstration at the Sand Ridge Cemetery inside the Mohican State Forest in Ashland County, near the now abandoned Sand Ridge Church where over a hundred people held a mock funeral protesting proposed logging. The Ohio Division of Forestry planned to sell 675 trees for $35,000 to make wooden pallets, explained Roger Clark of the Sierra Club's Akron chapter. Joseph Hazelbaker of the Buckeye Forest Council, now called the Buckeye Environmental Network, led the program. A local resident, out walking her dog in the woods, noticed trees marked for removal and discovered the plan. There had been no public comment period.

The demonstration felt more like an outing. Clark jokingly called the group "radicals, fanatics, and loonies," as some critics described us, also the favorite epithet: "tree-huggers." Three sheriff's cruisers and one state patrol car rolled slowly around the cemetery, along the narrow Township Road 3286, but officers remained in their vehicles and made no arrests. Leaning out the open window, one struck up a conversation with a demonstrator about the breed of his dogs. Participants supported two proposed state laws, House Bill 49, sponsored by Democratic state representative Frank Sawyer of Butler, and Senate Bill 51, sponsored by

Republican state senator Richard Schafrath of Loudonville, which would designate the forest as a "recreational wilderness," thus protecting it from logging. William Whitmore of the Department of Biology at the College of Wooster claimed that the area was well situated to become an old-growth forest. The gathering rated a story and color photograph on page one of the Monday, March 6, *Ashland Times-Gazette*.

The bills passed in the Senate but not the House, where the committee was headed by Republican Bill Harris, owner of a car dealership in Ashland and no environmentalist. After much discussion, the Ohio Department of Natural Resources allowed the acreage to be protected from logging.

Fourteen to twenty-four thousand years ago, in the area that is now southern Ashland County, meltwater from the retreat of the Wisconsin glacier carved an east–west gorge into sandstone bedrock. Hillsides continued to erode, exposing steep cliff faces and rocky outcroppings that reached depths of about three hundred feet and widths of about a thousand feet. The resulting stream came to be called the Clear Fork of the Mohican River and the valley the Clearfork Gorge or Clearfork Narrows. The old-growth white pine and hemlock are rare enough that about three acres have been designated a Registered National Natural Landmark. Barely discernable footpaths reveal that at one time trails descended the slopes; after the designation of the Gorge Overlook, which faces the ravine's northern side, a rail fence at the top of the ridge formed a boundary beyond which visitors were warned against venturing, as the cliff side is nearly vertical and the soil loose. Nevertheless, in 2020, a trail was forged that allows hikers to traverse the hillside to the river and back—unfortunately, as I believe the area should have remained inaccessible. A new swinging bridge, completed in 2021, spans the water at the site of the old Newville Iron Bridge (1913–38).

Because the gorge is too steep to farm, its forests were saved from the fate of the surrounding area where trees were cut down and the land plowed. The overlook presents an extraordinary vista, a smaller version of some of those in the Great Smoky Mountains of eastern Tennessee. Sycamore trees are more numerous along the riverbank, beech and ash on lower slopes, and oak and maple closer to the ridges. In early spring, before deciduous leaves open, lacy white clouds of dogwood are interspersed with darker hemlock. During summer, the visitor sees at least seven shades of green—from brightness of birch and beech to emerald, jade, and teal of maple, oak, hickory, and other deciduous trees to the viridian hemlock and blue-gray spruce. The best viewing season lasts from mid-September until the end of October, with its autumnal display of color from bright yellow, vermillion, scarlet, and carmine, to dark magenta. As dazzling in its own way as the spring, the winter takes on subtle hues, from the brown trunks of deciduous trees to blue and green of spruce to darker green of hemlock.

Archeological evidence indicates that prehistoric Adena and Hopewell people hunted in the area that is now the Mohican Park and State Forest; by the seventeenth century it was occupied by groups known as Delaware, Erie, or Erielhonoan, "the people of the long-tailed cat," thought to be the now extirpated mountain lion. The first European man in the area, who bore the quintessential English name of James Smith, is said to have been captured by Delaware and adopted into their tribe. Large numbers of European Americans began to migrate into the region after the War of 1812, when treaties favored them. One famous native warrior, called Tommy Lyons by settlers and infamous for retaliatory killing, became a villain in Hugh Nissenson's 1985 novel *The Tree of Life*, a finalist for the PEN-Faulkner and National Book Awards, about Johnny Appleseed and settlement of the Ohio country. It is rumored that the name John Chapman, or Johnny Appleseed, was carved into the rock at Lyons Falls—but if so it has been eroded by weather and replaced by less notable appellations. Tommy Lyons may have given his name to the falls, but another legend says that they memorialize settler Paul Lyons, who built a cabin near the location and either fell to his death or died in a logging accident. The folklore explaining the nomenclature of Hog Hollow is that a farmer rescued his prize pig—which had become stuck in a tree—after flood waters that had carried the hog away subsided.

Employing a carpenter from Pennsylvania named Peter Weirick, pioneer John Frederick Herring (1767–1832) built the second grist mill in Richland County, where Fredericktown Road crosses the Clearfork Creek of the Mohican River. In 1823, Herring founded the town of Newville near Slater's Run and the Clearfork. He was the great-grandfather of Clement Herring (1867–1939), who owned land that was to become part of author Louis Bromfield's world-famous Malabar Farm. Clement's wife was a descendant of the Ferguson family that owned another of the farms Bromfield purchased. Although the town was abandoned in 1940, some buildings still stand.

The Sand Ridge Church, once home to an Evangelical Lutheran congregation, where we held our demonstration, was built in 1898. According to that year's Thursday, May 5, *Bellville Messenger*, the cornerstone was laid the previous Sunday at 2:00 P.M. with "impressive ceremonies." Congregants donated the materials for the thirty-by-forty-foot structure designed by architects F. R. and I. L. McCollough. Reverend W. W. Criley, DD, of Wooster opened the event with an invocation; Reverend J. A. West of Loudonville, pastor of the Sand Ridge congregation read the scripture lesson; and Reverend Criley delivered a sermon based on a passage incorrectly identified as the First Epistle of Peter, chapter 20, verses 7 and 8. I Peter contains only five chapters, however, so the reporter clearly meant chapter 2, and the relevant message is contained in verses 6 through 8: "Behold, I lay in Zion a chief corner stone, elect, precious: and he that believeth on him shall not be confounded. Unto you therefore which believe *he is* precious: but unto them which be disobedient, the stone which the builders disallowed, the same is made the head of the corner, and a stone of stumbling, and a rock of offence" (KJV). This passage alludes to Psalm 118, verse 22: "The stone which the builders refused is become the head stone of the corner." An offering garnered a "substantial sum" before the cornerstone was laid, containing a Bible, bread and wine, a hymnal, church papers, a program of the day, and lists of charter members and of those present. The newspaper article contained the information that the previous Sand Ridge Church, built in 1846, although abandoned and decaying, still stood, and the "high old fashioned pulpit" could still be seen inside. Someone identified as Squire Vance held the deed. I have not been able to locate the foundation of the original church, but it may survive as one of the piles of stones on state forest land; nor have I been able to discover why the church was abandoned a second time.

Eventually, the hilly terrain that is now the Mohican Forest eroded due to insufficient ground cover, settlers left their unproductive farms, and the Ohio Division of Forestry acquired the land in 1928. Five years later, the Civilian Conservation Corps (CCC) was created as a response to the Great Depression, and in 1933 hundreds of underweight, malnourished adolescent boys and young men from the cities joined Company 1530, occupying tents at Camp Mohican near Perrysville. At first, the citizens of nearby Loudonville were suspicious of these newcomers, and so the boys of the "twig army" did not wear their uniforms when they traveled into the village. They mulched and seeded the fields around the river in white and red pines, which grow more rapidly than hardwoods. Over three years, the CCC boys planted more than 2 million trees—oak, hickory, beech, maple, aspen, ash, cherry, walnut, and others—on 122 acres. Ultimately, 4,500 acres became the Mohican Memorial State Forest; 1,300 acres along the river were set aside for the Mohican State Park, and 28 acres were protected for Clear Fork Gorge State Nature Preserve. The CCC camp was closed in 1937, but veterans of the Great War (1914–18) built bridges and trails in the new state forest, and Daughters of the American Revolution planted trees off what is now State Route 97. In 1947, sixty thousand members of the Ohio Federation of Women's Clubs created a living memorial of young woodlands, 270 acres that had previously been farmland; a chapel-like shrine of Ohio stone contains the names of twenty thousand servicemen lost in World War II, the Korean and Vietnam Conflicts, and the Persian Gulf War.

The Mohican Park and Forest are part of the Muskingum Watershed Conservancy District (MWCD), one of five created for flood control by the Ohio Conservancy Law, or Vonderheide Act, passed in response to the Great Flood of 1913, Ohio's greatest "natural" disaster. Three dams resulted in several small, deep lakes becoming two large, relatively shallow ones, Pleasant Hill and Charles Mill. The MWCD, established in 1933 to oversee the Muskingum River and its tributaries, includes Ashland, Belmont, Carroll, Coshocton, Guernsey, Harrison, Holmes, Knox, Licking, Morgan, Muskingum, Noble, Richland, Stark, Summit, Tuscarawas, Washington, and Wayne Counties. By 1939, the US Army Corps of Engineers had assumed responsibility for flood control, but MWCD administrators now manage conservation and recreational activities. Headquartered in New Philadelphia, the conservancy district is run by a five-member board of directors appointed by common pleas judges from the counties within it; the five members appoint seven executives to oversee daily operations. One member of the board of directors, Gordon T. Maupin, is a naturalist with over thirty years of experience teaching in the Wilderness Center in Stark County. The current chief of natural resources and land management was oil and gas operations coordinator from 2015 to 2020 and worked for sixteen years with five drilling companies, including Chesapeake Energy, renowned as the ninetieth most polluting company in the world. While the minutes of the executives' meetings are open to the public, few people are aware of them, and I have never seen them announced in any local newspaper (when such things existed) or online resource.

Local people claim that disasters created the park, state forest, and lakes: bad farming practices resulting in soil erosion caused people to leave the area; the Great Flood of 1913 preceded the creation of conservation districts tasked with flood control; the depression of the 1930s led to the Civilian Conservation Corps. The restored hillsides are now home to rare species such as the blue-headed vireo, magnolia warbler, Blackburnian warbler, Canada warbler, hermit thrush, cerulean warbler, ovenbird, and winter wren—birds that need mature forests in order to survive. In his twelve-minute video *Mohican: The Long View*, filmmaker Timothy McKee calls preservation of the park and forest "a second chance gone right."

That second chance may have proved too successful. Preservationists were concerned about state legislation passed in 2011 to open state parks and forests to increased logging and natural gas development. In January 2015, however, the Department of Natural Resources denied any intention of drilling in the park: "There are no plans for hydraulic fracturing in Mohican State Park or State Forest," declared spokeswoman Stephanie Leis. MWCD has, however, leased land and sold water for fracking at some of the lakes it oversees. More recently, House Bill 507, signed into law in 2023 by Republican governor Mike DeWine, not only allows fracking on state forest and park land but also mandates that Ohio Department of Natural Resources "must" grant leases to drilling companies that meet its criteria, eliminates or shortens the public commentary period, and defines natural gas as "green energy," which it is not. The bill, one that began as a law focused on poultry farming, was voted on during the lame-duck session in December 2022 without a public comment period and with only one hearing. A dark money group named Empowerment Alliance, established in 2019 to promote oil and gas development and oppose sustainable energy, helped to fund the initiative. Its executive director, Matthew Hammond, serves on the Executive Committee of the Ohio Oil and Gas Association as a lobbyist for Chesapeake Energy. Its treasurer, Eric Lycan, also serves as treasurer of Generation Now, a nonprofit organization implicated in the racketeering and bribery scandal involving convicted former house speaker Larry Householder to secure passage of House Bill 6 (2019), which included bailouts for failing coal and nuclear power plants, paid for by rate hikes to customers.

Rewilding is a progressive approach to conservation in which nature is left to restore itself, with some help from *Homo sapiens*— such as removal of nonnative species and restoration of corridors between habitats. The 1995 reintroduction of gray wolves into Yellowstone National Park may be the most famous example of a keystone species being employed to bring an ecosystem into balance: after thirty-one wolves were released into the park, numbers of deer and elk decreased, trees and grasslands along with bird populations flourished, erosion of streambanks nearly ceased, and many native populations returned, such as beavers, eagles, and foxes. The Rewilding Institute, developed by environmentalist and author Dave Foreman, defines the Mississippi River Watershed as a major flyover route for migratory birds; thus, he considers it a national priority. Reaching from western New York State to Tennessee, Minnesota to Louisiana, Montana to New Mexico, from the Adirondack and Appalachian Mountains to the Rockies, it includes thirty-two states and two Canadian provinces, 1.2 million square miles, and nearly one third of the entire North American continent. Home to more than four hundred species of birds, mammals, reptiles, and trees, the Mohican Park and State Forest are part of that watershed.†

In 2023, I returned to the decaying Sand Ridge Church. The padlocked door faces southeast toward a vista of hills and valleys. A small frame structure nearby perhaps served as an outhouse. The church's foundation stone reads "Pleasant Hill Evan. Lutheran Church 1878." Each long side has three large windows, now

---

† According to an article published in the March 27, 2023, issue of *Nature Climate Change*, reintroducing just nine wildlife species—African elephants, American bison, sea otters, wildebeest, and others—would contribute substantially toward reducing the amount of carbon dioxide from the atmosphere by 2100 and thereby help to prevent global temperature rise. The report states that animal behaviors distribute seeds and nutrients that keep carbon in the soil by affecting microbial activity in ecosystems. Natural grazing patterns of wildebeest, for example, helped to prevent wildfires and restore the ecosystems of the Serengeti Plain.

boarded up. Some roof tiles have fallen to the ground. Flat stones grown over in grass may have been a footpath. At the entrance from Township Road 3286, a large oak tree rises prominently beside a polished granite marker which declares that the cemetery was founded in 1803. An outline of a church with a belltower is etched into the surface, but no belltower now rises from the church roof. Some quite recent memorials stand next to graves so old the headstones are weathered nearly to rubble.

To the north, beyond the cemetery, in what had been part of the area preserved against logging, huge trees lay on their sides. These were uprooted by a storm on June 14, 2022, called a *derecho*—tornado-strength wind moving directly rather than circling—which tore through the park, toppling many of the old trees. Instead of leaving them to decompose naturally, the Department of Forestry drew up plans to sell the lumber and ostensibly designate the money to local school districts. Some conservationists believe the incident is being used as an excuse to log the forest. Fortunately, the vista at Clearfork Gorge was undamaged by the storm. It remains to be seen whether there will be third chance for the forest and whether the direction will be toward conservation or exploitation.

Three

Heritage

The official historical structure of Ohio is now the timber-frame barn, having been so designated by the 132nd General Assembly on March 20, 2019, with the passing of Senate Bill 86 and House Bill 12 (2017). Representative Anne Gonzales (R-Westerville) proposed the legislation at the request of school pupils in her district (one that has been losing historical structures to development and increasing population) in order to promote the preservation of barns in the state. No doubt those children had in mind antique barns rather than newer ones, but as the bill reads, a barn is defined as "an agricultural building located on farms and used for many purposes."

The barn joins the ever-lengthening list of state symbols, including the buckeye (tree), red carnation (cultivated flower), white trillium (wildflower), cardinal (bird), tomato (cultivated fruit), pawpaw (native fruit), white-tailed deer (mammal), and many others—including gemstone, insect, fossil, reptile, amphibian, frog, bicentennial bridge, prehistoric site, historic artifact, and drink (yes, we do have a state drink: tomato juice). By the time of this writing, there may be more.

Superfluity aside, symbols possess certain power that may preserve something in addition to history: not merely the image but the essence behind it, what we mean by heritage. Emblems such as flags represent something conscious and definable. The triangle and stripes of the state flag commemorate hills, valleys, and waterways; seventeen stars remind us that Ohio was the seventeenth state to enter the union; a white circle is the letter O. The state seal contains an image of Mount Logan in Ross County, the Scioto River, a wheatfield and sheaf declaring the importance of agriculture, seventeen arrows for the native people (driven out of the state by European immigrants), and a rising sun with thirteen rays, for the original American colonies. Unfortunately, the canalboat that represented an early form of transportation was removed. Symbols hold more than sentimental value; they stand for something elemental and universal, something perhaps even beyond consciousness.

With good reason, preservationists usually focus on houses and churches as examples of the greatest architecture. No one denies the grandeur of Notre Dame (1345), Westminster Abbey (tenth century), or Chartres (1194) or the imaginative quest fulfilled by Frank Lloyd Wright's Fallingwater, the weekend residence designed in 1935 for the Kaufmann family in the Pennsylvania woods. Ohio contains many interesting Victorian mansions, nineteenth-century churches, and antique courthouses, often in small towns on less-traveled roads. The State House is an example of neoclassical design. Barns, however, represent a different historical narrative.

In February 2020, the Ohio Humanities Council sponsored a lecture on these iconic structures, at the Cleo Rudd Fisher Museum in Loudonville. The conference room was filled to capacity with listeners standing along the sides and back of the room and squatting before the front row. Tom O'Grady, of Friends of Ohio Barns, explained that the three principal types of antique barns found in Ohio include the German-style bank barn, the New England–style flat barn, and the southern-style beaked barn. The first two have principal entryways, usually double doors, on the higher sides, beneath the gutters. Bank barns, constructed to allow wagons to be driven up to the doors on the raised sides, are distinguished by the presence of the forebay—cantilevered walls extending a few yards farther out over the foundation, providing shade for animals beneath—and the single-panel wind door on the side facing the lower slope.

The most numerous and widely distributed type, bank barns were built between 1790 and 1890; they are also distinguished by symmetrical gable ends—both front and rear side walls reaching the same height. The Sweitzer barn, from Switzerland, a variation on the German design, is a log-crib barn mostly built between 1730 and 1850 and retaining the forebay but having asymmetrical rather than symmetrical gable ends. Like the German barns, their entrances are over one of the long sides, beneath the gutter. The New England barn, often smaller than the German, is built on flat ground, also with doors under the gutter. Most German-style barns have gable roofs, meaning one angle with two straight sides;

Bank barn at Wedding Pines (Photograph by the author)

Sketch by M. Margaret Geib of Pennsylvania German bank barn with forebay. Ridgeline centered over floor instead of foundation may indicate that it is a variation called a Switzer barn. (Used by permission of Old Barn Post)

less-common gambrel roofs have three angles with four straight sides. Many barns are louvered, with horizontally slatted windows, accenting the antique appearance. In the southern part of the state, where the bank style is less common, barns frequently have entryways below the gable and sport a hay hood or beak that extends from beneath the point of the roof above a high door.

A *bay* is the space between two bents—upright posts or beams—located from front to back; thus, a four-bay barn contains five structural beams. New England barns typically have three bays. Holes called *owl doors* bored into the upper story allow predatory birds to fly in and out and so control the rodent populations. Numbers of owls and swallows increased with the proliferation of barns, and thus the arrangement proved mutually beneficial to farmer and fowl. As grain was the principal crop, the main floor of the barn was used for threshing, and hence called the *threshing floor*. Because the weather almost always blows in from the west or southwest, the back door, also called the *wind door*, slid open along the east wall opposite the main entryway, so chaff could be carried outside on the breeze. The forebay reached over the eastern side.

Sketch by M. Margaret Geib and Hubert G. H. Wilhelm of New England three-bay raised barn with stone foundation (Used by permission of Old Barn Post)

In *Ohio: A Bicentennial History* (1976), Walter Havighurst, (1901–1994), Miami University professor, described how pioneer farmers usually plowed and planted alone or with family members but harvested with help from neighbors using *cradles,* wooden handles attached to a row of scythes. As harvesters swung their blades, grain from severed stems landed in baskets attached to the implements. A leader called out the time. Before cutting, farmers herded their hogs along rows to kill copperhead snakes. Threshing waited until fieldwork ended. One farmer could flail ten bushels of wheat in a day, or twenty-five by using a horse.

Barn decoration had practical function as well as aesthetic appeal. Window frames were painted white, as the color was thought to keep witches away. Other apotropaic practices included placing piles of grain or horseshoes near doorways because, some frontier people believed—in the tradition of their European ancestors—goblins were compelled to count individual grains and hoofprints made by horseshoes, keeping the malevolent spirits busy until dawn attenuated their power. Heart shapes and swastikas (from the Sanskrit word for "well-being") similarly warded off malign intentions. One interesting stone in a Perry County barn includes the year of construction, 1819, below a heart and above the date, September 22. Beneath the name are two emblems containing four petal-shaped arms—one turning clockwise and the other counterclockwise—as well as vertical and horizontal lines, thought to indicate the temporal within the infinite.

Barn style reflects not only utility and custom but also Ohio's history of migration and settlement. Early fur-trading French immigrants left few structures, because they never intended to stay. Following the end of the French and Indian Wars (1754–63), the lands south of the Great Lakes became British colonial possessions; after the American War of Independence, the region was incorporated into the US Northwest Territory. New Englanders migrated to the area south of Lake Erie along the North Trail. The Western Reserve, initially set aside for veterans of the War of Independence, was settled largely by English immigrants from Connecticut, Massachusetts, New York, and Vermont. They lived in or near small towns, attended mostly Congregational churches, built cottages, and raised cattle and sheep. With their New England barns and threshing floors, they created the grain surplus that enabled construction of the Ohio & Erie Canal (1820s and 1830s) by later immigrants from Ireland and Germany. The Congress lands were settled by the Dutch and Germans from southeastern Pennsylvania, mostly wheat and livestock farmers, who traveled westward from Pittsburgh on the Great Trail into the forests north of the watershed divide and on into western Ohio. Other settlers migrated from Pennsylvania, the mid-Atlantic states, and Virginia along Zane's Trace. German immigrants numbered about seventy thousand while the Irish numbered less than half that, close to thirty-three thousand. Most Ohio barns influenced by German construction techniques are found in areas designated Congress lands. The Firelands were tracks given to Connecticut residents whose houses had been burned in the War of 1812; few actually moved there but instead sold their land to would-be settlers. Migrants from Massachusetts traveled downriver from Pittsburgh, occupied what are now the southeastern counties, and established

Marietta. Others headed up the Muskingum River and settled in the Hocking Valley. Barns built with hay hoods testify to the movement of immigrants from Virginia and the Carolinas who carved homesteads in the hilly land north of the Ohio River.

※

Antique barns figure in the state's turbulent political history as well as its migration and architectural history. Farmsteads often served as Underground Railroad stations, because larger groups of people could hide in barns than could in attics or cellars. The first state to create a charter prohibiting slavery, Ohio possessed the second-largest number of safe houses, after New York. The farthest northeastern county, Ashtabula, which lies along Lake Erie, was termed a hotbed of abolitionism, possibly because of its proximity to Canada. US Representative Joshua Giddings and US Senator Benjamin Wade, both from northeast Ohio, called themselves abolitionists, and thirteen of John Brown's nineteen recruits came from Ashtabula County. While some historians identify the Western Reserve as the most antislavery region in the country, others debate whether the sentiment arose from moral outrage over human bondage or from small farmers' not wanting to compete against large planters.

Tom O'Grady records that a woman who died in 1942 at the age of ninety-five related that as children she and some friends found a stash of weapons when they were playing in a barn belonging to a family named Forbes. The weapons included rifles, revolvers, powder kegs, swords, bayonets, and pikes. Boxes marked "fence castings" were hauled in wagons across the state line from Ashtabula County to Hartstown, Pennsylvania; by canalboat to Johnstown and Harrisburg; and by wagon to Chambersburg, where they were stored until used in the raid at Harpers Ferry (1859). Barns along Route 61 housed people fleeing to Lake Erie where they could be ferried to Canada, but it is not clear which; owners kept no records because the Fugitive Slave Acts (1793, 1850) outlawed helping slaves to escape.

The Granville Riot in Licking County took place because of opposition to an April 27, 1836, meeting of the Ohio Anti-Slavery Convention, in a barn owned by Ashley Azariah Bancroft. Even though they held their meeting outside the village boundaries, the abolitionists encountered resistance from a mob whose origins are not clear. The Bancroft House became a station on the Underground Railroad, as did several other houses on Pearl Street (State Route 661). The "Hall of Freedom" barn, built in the 1830s, was a New England–style structure with stone foundation walls and wooden silo (as evidenced from photographs). While the barn has, unfortunately, been torn down, the farmhouse, built in the Federal style between 1832 and 1834, still stands on the campus of Denison University, which acquired it in 1917. Historian Hubert Howe Bancroft was born there, the son of Ashley Azariah, whose ancestor was Samuel Bancroft, founder of Granville, Massachusetts, in 1754. Shaded by an old black maple, the house now serves as a women's residence; its horizontal gray ashlar facade, made of locally quarried stone, distinguishes it from other houses on Pearl Street. The house faces the road, while the backhouse, a single-story addition typical of New England dwellings, extends perpendicular to the main structure. The farmland has become playing fields and an athletic complex. To the north is a smaller antique gray stone residence referred to as "The Cottage"; beyond that stand a venerable old white farmhouse constructed in the colonial style and an antique, New England–type red barn, where the university stored machinery and later (in the 1980s) housed its recycling center. Even against a frenzy of building during the last thirty years, residents of the village guard its antique houses and heritage. While they regularly celebrate its founders' history of migration as a group from Massachusetts, and establishment of a temperance community in 1805, however, in the eight years I lived there (1986–93), I never heard anyone from the local historical society proclaim the village's considerable participation in either the Underground Railroad or the abolitionist movement.

Springhouses, antique rural structures made of wood, stone, or brick built just over or downstream from natural springs, also tell part of the history of settlement. They kept leaves, sticks, and animals out of drinking water and provided the earliest form of refrigeration, primarily for milk and cider. Iconic buildings that have all but disappeared from the landscape—because rural electrification and delivered ice made them obsolete—they are smaller than most rooms, no bigger than a closet or playhouse. Springhouses sit prominently on two of my neighbors' farms, one directly adjoining our pasture and one about a mile south, which bears the insignia of a designated historic structure. The water (about 55° F) modulated the temperature and kept the interior cool in summer and above freezing in winter. Sometimes springhouses had second levels for keeping ceramic crocks and jars of produce. At Malabar Farm, famous novelist, essayist, screenplay writer, and agriculturalist Louis Bromfield built a springhouse that faces Pleasant Valley Road close to the intersection of Ohio Route 603; it plays a prominent role in several of his books. (See chapter 10 for further discussion of Bromfield.)

My fascination with barns and stables began in childhood, when I desired nothing more than to own a horse. I designed barns on paper, created models out of cardboard, and studied books with photographs and drawings of old barns and stables. I reconstructed every dilapidated structure I saw—and there were many in Jefferson County. I favored a single-story stable with a cupola on the roof, double doors on each stall, and cobblestone courtyard.

Finally, I bought a place near Perrysville in Green Township in Ashland County called The Wedding Pines, with a large old barn that had housed beef cattle, hogs, and horses. Most stables I had seen were pole barns or newer wooden structures with fitted stalls. I cleaned out years-old manure and repaired paddock and pasture fences. Set away from the county road, the barn is one of the most distinctive features on the place, in addition to two large spruces in the front yard. In the heavy fog of an autumn morning, the barn appears to float above the undulating landscape. Under a full moon, it resembles a ship's prow forging through waves. Although the silo and all of the outbuildings except the carriage house and henhouse have fallen or been torn down, the barn survived because the builders intended their work to last for centuries. The year 1878 had been traced into one of the concrete footers, so I assumed my barn dated from then.

When a visitor from the local historical society wanted to feature it on a tour, my husband told her she would have to talk to me, saying, "That barn is her baby." The expert explained that mine was a German-style bank barn and probably older than I thought. "The primeval forests of Ohio reside in its barns, and each barn contains a wood lot," she said. Many of the largest trees in the state, cut down to build barns, were over four hundred years old.

My gable-roof barn is approximately seventy-three by thirty-eight feet (including the forebay) on the main floor and seventy-two by thirty feet on the lower level. The foundation was carved out of a natural slope above a stream flowing northwest to southeast across the pasture. The springhouse on my neighbors' land once belonged to my farm. Wide doors open under the long gutters on the western side; high above the foundation, a wind door slides open to reveal the view of fields stretching eastward to the banks of Honey Creek and rising to wooded hills beyond. Inside the upper story, two rows of four bents connected by tie beams create three bays. Many of the floorboards measure twelve to eighteen inches wide, indicating their age: boards installed after 1900 measure about four inches in width. Timbrel braces connect the east–west beams at forty-five-degree angles beneath rafters that allow space for several thousand bales of hay that are called "square" but are really rectangular. A section on the south side is separated by a half-wall, or waste wall, constructed to keep seeds from blowing away. Splines—long, thin wooden strips—beneath and between boards of the threshing floor also prevent grain from falling into the lower level. Several built-in ladders reach to the overhead beams, where a hay track traverses the length of the roof. A rake hanging from a cable in one corner may have been used to collect mounds of loose hay. Gazing toward the rafters reaching more than fifty feet above the threshing floor, a visitor realizes that mass production unfortunately sometimes means the loss of ancient skills, such as timber framing.

A large room in the north section of the upper barn served as the granary, with five separate compartments, spaces I use to store feed, tools, and horse equipment. One of the shelves in the feed room, perhaps pilfered from some demolished structure, contains part of the name of a business, but because the board was sawn in half, I have been unable to identify it, its location, or the type of merchandise the proprietor sold. I can make out *To You* and part of a name, *Sch,* and the Roman numeral *VII* painted in yellow Gothic letters. Tattered remains of old maps line some of the walls, and the headboard of an old bedframe, complete with mirror, hangs on a wall. The farmer's purpose in hanging the old mirror in a barn remains a mystery.

Descendants of the original German settlers, named Weirick, who live in Mansfield, presented me with a photograph of the barn with the year 1875 painted on the front, but I now know that notches in the beams of the understory indicate that they were hand-hewn, and so the barn is probably dates from before the Civil War (1861–65). The understory is only about fifteen feet high, with twice as many oak support beams as necessary, according to two contractors, providing further evidence that the builders meant that their work should last. Some of the shorter braces contain parallel, shallow curving grooves like machine-sawn wood; they must have been added after the war, when sawmills proliferated, converted from portable steam engines built to manufacture armaments. Another more recent addition is the staircase leading down from the feed room to the lower level onto a concrete dais about three-quarters of the way to the southern wall. The farmer would have used it to carry feed from the granary to the animals stabled below, whereas his predecessors would have walked outside in order to get to the lower story. A horse stall took up the space on the north side of the lower barn where the original foundation stones are still visible; the rest of the interior wall is more recent, made of reinforced and mortared cement block. Bolted to the side beams on the upper story and driven horizontally into the earth on the bank side, metal rods prevent the structure from falling forward down the slope. Three hand-hewn oak beams laid north–south that support the floor of the main level measure two feet in width and height and seventy-three feet in length, revealing the size of the trees they were made from. Twenty-one hand-hewn crossbeams, each approximately a foot in diameter and retaining the trees' outer bark, undergird the second floor from east to west, joined to the long beams with wooden pins rather than nails. Anyone who has ever used an axe knows how hard those people must have worked to fell the trees and build these barns.

The descendants' photos also reveal that our house once included a summer kitchen—a long, low attachment extending from the first floor, where the farm wife would have done her cooking and canning. That summer kitchen explains the reason our present one is so small: long ago, most of the food was prepared outside the main house. A large rectangular stone marks the north side of the foundation. I regret that the structure was torn down, partly because it would have provided more space but more importantly because it would have preserved evidence of an older way of life. A back porch that ran the length of the house has now been enclosed into a room we use for storage and laundry. Fortunately, the contractors provided windows along its entire outer wall, affording us access to the best view, toward the wooded hills to the east. I have seen no photograph of that side of the house before the porch was enclosed, but the door opening to the back is elaborately carved, with long, curved windows at the top. Someone cared to make an impression on visitors. A step on the south side of the porch was quarried from the same type of stone as the foundation of the summer kitchen.

Back of house at Wedding Pines (Photograph by the author)

Cabinets at both ends of the third floor and covered circular holes where pipes from wood stoves or fireplaces would have been vented testify that at one time the house had a chimney on each end. This type of pioneer dwelling is called an *I house* because of its frequency in states beginning with the letter *I:* Indiana, Illinois, and Iowa. A brick chimney rises from the middle of the roof, but, interestingly, it takes a right-angle turn in the "true" attic above the third floor, possibly to situate it aesthetically in the very center of the roof. No longer in use—because we installed a side-venting, 98 percent–efficient furnace during the frigid winter of 2014—the chimney now provides a home for swifts and other roof-nesting birds. Wooden pins in the attic beams reveal that the house, or part of it, also probably predates the Civil War. In the lower floors and in the barn we found metal nails of the

Sketch by M. Margaret Geib of I-house (Used by permission of Old Barn Post)

type made between the late eighteenth century and 1900: manufactured from strips of iron, they were square and tapered from a large oval end called a *rosehead*. The house contains only one closet, a modern invention. Prior to the twentieth century, people used clothes hooks, chests, and wardrobes to store clothing; five rooms in our house contain antique nails that would have served to hang clothes.

One of our Weirick visitors explained that the family members did their "living" in the dining room, where there had been a large wood-burning stove, and that the grandkids swam and fished in Honey Creek. A handpump outside served as the house's main source of water. The rusted hydrant still stands. No evidence remains of an orchard, which had been planted behind the house.

When we had the barn, garage, and henhouse painted dark red (it was a pale yellow), we preserved the white trim, although I have no fear of witches. My present concern involves another fairytale: the belief that "progress" means only more building, population, and increased traffic on the county road. The result of this contemporary sorcery is that farms are sold off and the rural character of the township is lost.

Because many records in the county offices were burned in a 1900 fire, dating the homestead precisely is difficult. When we bought the place, the previous owner told me that the house was believed to be situated on the site of a log cabin that had been built by German immigrants named Weirick in the 1860s and that the house had been owned by only four families. An old tax map in the lower reaches of the county courthouse, however, shows that the farmstead already existed in 1830, with at least two buildings. The owner's name is indecipherable, but other records reveal that as early as 1837, a man named William Taylor sold 160 acres—which included our land—to William McCleary, who sold it to Jacob Churchman, who sold eighty acres of his homestead to William Priest in 1842. Five years later, Priest sold the land to Thomas Robinson, who held most of it until 1887 but sold some acreage, house, and barn to Joseph Weirick in 1861; he and his descendants owned the farmstead for more than a hundred years, until 1968, but it is unknown which individuals occupied the house and for how long. Family members informed me that their grandparents, G. Elzie and Maud D. Weirick, lived here twenty-eight years, from 1940 until 1968. They farmed with teams of horses and mules, two of which were named Frank and Ned, and bought supplies from a peddler who drove a wagon. In the Greenlawn Cemetery on State Route 39 southeast of the village of Perrysville, I found the gravestones of Joseph (1854–1933)—probably a second-generation descendant of the original settler Joseph Weirick, whose grave I never discovered—and his wife, Amanda E. Weirick (1856–1940); J. Henry (1881–1967) and Maude I. Weirick (1886–1988); and Elzie (1880–1969) and Maud

(1883–1970). Since 1968, the farm has been sold five times, to Daniel A. Huffman in 1968, Harry and Betty Thomas in 1971, Robert Thompson in 1984, and Jack and Pat Stevens in 1990. My husband and I purchased it in 1993.

According to Robert A. Carter and Michael C. Cullen in *Water-Powered Mills of Richland County* (2016), Joseph Weirick owned a grist mill on Honey Creek (in what was then Richland County), near the intersection of Township Road 2475. A man named Jack Royer, whose land lay to the east of the Weiricks', also operated a grist mill where Township Road 827 crosses Honey Creek. Caldwell's *Ashland County Atlas* of 1874 verifies that there were two mills in that area.[†] Since the Weirick property produced mostly grain, the farmer would have had incentive to increase his income by operating his own flour mill. I found no evidence of a mill near Township Road 827, which runs along the southern border of my pasture, but a large pile of cut stones lies on the banks of the creek near Township Road 2475, north of our place, the location Carter and Cullen describe as Weirick's mill. The book places the two mills about three-quarters of a mile apart—approximately the distance between the two township roads—and explains that after the structures were torn down in 1915–16, the millponds would have been drained, making the field more productive because of nutrient-rich sediment. Certainly the low-lying area west of the creek is the only land between it and the county road that is entirely level. During early springtime, the fields are often covered in water, but after the flood subsides, the dark, rich soil produces abundant crops.

I have not been able to discover which inhabitants planted the two Norway spruces (*Picea abies*) in the front of the house and named the place The Wedding Pines. It was a custom among pioneers to plant two trees of the same kind when they founded a

---

[†] Caldwell's 1874 *Atlas of Ashland County* also includes the information that Perrysville was laid out by Thomas Coulter and contained a population of 160, a post office, one church, two stores, a hotel, a blacksmith shop, a shoe store, a depot, a foundry, one physician, a "good academy," several new houses, and "spirited people."

homestead, and they sometimes celebrated the births of children by planting trees. According to Louis Bromfield, Norway spruces were a favorite for midwestern windbreaks as they grow fast (about one foot per year) and are hardy: their flexible wood and spreading root system enable the trees to stand up to strong winds, pendant branches shed ice and snow, and they survive well in cold climates. My spruces have never lost limbs, even in a strong storm in 2009 and the derecho of June 14, 2022, when venerable trees planted near them, a red cedar and pin oak, dropped several very large branches. Our trees stand about 150 feet in height and about five feet in diameter; if they grew one foot per year, they were planted about 1873, perhaps by the original Weirick or his son.

※

The Ashland County Barns and Rural Heritage Society, active between 2003 and 2018, recorded 1454 barns in fifteen townships, photographing them, recording their type, and grading their condition as "good," "fair," "poor," or "ruin." In Green Township, 119 barns were surveyed, the vast majority (66) in good condition, predominantly bank barns (69), mostly with gable roofs (101). The society's records, housed in the Ashland County Historical Society building (itself an antique structure) on Center Street, are stored in a cabinet constructed in an old style from timbers salvaged from a historic barn.

State and national organizations demonstrate that old structures can be preserved for more than sentimental reasons. The Barn Again! program launched in Denver in 1987 by the Regional Office of the National Trust and *Successful Farming* magazine showed that renovating historic barns for current use (including dairy and hog operations as well as grain and machinery storage) could be more economical than building new structures.

On our road between Loudonville and Ashland, a distance of about twenty miles, there are eighteen barns, thirteen of them the German type. Eight contain extensions, while three have awnings with no forebay. All but three have gable roofs. The barn directly south of ours is a white German-style bank barn with a gambrel roof and the names of the farmer and his wife (now deceased) proudly emblazoned in green on the long side. Four of the barns have siloes still standing. Also on the road there are three corncribs, two sizable henhouses, and two springhouses. A large corncrib about three miles south caught fire and burned several years ago; the blackened beams and slats were finally torn down. Northward from our place are two bank barns, one white and one red, a red New England–style barn, and a red southern-style barn with characteristic beaked hay hood, unusual in this part of the state. Six miles farther, a red-brick Victorian house dwells in the shadow of an ancient red oak and gazes across the road to another working farm. An old bank barn stands behind the house along with silo and several long, connected outbuildings. The farmer could walk from one area to another without going outside, a unique benefit during harsh winters. That farmstead is now endangered, as the windows are boarded up and the barn is being allowed to decay. One mile south of our place, an ancient schoolhouse—another type of antique structure that is disappearing—sits near the road on the property of a man who sells mowing equipment. Some neighbors attended that school as late as the 1940s. The owner is not tearing it down, as he values historical buildings and has already restored an attractive old colonial saltbox-style house on his property.

The Friends of Ohio Barns hosts an annual tour and conference with the object of educating the public and saving as many old structures as possible. One method of preserving the heritage of antique barns is to change their use, or *repurpose* them, as the organization terms it. Mohican Gardens, near Mohicanville, is a working nursery that rents out its antique German-style bank barn for weddings, reunions, and other events. The greenhouses lie in a swale behind the barn and are surrounded by fruit trees and ornamentals. Barberton Farm near Akron and Woodside Farm in Belmont County serve as tourist attractions. The state's earliest known barn is on the Carter farm in Ross County. A beautifully preserved antique barn in Greene County, distinctively painted in red and white, serves as the central building of the nonprofit Agraria Center for Regenerative Practice.

The four-bay bank barn at Sugar Grove Farm on a township road west of Ashland in Mifflin Township is said to be the oldest in the county. The farm dates from 1823, when Peter Brubaker bought land from his father, Benjamin Brubaker, originally from Lancaster County, Pennsylvania. Peter's daughter Susan Whistler inherited the farm, as did her daughter Evelyn Whistler. Owned by six generations of the same family, it passed in 1976 to descendants. The farm is now a profitable tree nursery where the barn is used for storage. The structure sits on a foundation of local stone, and the characteristic wind door faces the east. Although the hand-hewn beams have been left in place, the sides are now covered in white aluminum siding. Coverings of this sort protect the wood but prevent structures from being designated as historic buildings.

In spite of local and private efforts, antique Ohio barns are being torn down or bought up by brokers, disassembled, and shipped out of state. Looking at an old barn, the developer sees an impediment to profits; an owner imagines exorbitant maintenance costs; aficionados of new houses complain of an eyesore. Someone who appreciates the rural landscape, however, admires a beautiful vista, while a lover of history contemplates an opportunity for preservation. Due to suburbanization and the high cost of maintenance, the state is losing old barns at about fifty per decade: in 2003, there were approximately 1400 barns in Ohio; by 2012 the count was 1350. In trying to build a tourist industry, Hocking County calls itself the "Gateway to Ohio's Scenic Wonderland" (the Appalachian foothills), but a bicentennial barn—one decorated with a flag and the date 1803, Ohio's entrance into statehood— was torn down to make way for a gasoline station and convenience store. A decaying bank barn on the township road immediately north of our place, with many boards missing and holes in the roof, was demolished in January 2021. The farmhouse that must have stood nearby had been torn down long before, and a newer house built facing the county road. In my time here, I have seen two other barns northward on the county road and one directly south of ours demolished because lack of care caused them to become derelict.

Country Living, a monthly magazine published by the local electric cooperative, contains this advertisement in nearly every issue:

> OLD BARNS WANTED
> Buying barns, bank barns,
> and granaries.
> Insured, 20 years experience.

A company called All Ohio Barn put an ad in the January 2022 issue that reads "BARNS WANTED FOR RECLAIM. We pay up front." Another business, Ohio Valley Barn Salvage, bills itself as a company that "preserves the past" by tearing down old barns and using the timbers for newer structures. Its website features photos of large forklifts and other equipment. The family-owned Ohio Valley Reclaimed Wood in Bellville once repaired barns but found that there was more money in disassembling them, not for rebuilding but for cabinets, countertops, furniture, and floors, because "Ohio has the best hardwoods in the country." Many of these reclaimed barns are shipped to the West, where there are few antique barns and almost none in the style of the early settlers.

The Federal Historic Preservation Tax Incentives Program, established in 1978 and administered by the National Park Service, provides up to 20 percent of expenditures for preservation of historic structures, but to qualify, a barn must be "income-producing," or used for some commercial purpose, and must be listed with the National Register of Historic Places. A federal bill sponsored by Senator Jim Jeffords of Vermont to establish a National Historic Barn Preservation agency (Senate Bill 1628, Agriculture, Conservation, and Rural Enhancement Act of 2001, section 639), would have authorized money to save antique barns. The bill did not receive a roll call and was never brought to a vote. In 2002, Governor Bob Taft and the Ohio legislature authorized $25 million in farmland preservation, but no money was set aside specifically for barn preservation. The Ohio Historic Preservation Tax Credit Program, however, offers state tax credits up to 25 percent of expenditures for rehabilitation (not to exceed $5 million) of historic structures as defined by listing in the National Register of Historic Places, contribution to nationally registered historic districts, or designation as a landmark by local government. As of 2023, the program had assisted in funding for 819 buildings.

❧

At the time many of our antique barns were being built in the New World, English essayist John Ruskin (1819–1900) articulated in "The Seven Lamps of Architecture" (1848) that builders should create structures intended to last and bring credit to the age in which they are built. In "The Lamp of Sacrifice," he declared that architecture should emulate what is natural and express "some great truths commonly belonging to the whole race." Viewers should be able to "read" buildings, whose architecture must be interesting and intelligible. The "soul" of the Gothic was comprised of balance among parts.

People today cannot read the soul of a metal pole-building, because it has none; balance and harmony do not inform structures thrown up as hastily and cheaply as possible, with no concern for aesthetics or heritage. Nineteenth-century barns were built to last because the carpenters expected that descendants would inherit the land and that farming would always be the primary occupation. The old barn says to the onlooker, "I represent abundance, prosperity, thriftiness, and home." While we may blame pioneers for stripping the frontier of trees, the settlers left these noble structures—barns and houses—for us to learn from by reading our history in the landscape.

In *Pleasant Valley* (1945), Louis Bromfield compares the building of barns in this country with that of constructing cathedrals in Europe: "The old barns built in the time of the great tradition of American agriculture when the new land was still rich and unravaged by greed and bad farming, had each one its own character, its special beauty born of the same order of spirit and devotion which built the great cathedrals of Chartres or Rheims or Salzburg." The barns boast of their specialness with "splendor and nobility about them which no modern hip-roofed, standardized, monstrosity can approach." Ohio possessed all types, including what he termed *Gothic, Pennsylvania Dutch, New England,* and "stone-ended barns of Virginia." Many were decorated with weathervanes and cupolas, and many were hand-painted with pictures of animals or hex symbols. Moravians painted theirs with whole farm landscapes.

In writing about barns, Tom O'Grady echoes this philosophy:

> To preserve the barn is to preserve a tangible part of the American heritage. To preserve the barn is to preserve our sense of place and a sense of who we are, where we came from, and how we got here. The barn represents the people who built it and the way of life it supported. It represents the frugality, stewardship, and ingenuity of its former owners. Such a link to the past might yet be a guidepost along the road to economic stability as it was in days gone by.

We in Ohio do not have ancient theaters or medieval cathedrals, but we have nineteenth-century barns, houses, churches, and courthouses. Once they are demolished, they are gone forever, and our history, identity, and intrinsic aesthetic selves with them. Most houses and industrial buildings constructed in the late twentieth and early twenty-first centuries are not created to be aesthetically pleasing or to leave a legacy. Cost and convenience make up the primary concerns, even when the corporations building them make millions in profits. Beauty, balance, and effect on local communities is seldom a factor in determining what kind of building is put up. Failure to protect antiques structures results in loss not only of skill and craftsmanship but also of identity and character.

To the argument that people cannot afford to repair old barns, O'Grady writes that while doing so is expensive, we could at least stabilize them so to preserve them for a time when someone else may afford to make repairs. Such buildings can never be replaced: it would cost a half a million dollars to build a timber-frame barn; it would not be made of old-growth trees, nor would the timbers be hand-hewn. Estimating the cost is impossible because we cannot calculate the value of our culture.

While we need to remember the dark parts of our history—the cutting down of the ancient forests, ruthless genocide of indigenous people, unspeakable atrocity of slavery—we should also preserve the good parts, the houses and barns that tell the story of brave, adventurous, and energetic people who built them. As it is impossible to put a monetary figure on Notre Dame Cathedral or Westminster Abbey, we should value our own antique structures not by their retail price but by what will be lost of our collective memory—the hard work of farmers, skill of builders, courage of those who assisted slaves to escape, strength of the ancient trees, beauty of the primeval forest. Perhaps the old barns and rural landscapes of Ohio should be considered the museum of our heritage.

Four

Barn Burning

LOUD TRAFFIC ACCELERATES past modern office complexes on Trimble Road south of the Millsboro intersection in Mansfield in Richland County. On the other side, however, acres of sloping, mature grassland stretch toward elegant yellow and white farm buildings. Raemelton Therapeutic Equestrian Center, once part of Raemelton Farm, a 650-acre estate, represents the true rus-in-urbe experience for the twenty-first century. While the property faces businesses and strip-mall–type offices, large and elegant houses line Marion Avenue behind it. Until 1918, however, the farm stood in the country, on roads not yet paved.

The estate's founder, Franklin "Frank" Blymyer Black (1865–1937), named it for the town of Ramelton, Ireland, even retaining some of the Gaelic spelling, Rae Mealton. His father, Moses Black (1836–1904), emigrated from the village of that name in County Donegal to settle in Zanesville, Ohio, where he opened a dry goods store in 1858. He married Elizabeth Blymyer of Pennsylvania and later moved to Mansfield. Inheriting or acquiring his father's business acumen and entrepreneurial talent, Frank Black founded Ohio Brass in 1888 with ten workers. Originally a foundry that manufactured brass buckles for horse harnesses, the company diversified to include plumbing fixtures, and by 1906 it employed six hundred. In 1954, its workforce numbered eleven hundred people in Mansfield and other locations, even outside the United States. The business did not close until 1990. During the Panic of 1893, board member Reid Carpenter recognized the need to expand the company's production range and hired engineer Charles Kelly King from Indiana, who designed brass parts for the newest transportation technology: electric streetcars. Later contracts led to the manufacture of transmitters for power companies near Niagara Falls and brass parts for two battleships, the USS *Kentucky* and USS *Kearsarge*. King became a partner who eventually created Kingwood Estate, now the Kingwood Center and Garden, thirty-five acres of the original property open to the public, another rus-in-urbe setting not far from Raemelton. The mansion stands at the head of a walkway that leads to the garden, a pond where swans glide, and a large greenhouse at the far end. The Kingwood Foundation hosts tours of the grounds, where plays and operas are performed outdoors during summers.

Frank Black founded Raemelton Stable in 1918 at 569 Trimble Road and in 1929 created Raemelton Equestrian Center for his own show horses and polo ponies after remodeling the original barn, built in 1850. Frank's favorite mount was a fifteen-hand (sixty inches at the withers), dapple-gray American Saddlebred mare named Quaker Lady; after she died he honored her with a quarried stone memorial to mark her burial site behind the riding hall. Brick walls descend a slope from the archway of the current stable and outline the place where an annex stood before being destroyed in a fire. An alcove leads into the stable, which contains a cobblestone walkway and ten spacious, wood-lined box stalls with wrought-iron railings around the top allowing horses to see but not reach each other. Each stall has a window for natural light and a plaque with the resident horse's name, breed, and birthdate. The barn also contains a tack room and washing rack. Signs ask visitors not to feed the horses; they *are*, however, permitted to feed the volunteers. A cupola with a horse weathervane crowns the roof.

In addition to the main barn, the farm includes twelve buildings designed by landscape architect Marian Cruger Coffin in Greek revival and colonial style, most painted in yellow and white, the favorite combination of the founder's wife, Jessie. An octagonal brick building in front of the barn held a water pump. A long shed built in 1910 and remodeled in 1929, referred to as the polo barn, housed horses from visiting teams, including one from Firestone Farms near Columbiana and another from Kenyon College. The polo field stretched along Trimble Road. The indoor riding hall, built in 1930 for the Raemelton Riding Club, provided a place for polo practice three times a week. An attached lounge, separated from the arena by a glass wall, allows guests to observe horses and riders at work. One unusual light fixture is made from stirrups and riding bats. Other buildings include two cottages, a brick potting shed with a greenhouse, a smaller riding hall, two hay sheds, an older bank barn, and two storage sheds. The horse pastures stretch from behind the barns to Marion Avenue. Across the farm lane are an enclosed outdoor arena and fifty-foot round pen for training. The Raemelton Farm District was added to the National Register of Historic Places in 2003.

Frank Black also built Raemelton House, a large, elegant brick mansion at 818 Marion Avenue, next door to the farm, that took two years to complete. The house passed to Joel Black, grandson of Frank and his wife, Margaret, and then to Joel's son Donald Black, the last of the family to live there. The house was sold in 1970. Pictures published in *Richland County Source* show some of the interiors, including the walls of the dining room painted in classical style to represent the four seasons. The residence included guest quarters and even an indoor swimming pool. It was not turned into a museum or made part of a public park as was the mansion at Kingwood Gardens; a chain across the entrance to the circular driveway notifies inquisitive would-be visitors that the property is privately owned. Its grandeur is visible from the road only after the leaves have fallen from trees evidently planted to obscure it from sightseers.

The farm's Irish namesake—now one of five heritage towns in the northwestern county of Donegal—boasts some of the best Georgian architecture in the region, and locals refer to Ramelton as "the jewel in Donegal's crown." Originally a tenth-century Viking settlement, it lies near the river Lennon, eleven kilometers north of Letterkenny, near picturesque Lough Swilly. An antique lighthouse stands on Fánaid Peninsula between Lough Swilly and Mulroy Bay. Originally called Rath Mealtain, or Fort Mealtan, the town was occupied by the twelfth-century O'Donnell (O Domhnaill) clan of Tyrconnell that built Donegal Castle. In the eighteenth century, the present village, established between 1609 and 1622 by William Stewart from Wigtownshue, Scotland—who also founded Letterkenny—became a busy industrial center, especially for manufacturing linen.

Dún na nGall means "fort of the foreigners," and the county witnessed many battles against English incursion. Arsonists burned Rossreagh Castle and Donegal Castle (1474) in the 1640s in protest against English and Scottish planters. Referred to by its own politicians as "the forgotten county," Donegal was the province most ravaged by the Great Hunger of 1848–49. As a boy, Moses Black would have witnessed the devastation of the Famine and the mass migration that followed. One third of the Irish people either starved or emigrated, and a further 20 percent of emigrants died during the journey. Shortly after he arrived in the United States, Moses would also have known of the most catastrophic event in its history, the American Civil War (1861–65), although he did not serve in the conflict.

Similar conditions that brought about Ireland's Great Famine led to the destruction of the stable at Raemelton. The structure burned in 1932 and again in 1937, acts of arson because workers left unemployed by the Great Depression believed the horses ate better than many Mansfield children. Powerlessness inspires rage that leads to violence. In agricultural societies, torching a barn means more than destroying a dwelling, because the barn stands as the symbol of wealth. In a meaningless act of spite, furthermore, someone who gained access to the stable in 1937 cut the tails off the expensive show horses. Although the immediate cause of the Famine in Ireland was the potato blight, larger causes were the indifference of authorities—most notably Sir Charles Edward Trevelyan, assistant secretary to the Treasury under Queen Victoria—to the plight of the poor and the landlord-tenant system which left destitute the very people who grew the crops. Trevelyan stated his devotion to free trade and employed British garrisons to keep Irish ports open: more than 39,000 tons of wheat; 98,000 tons of oats; vegetables (peas, beans, onions); seafood (salmon, oysters, herring); 822,681 gallons of butter; and record numbers of livestock (including about 4000 horses) were exported from Ireland to Great Britain and Europe, where bad harvests had increased the demand for food. The British government left in place restrictions on trade in the form of the Navigation Act and Corn Laws, which kept prices high to benefit landlords.

In the United States, the immediate causes of the stock market crash and decadelong Great Depression (1930–39) were greed and lack of regulation, but starvation was the result not only of indifference but also the fact that transporting some of the available harvest would have cost more than farmers would have earned from selling it. When Frank Black began building his opulent house, in December 1929, just after the financial debacle, friends warned him that he should discontinue the construction, as they feared class warfare similar to the Russian Revolution of 1917. He decided instead to carry on with the project, claiming that he could keep more workers employed if he did so. Black would have known about the violence in Cleveland during the May Day (International Workers Day) riots of 1894, which resulted in part from careless speculation that led to the Panic of 1893. He may have heard of the Great Railroad Strike of 1877, which began in West Virginia on July 17. Strikes and violence occurred in Cleveland and Columbus but also smaller cities like Newark, Lancaster, Zanesville, and Steubenville. As the son of an Irish immigrant, he may have read about one of the most violent strikes, the labor protest that began on January 29, 1834, when Irish immigrants lured to the United States by misleading recruitment posters from the Chesapeake & Ohio Canal Company attempted to organize labor unions. The company had promised more pay and benefits than were ever provided; many workers, moreover, did not survive the strenuous labor. It is estimated that about a thousand Irishmen died working on the canal, most from accidents caused by gunpowder used to move earth. One letter sent to Ireland included this comment: "The rarest sight in America is a grey-haired Irishman." President Andrew Jackson, himself the son of Irish immigrants, employed federal troops to suppress the organizing.

No worker revolution occurred in Mansfield in the 1930s, however.

Rebuilt after the arson attacks, Raemelton Equestrian Center remained, its operation taken over by Raemelton Therapeutic Equestrian Center in 1995. Local stables and individuals lend horses through special programs. The center provides equine therapy to assist children and adults with physical, mental, social, emotional, or sensory handicaps or special needs to improve gross and fine motor skills through riding and caring for the horses. In 2016, the Raemelton Therapeutic Equestrian Center acquired the buildings and thirty-four acres. Funded by grants, donations, and fees, the organization supplies scholarships to people in need.

Horses' gaits have long been thought to enhance sensory input: in 460 BC, Hippocrates wrote about the benefits of horse riding to human health, as did Merkurialis of Italy in 1569 and Tissot of France in 1780. In 1875 Charles Chassaignac wrote that he found riding therapeutic for neurological disorders. In the United Kingdom, Olive Sands worked with wounded veterans of the Great War in therapeutic riding. In 1952, Liz Hartel won the Olympic silver medal in dressage after her legs had been partially paralyzed by polio. The Disabled Riding Association was formed in Great Britain in 1969, the same year the North American Riding for the Handicapped Association was organized in the United States, later known as the Professional Association of Therapeutic Horsemanship, which provides safety guidelines and certifies instructors. All of Raemelton's instructors hold this qualification.

During the 2012 presidential campaign, Americans were informed about Senator Mitt Romney's wife, Ann, who rode dressage horses as part of her therapy for multiple sclerosis. An item on National Public Radio's business report recited the costs, giving the most expensive totals, but those who actually ride and show dressage horses know that there are many ways to engage in the discipline without being a multimillionaire. Dressage saddles and equipment can be expensive or moderately priced, and equestrians can ride many different types of horses, some expensive and some less so. I belonged to the Mid-Ohio Dressage Association in the late 1980s and knew not a single millionaire. One member, a woman diagnosed with multiple sclerosis, competed in combined training events, which include dressage, stadium jumping, and cross-country jumping. Riding was part of her therapy, although she rode primarily because she loved horses.

Dressage horses perform precise movements initially used in war: while every one of these maneuvers originates in actions natural to horses, executing them on command requires extensive training. The levade, capriole, and courbette—the most difficult exercises in the "airs above the ground" of haute ecole horsemanship—were all originally taught to war horses to protect their riders from spears, arrows, and swords. The training evolved to become a performance for audiences (most notably by the Lipizzaner of the Spanish Riding School in Vienna and the Andalusian horses of Spain) and a therapy that enables people to overcome disabilities in learning, muscular control, and self-control.

Since the invention of the internal combustion engine, people have prophesied the horse's demise. Its history is well recorded: *eohippus,* the dawn horse, now termed *Hyracotherium,* evolved on the plains of what is now North America about 59 million years ago; extinct in its homeland by 8000 BC, the animal and its descendants flourished in Asia and Europe. The *Iliad* (seventh or eighth century BC) lauds its hero Hector and *Aeneid* (30 to 19 BC) its heroes Lausus and Messapus with the epithet "tamer of horses," the final words of the *Iliad*. In the sixteenth century, Spanish explorers brought horses to the New World, where some escaped from their owners and became the mustangs of the American West. Others, pastured on islands off the coasts of Virginia and Maryland, were ancestors of the feral ponies of Assateague, now a wildlife preserve. In spite of the prophecy that they would become obsolete—like harness-makers, carriage-builders, and manufacturers of brass buckles—horses are now more abundant than they were in the nineteenth century.

Frank Black was a capable and imaginative entrepreneur. He was fortunate that manufacturing was expanding and his product was needed, but he was also fortunate to live in a country that allowed him to thrive and develop his talents. His love of horses translated to a polo center where people of Mansfield as well as his wealthy friends could gather for equestrian events, flower shows, and other celebrations. He funded or assisted in the funding of Mansfield General Hospital, Renaissance Theater, Arts Center, Richland County Foundation, and Mansfield Symphony. He embodied the ideal of an Irishman nearly his exact contemporary, the poet W. B. Yeats (1865–1939), who believed that wealthy and educated men should serve as benefactors to society by providing people with the best examples of generosity and culture while remaining independent of popular opinion. Yeats's ideal included the difference that his "aristocracy" was one of birth and inherited—not earned—wealth, even though his own maternal grandfather, owner of a shipping company in County Sligo, just south of Donegal, had been such an entrepreneur. In Yeats's poem "Ancestral Houses," first of a series called *Meditations in Time of Civil War* (1928), he mentions that a "powerful man" called "architect and artist in" to "rear in stone" the beauty of a great house where against an elegant backdrop—the lawns of an estate—the owner finds the leisure and contemplation necessary for the patronage of great art. The poem questions the likelihood of the survival of the ancestral house and the customs it represents, however, due to the uncertainties of the time and unproven abilities of the creator's descendants, as it will be their responsibility to perpetuate their heritage. Concerned with the chaos and destruction of war, the series examines the fact that meditation requires time, concentration, and stability, and the initial poem takes as its central subject an image of continuity—a large house that only a wealthy person can afford to build. Although "violent and bitter," the powerful man, his architect, and artist succeed in their vision: in spite of the chaos of war or conflict, they create beauty—described as "sweetness" and "gentleness." The wealthy man not only patronizes great art but also provides the emblem that serves as the embodiment of the culture.

Whether Moses Black emigrated from Ireland in search of opportunity or escape from poverty, he found a place where his gifted son realized a dream of what was elegant and beautiful but also useful. I am not aware of any major biography of Frank Black, so Ohioans have only the accolades accorded him in picture books and websites that describe him and Charles King as visionaries, inventors, and philanthropists.[†] Perhaps he is less interesting because his story lacks the ruthless strikebreaking and exploitation of workers that scar the legacies of industrialists Andrew Carnegie (1835–1919) and Henry Clay Frick (1849–1919); the adventurousness of railroad magnate Robert F. Stockton (1795–1866); or the literary creations of Louis Bromfield (1896–1956), another famous Mansfield son whose farm has become a place of historic preservation. Frank Black's legacy is smaller than theirs: an elegant stable and riding hall surrounded by pasture in a small city

---

[†] John Baxter Black (1924–2014), historian and great-grandson of Frank Black, compiled the two-volume *A History of the Family of Mr. and Mrs. Frank Blymyer Black of Mansfield, Ohio*, in 1995. His diaries and papers are archived in the New York Public Library.

not known for beauty, one of its emblems a historic carousel in the middle of town.

While the city presses in upon the Raemelton Equestrian Center, the pastures and barns provide a respite from the relentless onrush of industrialism of which Ohio Brass was part. When I last visited (in 2022), the ancient maple and oak trees enabled me to imagine that I was in Ireland. I listened to the cadences of goldfinches, song sparrows, and field sparrows. Even if we are not conscious of the details, however, history reminds us of our heritage. The farm was established over a century ago (1918), and the equestrian center will soon celebrate its hundredth year (2029), still in use and available to the public as the founder envisioned.

Five

Time and the Stream

AT THE SOUTHERN END of my pasture, a small pond sustains a little community. The story goes that when the gas company dug a pipeline that crossed the property, it left a depression that subsequently filled with rainwater. Over the years, the area evolved through geotropism into a wetland, or "wet meadow," except in early spring, when the area expands into a pond. Evenings from late March to early October are filled with the music of spring peepers, green frogs, treefrogs, and bullfrogs. Dragonflies, especially the white tail and twelve-spot skipper, hover over lily pads and poise on the blossoms of bulrush, spike rush, and bur-reed and the red spines of cinnamon fern. They will fly quite close to me, while frogs and turtles, hearing my step, seeing a shadow, or feeling the presence of a noninhabitant, plop into the water from the bank, where sedge, rush, milkweed, and nettle thrive.

Tree swallows and red-winged blackbirds cling to broad-leaved cattails, the most abundant plant in the boggy area surrounding the pond. I put up a birdhouse for swallows, which will nest over water, but none ever chose to live there. For several years, a pair of Canada geese built their capacious home on a bluff that reached over the surface. After a brood hatched, goose and gander strutted along with their goslings—usually about seven—in a line. I tried to keep a respectful distance, but even so, if I stepped too close, their loud honking created an ear-splitting racket. A few times I have been able to observe the courtship behavior of geese facing each other while dipping their beaks repeatedly into the water. A family of white egrets once visited the dry ground above the pond, but I have not seen any since. Sandhill cranes, a threatened species in Ohio, sometimes investigate nesting locations in the pasture or surrounding fields while calling to each other with their distinctive rattle.

Morning is the best time, when the cloak of fog rises just as the sun emerges from the rim of the eastern hills. Watching it disappear into the brightness of day, I understand the ancient Shawnee belief that God walked in the early hours, concealed in the mist from human eyes. Larks and thrushes embodied the living spirits of departed ancestors, and lakes and streams listened to human prayer.

Sometimes I see a great blue heron stepping around the edge of the water, the *S* shape of his head and neck resembling a shepherd's crook. Eventually he lifts himself into the air on expansive gray wing-capes and sails over the fields, long legs stretched out behind, to land on the border of my neighbor's pond, about a hundred yards away, or farther on the banks of Honey Creek, about a tenth of a mile to the east. While numbers of Canada geese appear to have remained stable for three decades, I believe the population of herons has actually increased. Aldo Leopold described them in prophetic terms in "Marshland Elegy": "When we hear his call we hear no mere bird. We hear the trumpet in the orchestra of evolution. He is the symbol of our untamable past, of that incredible sweep of millennia which underlies and conditions the daily affairs of birds and men."[†] Their size and elegance inspired myth:

[†] Although Leopold refers to them as cranes, the birds he described were probably herons, as he further identified them with the colloquial name *red shitepoke,* a term for herons, which acquired a russet color in August. Because herons and cranes are long-legged, carnivorous wading birds, they are sometimes thought to belong to the same family, but herons fly with necks retracted and legs held out behind them. Cranes, however, fly with necks extended.

some indigenous groups believed they represented the spirits of sages; for the Greeks, herons served as messengers for Athena, goddess of wisdom; Buddhist mysticism associated them with purity; ancient Egyptians identified them with the sun god Ra and cyclical renewal, and the herons' raucous cry was thought to have announced the beginning of time. Their ancient genealogy reaches back to the Eocene (55 to 35 million years ago).

My neighbor's pond takes up about a quarter of an acre in a lower field; most of the time, the glassy surface appears dark gray, shimmering in sunlight or rippling with wind. It provides an early spring stopover for geese; mallards; and buffleheads, with their distinctive black and white feathers. Although he constructed nest boxes for wood ducks, I have never seen any taking up residence. Mist-shrouded in early morning, a row of tall, slender cottonwoods borders the southern edge. Members of the poplar family, they are not beautiful up close but from a distance create a vista like one of Poussin's idealized pastoral landscapes. In sunlight, their leaves shimmer in displays of bright and dark green.

Enhancing my wetland would attract more birds, but I do not want to disturb the painted turtles that dig their nests into the banks and bask in the long grass. Drainage ditches that flow along the township road and empty into Honey Creek make an ideal home for snapping turtles. Several times I have seen one occupying a rain-filled swale on the township road. With their wise, ponderous expressions, turtles and tortoises first appeared 230 million years ago, long before human beings, newcomers of only about 300,000 years. The strong current of the creek forms a highway for beavers, while noisy kingfishers dwell in the thick brambles.

April brings the opening of the marsh marigold in the pasture and later the white swamp mallow and yellow St. John's wort. Earliest flowers along the stream banks include bluebells and May apples. Dandelions, sometimes the bane of urban landscape designers, provide important early food for bees. A few weeks later, royal purple violets bloom profusely in the lawn and field north of the house, amid the lime green of early grass. They last about a month, when purple and white standing phlox create a spectacular show along the slopes near my stream and Honey Creek. Jerusalem artichoke grows on the drier upland side of the pond, its name a corruption of the Italian *girasole:* to turn to the sun. Canada white anemone and southern blue flag appear in the pasture in late May along with the white flowers of the common elderberry. In long grass I am likely to see the dragonfly called the green darner (which is more often turquoise) and iridescent, cobalt-colored damselflies called bluets, like an exquisite gem, barely more than an inch long. Perhaps to them we are shadows that float across the landscape.

Fed by 250 acres of watershed, the stream flows from a culvert beneath the county road, pools near the fence line, meanders alongside a steep slope, widens at a level place where bolder horses crossed, and cascades over large rocks to become a creek that runs between steep banks before emptying into the drainage ditches. Swamp willow, pussywillow, common elderberry, and grasses along the slopes help to prevent erosion as the water rises and falls with the seasons. Spring rains often cause the stream to overflow its banks, one year washing away so much soil that a new gully formed near the fence line. I had to replace one post that had been left hanging in midair, still attached to the wires. Some trees died in the inundation, but I do not cut down the dead trunks: they make ideal perches for hawks and homes for cavity-nesting birds. A red-tailed hawk we refer to as Herman often perches on the topmost point of a dead tree in the stream valley and surveys the territory with the acuteness of a sentinel. Reed canary grass, an invasive species, took over part of the shallower banks nearer the culvert but during the last two years has been less abundant. When pulled up and dried, its broad leaves create excellent garden mulch.

Feeder calves previously pastured on the place kept the hillside bare of trees before we took up residence. My horses would not climb steep slopes, so the vegetation thrived: first briars, multiflora rose, and wild blackberry. Year by year, the incline became a thicket and then a copse with a paw-paw tree and red maple as well as several oak, beech, white and pink dogwood, and locust. Finding multiflora rose conducive for their homes, sparrows shriek as I try to cut down some of the aggressive European hedgerow that springs back every year, creating in its thorny shadows a perfect home for wild cherry saplings. Although indigenous and useful for revegetation of despoiled land, wild cherry sprouts leaves that are poisonous to horses when dry. Wearing leather gloves and canvas coat and leggings, I have to forge my way into the thicket to cut the stems down. Lopping them off at ground level merely enables them to propagate elsewhere, sometimes far from the parent root. I tried to contain this many-headed Hydra by girdling, which prevents the plant's energy from descending into the soil as well as ascending into new branches, but without success.

One summer I left about two acres of my pasture unmown to allow butterflies and other pollinators to live there. Doing so did not increase the number I observed, but at a time when the monarch butterfly numbers were dwindling, I saw as many as in previous years. The first butterflies to emerge are the brown elfin; spring azure; and Baltimore checkerspot, with its distinctive black-and-white markings.

The populations of honeybees and bumblebees appears stable, but I estimate about 90 percent reduction in the number of fireflies over thirty years, due largely to habitat destruction; artificial lighting, and insecticides, especially neonicotinoids and organophosphates. Of more than two thousand species worldwide, about twenty-four live in Ohio, most commonly the eastern firefly, *Photinus pyralis,* the genus name that of a fourth-century heretical Christian bishop, the species appellation borrowed from a mythical fly born in fire.‡ During the 1990s, the pasture and field vibrated like galaxies on midsummer evenings, with num-

---

‡ Photinus of Sirmium (d. 376 AD) is believed to have denied the divinity of Christ as well as the preexistence of the Incarnation. His name (from Greek) means "light" or "radiance." *Pyralis* comes from the Latin for "fire"; hence, the fireflies' scientific name means "firelight."

bers greatest during the last week of June. Their habitat—moist, rotting vegetation—is threatened by wetland drainage, and artificial lighting disrupts reproduction, as they use bioluminescence to attract mates. Insecticides remain in soil, where firefly larvae live, for four to five years, longer in dry and cold climates. Firefly populations could recover, however, with protection for their ecosystems. We leave leaf litter beneath a copse of white pine, honey locust, eastern hemlock, maple, and walnut, but the insect populations continue to decrease.

When we first arrived, bluebirds appeared every day on the electric wires, white pine branches, and clothes poles, but with time they migrated, even though I mounted nest boxes. A pair took up residence a few years ago, and more subsequently returned, easily seen perching on fenceposts. Infrequently, a brown thrasher perches in view, but I have, unfortunately, never seen or heard a scarlet tanager on my place. Although they are shy and secretive, one year a pair of house wrens chose to build its twiggy nest in one of my bluebird boxes. I see and hear tree swallows but have not discovered where they nest.

Hummingbirds are ubiquitous spring and summer inhabitants. If I do not have my feeder out early enough, one is sure to light on the dining-room windowsill and tap its beak on the glass. Orioles, both the bright-orange northern, or Baltimore, and the subtler-hued orchard species, returned about ten years ago and have taken up residence ever since in a beech tree on a bank above the stream. Sometimes the orioles engage in an unusual practice of fluttering against the south windows on the first and second floors of the house with so much force I am concerned they might injure themselves. I have no idea what this behavior represents, but it ceases after a few days. Orioles raise their young quickly and migrate by mid-July.

Watching activity at the bird feeders, I observe both intolerance and coexistence. Orioles will drink together at the same feeder; hummingbirds tolerate orioles but chase away their own kind, squealing in indignation. On the north side, opposite the nectar feeders, seed-eaters engage in continuous social display. The resilient nonnative house sparrow (really a finch) appears in all seasons. Red-bellied woodpeckers, which have been migrating northward since the 1980s, are numerous all year, along with cardinals, robins, song sparrows, goldfinches, and field sparrows. Chipping sparrows live here in summer. Carolina and house wrens keep to themselves, mostly in bushes and shrubs. Red-bellied woodpeckers, the largest residents, chase away the smaller downy woodpeckers and sparrows and at the same time provide for the ground feeders, as they discard much seed in their greedy search for peanuts. Mourning doves puff out their feathers, trying without success to intimidate chipmunks. Starlings and grackles fly in, usually in flocks, and feed mostly in the grass. Although they don't stay long, they are even more aggressive than the red-bellies. The most frequent bullies are the red-winged blackbirds, which used to keep to the pasture but now spend much time at the feeders. Once I witnessed a standoff at the peanut feeder between a red-wing and a red-belly, which faced each other with beaks open; the red-wing emerged the victor. I witnessed a red-tailed hawk descend suddenly from the one of the white pines and swoop away, although I did not see whether it caught a songbird as it did so. Hawks are known to frequent bird feeders for easy hunting, although I have observed this strategy only once. Family members, however, display behavior that appears solicitous: sparrow mothers feed their fledged chicks even when they have grown nearly as large as the parent. One spring day, far too early for nesting or fledging, I observed a male cardinal feeding its adult mate.

Killdeer do not visit feeders and prefer camouflage to privacy. Nearly every year, a killdeer mother lays her speckled eggs on the driveway and valiantly defies any animal or person who ventures too close. I mark the nests with a surveyor's flag until the young hatch, usually in early summer.

While I rarely see barn owls, in early hours I have heard the hooting of the great horned and during evenings the rapid chatter of the common screech owl. Early one winter morning, I was awakened by the barred owl's *secundus* paeon followed by diamb ionic (short-long-short-short, short-long-short-long) hooting in my neighbor's pine trees. Kestrels are frequent visitors in the barn, loudly fluttering from one end to the other. Bats colonize the rafters—in large numbers, to judge from what they drop on the floor. Sometimes I have to rescue robins and gray catbirds that find their way into the granary but cannot figure their ways out.

In the lower story, barn and cliff swallows dominate, building their cup-shaped and igloo-shaped mud nests in the spring. Naked chicks sometimes fall to the sawdust on the floor; if they are alive, I return them to their homes, but every year some are lost. The mothers shriek when I walk into the barn, but they remain on their nests while I work right underneath them. Fledging begins in July and continues through August, when little, round, dark-blue heads with yellow beaks peer eagerly out over the edge. By the autumn equinox, adults and fledglings migrate, and the lower barn grows suddenly silent. Swallows repay me for their summer tenancies in the barn by scooping up insects on the wing, especially when I mow.

In 2021, for the first time, a pair of rock doves made a home in the rafters until about mid-May; loud beating of wings announced their displeasure when I invaded their space to throw down hay. That same spring, several pairs of least flycatchers nested somewhere near the barn and rested on fences and gates. Although they do not visit feeders, they seemed remarkably comfortable with people as they flew inside the barn and perched on wooden beams and even the handles of my wheelbarrow, letting me get within about four feet. The chicks fledged by mid-July. In subsequent years, I have seen the flycatchers on the pasture fence and heard their distinctive three-note calls, but they have not ventured into the barn again.

In the past two summers, mockingbirds have migrated northward from their southern homes, often nesting in multiflora rose. Due to climate change, they are expanding their range. Large birds, they are easy to identify by their white wing-patches, long tails, and erect stature. At fledging time, I observed them harassing one of the barn cats, diving quite close and finally chasing him away. In addition to their distinctive, varied melodies, they imitate the calls of other birds, remembering those borrowed notes for as long as seven years. Their scientific name, *Mimus polyglottos*, could refer to us, for we also mime the sounds we hear and speak many languages. Mockingbirds also share our tendencies to migrate for comfortable weather and make beautiful music out of tragedy: their trills delight even as their presence warns us of the most serious threat to the ecosystems we inhabit.

Gray squirrels and even a few red squirrels have made homes in the pines north of the house. Squirrels seem to limit their populations to one area, but the chipmunks have established extended families, larger in some years than others. To judge from their numbers, I estimate that they have an extensive underground network of tunnels. They scamper from trees to participate in the usufruct fallen from bird feeders and then to the concrete stoop, where they dig entrances to their underground bunkers. They connect these locations with what we call chipmunk paths, which become well-worn throughout the summer. They even extend across a field to a small patch of rough weeds, dead wood, and rocks. Rabbits, raccoons, and groundhogs also use that pile.

As evening darkens the lawn and field, night visitors creep stealthily closer—raccoons, possums, and sometimes skunks. In 2021, a family of white-tailed deer inhabited the neighbor's cornfield; in the evenings they came out of the cover and foraged along my riding area. We have counted as many as thirteen. When my neighbor plants soybeans, which leave no cover, they live in the woods near the creek. For many years, a doe hid her fawn in tall grass near the stream in my pasture, but after I kept cattle in 2019 and 2020, she did not return. When I owned hens, I sometimes spied red foxes in the field. Once I stepped outside the barn and surprised one, which apparently had not heard me, drinking from the horse bucket. Foxes frequent the place at night, as I find their tracks in the snow on my riding arena in winter and in mud during spring and summer.

One year, a family of raccoons occupied a den in the white pine windbreak north of the house. Unfortunately, one of the young was killed on the road. While they have not returned to the same den, they patrol the lawn after sundown. I kept the oriole and hummingbird feeders secured under large flower pots weighted down with heavy stones during the night, as raccoons and squirrels will raid them; the technique worked until recently when someone—I suspect a raccoon—figured out not only that he or she could remove the stones but also unscrew the feeders to drink the contents. Now I keep the feeders in a tub with a secure lid at night.

At midsummer, the cicada begin to sing. Bull thistle, ironweed, Shasta and oxeye daisy, Queen Ann's lace, and goldenrod create an impressionistic purple, white, and yellow display on the upper slopes of the pasture. Bulrushes and spike rush produce less impressive brown sprays, and orange tiger lilies and pink swamp milkweed open along the roadside, taking over the space where phlox had bloomed earlier. Bladderwort and bird's-foot trefoil grow partly concealed in tufts of grass, while white clover thrives, another favorite of the bees. After midsummer when the colorful zinnias open in the garden, I see the greatest profusion of butterflies, including American copper, Harris' checkerspot, black and orange pearl crescents, little wood satyr, wood nymph, eyed brown, painted lady, question mark, white and red admirals, silver-spotted skipper, and the swallowtails—tiger, eastern black, giant, and spicebush, the last being the rarest, although recently their populations appear to have increased.

In August and September, the slopes and roadsides are blue-purple with New York asters. Pink lady's thumb flourishes alongside the bright red berries of the bittersweet nightshade and the white flowers of the flat-topped aster, snake root, and bladderwort. At the streamside, yellow St. John's wort blooms along with blue vervain reaching on long stems and orange flowers of spotted touch-me-not, also called jewelweed, for the translucent stem and silvery aspect of the leaves in rain. In late summer, a mass of great lobelia dazzles with profusion of deep purple blossoms.

Autumn arrives with the change in the plumage of the goldfinches, the turning of a maple leaf at the end of August, or the warmth of sun that is not the heat of summer. Although increased temperatures have decreased the intensity of the display, the peak of the fall colors usually occurs on October 17, following at least one hard frost. In October, I see the Milbert's tortoiseshell, pearly eye, and buckeye butterflies. Starlings begin their elegant dancing when large flocks fly in formations called murmurations above the harvested soybean fields.

Old residents return in winter, including chickadees, white- and red-breasted nuthatches, white-crowned and white-throated sparrows, and tufted titmice. Conspicuously absent are the eastern meadowlarks that used to perch on my paddock fences, especially in January. Their numbers are dwindling mostly due to habitat loss, as they need large meadows in order to breed. Slate-colored juncos, with distinctive smoky black upper side and bright white breast, are said to be increasing, as they have adapted well to climate change. Nuthatches and chickadees are always in a hurry, taking what they want from the feeders and retreating to the safety of the trees so rapidly that even the woodpeckers have no chance to bully them. Cardinals, resident year-round, and robins feed more leisurely.

The farm appears to be a natural place but is not. Multiflora rose and reed canary grass invade hillside and stream. The pond itself resulted from installation of a pipeline, and the drainage ditches where snapping turtles live were constructed to carry water away from the township road. Every year, the process of freezing and thawing thrusts remnants of previous inhabitants from underground to the surface: rusty nails, pieces of wire, shards of glass. The pastures where cattle and horses graze and fields of corn, soybeans, and wheat were once dense forest inhabited by timber wolves, mountain lions, and grizzly bear.

Blood, as well as labor, nourished the soil, as the region provided the setting for skirmishes during the French and Indian Wars (1754–63). Reconstructed in 2013 as a historical site, the village of Greentown stood five miles away, founded in 1788 by a Tory from Connecticut and occupied by Shawnee, Delaware, and Mingo people. In 1812, when rumors of alliances between the British and native people caused settlers to fear renewed hostilities, the inhabitants moved to the Mansfield Blockhouse for their safety. White settlers then plundered and burned the village. When the Reverend James Copus, who had assured residents that their property would be respected, and his family were subsequently murdered, settlers retaliated by killing all Shawnee who remained in the area.

Still, the same wind that brought the seasons to natives and settlers blows over the fields. "Time is but the stream I go a-fishing in. . . . Its thin current slides away, but eternity remains," Henry David Thoreau recorded in *Walden.* Rabindranath Tagore (1861–1941) wrote in *Gitanjali,* the "stream of life that runs through my veins night and day runs through the world and dances in rhythmic measures." The wild batters at our windows, feasts on our gardens, tunnels beneath our buildings, and springs up along our fence lines, for the most part ignoring us, for all our furious history and our grand philosophies.

Six

The Kreutzer Sonata

ONE DEFINITION OF *a truly natural place* is a location where a person can hear no human-created sound for fifteen minutes. According to that description, there are few natural places in Ohio. We live in a very noisy environment, which has become increasingly loud over the last decades because of industry, transportation, amplification, and power tools—until even in rural areas the grating mechanical cacophony is inescapable.

Nature preserves, remote forests, and mountains are all subject to the nauseating groan of airliners and the shrill whine of small planes. The same racket that permeates urban life penetrates the countryside and parks, which used to provide refuge from mechanical sound. Even during the few moments that are free of automobile and airplane noise, the grating of engines is audible in nearly every location in the aftermath of the Industrial Revolution. Omnipresent auditory clamor destroys or at least decreases the quality of experience. Pointing out that it is useless to launch a canoe among the whine of motorized watercraft, Aldo Leopold asserts in *A Sand County Almanac* (1948) that he regards the enjoyment of natural places to be a human right. With so much of our land devoted to paved roads, surely we can designate the parks and rural areas as places free of the continuous roar of automobiles, motorboats, and airplanes.

An atmosphere of noise makes work increasingly difficult. No task however large is unwelcome when I have the song of birds, music of insects, and rustle of wind in leaves. Any task however small is a chore with the grinding of the internal combustion engine or screeching of amplified music. On one occasion while I was cutting weeds, a flock of Canada geese flew overhead, but I could not hear the swishing of their wings or even their normally vociferous honking because of the revving engine of a car speeding up the county road.

Anthropogenic noise creates problems for not only human communities but also nonhuman ecosystems. Birdsong is said to be territorial, but birdcalls are about reproduction, and excessive discord has been shown to interfere with mating cycles in some species, according to studies conducted by biologists at the California Polytechnic State University (2020), funded by the National Science Foundation, and published in *Nature*. Ecologists at Boise State University (2017) found that the continuous roar of natural-gas compressor stations decreases the hunting abilities of the northern saw-whet owl, which uses its superior sense of hearing to detect its prey—rodents scampering under snow or forest debris. White-crowned sparrows must alter the pitch and length of their songs to be audible above human-created racket. Studies conducted in southern Idaho revealed that when traffic increased on a nearby highway, a third of migratory birds avoided a ridge that had been one of their traditional feeding grounds, even though the area was remote from human residential populations; birds that did remain failed to put on the weight needed to continue their migration.

Research by scientists at California Polytechnic State University in 2017 revealed that compressor noise discouraged scrub jays from feeding in areas in northwestern New Mexico where they are important in perpetuating the pinyon pine forests that provide habitat for many wildlife species. The jays bury fallen seeds for winter fodder, but those the birds fail to recover germinate into new seedlings. The forest dwindled in the acoustic zone of the compressor stations but flourished in quieter locations. Collaborative research (2018) by scientists from Cal Poly, the University of Colorado–Boulder, and the Florida Museum of Natural History (Gainsville) on western bluebirds, mountain bluebirds, and ash-throated flycatchers suggests that human-created noise can interfere with birds' ability to detect the presence of predators or locate food. Where noise levels were highest, researchers found greater stress in adult birds, reduced feather growth and body size in chicks, and lower hatching rates, especially in western bluebirds.

Even in the nineteenth century, Henry David Thoreau complained, in *Walden*, about the noise of the railroad. After train cars went by, his meditations were interrupted only by the rattle of a carriage or team on the distant highway. He liked, however, the ringing of bells from neighboring villages, which made "natural melody, worth importing into the wilderness." Distant sounds produced one effect, "a vibration of the universal lyre," as atmosphere made a faraway ridge more interesting "by the azure tint it imparts." The lowing of a cow sounded pleasant as the "natural music" of minstrels and became "one articulation of Nature." He described some natural sounds in anthropomorphic ways: the whip-poor-wills chanted "vespers" at sunset, and "doleful" strains of screen owls represented "the stark twilight and unsatisfied thoughts which all have." The shore of Walden rang with bullfrogs, "sturdy spirits of ancient wine-bibbers and wassailers." By morning, "a different race of creatures awakes to express the meaning of Nature there."

When I first visited Walden in 1971, it was September, and I was the only person walking to the site where Thoreau's cabin had stood. A solitary canoeist wearing a large, floppy hat paddled the still water. (I think it was Thoreau's ghost; friends insisted that I had been hallucinating.) Today, during the summer, the Walden shore is inhabited by swimmers shouting and playing, and portable bathhouses stand sentinel on the sand. A parking lot accommodates the many tourists who come to see a replica of the cabin, which, fortunately, was built close to the entrance to the woods, I suspect in order to keep people from trampling the undergrowth on the forest floor.

No doubt sounds related to farming can be intolerable to many, such as cattle bellowing, sheep and goats bleating, dogs barking, and horses whinnying. Tractors and combines roar and whir loudly, although their use is limited to certain times such as planting, cultivating, and harvesting. In 2021, after residents in France complained about rural noise, a law was passed protecting the sounds and smells of the country as "heritage." The initial case stemmed from complaints from urban dwellers recently residing in the countryside of Saint-Pierre-d'Oléron who objected to the early morning crowing of Maurice the rooster, owned by Corinne Iesseau. Minister of Rural Life Joël Giraud stated that there had been an increased number of conflicts between longtime rural residents and new arrivals from the city, most of whom visited the town only on holiday. Multinational news outlets carried the story, including CNN, *Marketplace*, *Travel & Leisure*, the *Guardian*, *New York Times*, and *India Times*. With law on his side, Maurice continued to crow until his death.

I. Voices

Anthropogenic noise includes vocal stimuli whether welcome or unwelcome, joyful or angry, spontaneous or amplified.

In an article published in the August 1, 2022, *Atlantic Monthly*, author Xochitl Gonzalez objected to rules against noise in her college town (Providence, Rhode Island, unidentified in the essay), calling them "oppressive." In "Why Do Rich People Love Quiet?" subtitled "The Sound of Gentrification Is silence," she described the noise regulations of the quiet, wealthy, and mostly white campus of Brown University as evidence of classism and racism. She wrote, "It took me years to understand that, in demanding my friends and I quiet down, these students were implying that their comfort superseded our joy. . . . Some white students resented that we self-segregated. What they didn't understand was that we just wanted to be around people in places where nobody told us to shush."

Gonzalez found the same phenomenon upon her return home to Brooklyn after college: her community was now filled with people who wanted quiet. Accusing the new residents of the same prejudice, she concluded, "Now the foreigners had come to my shores, with no intention of leaving. And they were demanding that the rest of us change to make them more comfortable." She did not convey what her attitude would have been had she been referred to as a "foreigner" in her college town, but she admitted sometimes wanting diminished distractions, so long as the rules were on her terms: "I find many city noises nerve-racking and annoying: jackhammers doing street maintenance, the beeping of reversing trucks, cars honking for no good reason. Yet these noises account for a small minority of all noise complaints. Nearly 60 *percent of recent grievances* center on what I'd consider lifestyle choices: music and parties and people talking loudly. But one person's loud is another person's expression of joy."

On the same date, author Nate Hochman answered, in his rebuttal in the *National Review* online:

> What is there to say about an essay like this? Some arguments are too absurd to address at length; by quibbling with every dubious line, one is taking the premise more seriously than it deserves. But two things stand out: First, the hilariously racist assumption that undergirds Gonzalez's piece—that minorities are, as a totalizing generalization, *loud*. (Has she spent much time in New York's Asian neighborhoods?) And second, the insistence that *every* community should be loud to validate Gonzalez and her friends. Ironically, this is the inverse of what she accuses her white classmates of: Gonzalez resents that "their comfort superseded our joy." In

response, she insists that *her* preferred mode of communication supersede *theirs*.

The differing editorial perspectives of these publications underscores the fact that the debate on noise pollution transcends political identification.

I suspect that Gonzalez would have found fault had her white colleagues and neighbors imposed segregation on her and her friends in order to have quiet, yet she eagerly insisted on her right to inflict noise on those who did not want it. Apparently no one in her group thought of expressing their joy in some location where people outside her crowd (and she *did* exclude those she perceived as other) would not be inconvenienced—soundproof rooms, auditoriums, stadiums, or rented halls, for example. Her article was notably short on details about where and how she and her friends chose to celebrate their culture. She also neglected to inform readers of *when* her group engaged in vocal exuberance: people may be more accommodating during late afternoons and on holidays than during the night and early morning. On college campuses, finding quiet places to study can be challenging, and even libraries no longer provide refuge from endless discord. In residential neighborhoods, people who spend most of their time working feel entitled to inhabit an environment of their own choosing during the limited time they have to themselves.

Irritation caused by loud voices is not new. In his essay "On Noise," Spanish essayist Seneca the Younger (3–65 AD), who lived for a time above a bathhouse, described in his humorous way the athletes' grunting as they lifted weights, masseuses' pummeling of bodies, ball players' shouting as they kept score, divers' splashing, and others' singing and brawling. He also complained about noise from the street: piercing voices of peddlers calling out their wares, rattling of horsedrawn vehicles, banging of carpenters, and racket of horn and flute players. Voices were more distracting than discordant sound, he stated aphoristically, because they caught the unwary hearers' attention more readily, and intermittent noise was more unnerving than that which was continuous. Claiming that the meditative person must have "quiet within," Seneca antithetically denied the existence of "peaceful stillness" because the individual experiences "commotion within": "The temperament that starts at the sound of a voice or chance noise in general is an unstable one and one that has yet to attain inward detachment. It has an element of uneasiness in it, and an element of rooted fear that makes a man a prey to anxiety." The quick-witted rhetorician, nevertheless, escaped from the din by moving away from the bathhouse and outside of the town.

In 44 BC, just before he was assassinated, none other than Julius Caesar enacted the first regulation against hubbub: "No wheeled vehicle whatsoever will be allowed within the precincts of the city, from sunrise until the hour before dark." Earlier, in the sixth century BC, the Council of Sybaris, a Greek colony in the Aegean, had ruled that potters, tinsmiths, and other tradesmen must live outside the city walls because of the tumult of their professions. The council also barred roosters from living inside the town.

II. Music

Music figures in many notable literary works in which authors are limited to onomatopoeia and synesthesia in order to create sound. James Joyce (1882–1941) described songs in the "Sirens" chapter of *Ulysses* (1922) and demonstrated poignantly the role of music and memory in "The Dead" (1907). James Baldwin (1924–1987) put the reader into the mind of the musician-composer of a jazz piece in "Sonny's Blues" (1957), after the first-person narrator states that all he knows about music is that most people never really hear it.

In Leo Tolstoy's famous novella "The Kreutzer Sonata" (1889), however, music becomes a culprit. The protagonist, Pozdnyshev, confides to the narrator, a fellow-traveler in a train carriage, that he murdered his wife, ostensibly because of adultery but really because he hated his own lascivious nature. Acquitted because of her proven infidelity, he is nevertheless conscience-stricken and searches for people sympathetic enough to listen to his arguments against sex and marriage. His wife's lover having been a violinist, Pozdnyshev articulates the significance of music to everyday life, impressing on his hearer the transformative role that sound plays in profound experience:

> They say music exalts the soul. Nonsense, it is not true! It has an effect, an awful effect—I am speaking of myself—but not of an exalting kind. It has neither an exalting nor a debasing effect but it produces agitation. How can I put it? Music makes me forget myself, my real position; it transports me to some other position not my own. Under the influence of music it seems to me that I feel what I do not really feel, that I understand what I do not understand, that I can do what I cannot do

Tolstoy's protagonist suffers under the influence of music while most listeners would probably appreciate what he finds oppressive: Beethoven's *Kreutzer Sonata* (1804) is one of his most beloved creations.

William James (1842) wrote, "I don't sing because I am happy; I'm happy because I sing." Many listeners would say that their favorite music puts them into a better frame of mind, perhaps the way Beethoven's "Ode to Joy" (1824) encourages exultation and a feeling of oneness with humankind, however brief, and Samuel Barber's "Adagio for Strings" (1936), sometimes called "the saddest music ever written," creates feelings of the inevitability of death and poignancy of loss. The marches played at the funeral of Queen Elizabeth II (September 19, 2022) inspired wistfulness at the end of an era as well as optimism for a new beginning.

Perhaps those who write that music deepens the perception are describing the process of learning to listen, as we learn to see more clearly when we undertake to know more about what we perceive. Woods are nothing but upright trunks until we learn what kinds of trees we are gazing at, how old they are, and what they can tell us about the history of the place where we are walking. Similarly, we know more about a place when we recognize the distinctive calls of the resident birds and insects.

Music, perhaps more than any other form of art, represents its time. Early musical instruments, such as the recorder, sackbut, wooden flute, cornet, mandolin, and viola da gamba mimic natural sounds—such as birds singing, frogs croaking, and insects chirping—and so remind listeners of a pond in springtime. Eighteenth-century compositions reflect the era's emphasis on balance and harmony. Rock music and heavy metal, especially when amplified, often imitate mechanical pandemonium like the assault of revving engines.

Do not believe that this essay is about good or bad taste in music. My concern is that our environment envelops us with so much discord that we can no longer really listen to anything, whether we want to or not. Duke Ellington's dictum that "If it sounds good, it is good" leaves us with the unanswered question of what "sounds good." My own variation of Ellington's notion is "Good music is music I want to hear; bad music is music I don't want to hear." The same is true about all auditory stimuli—musical, conversational, mechanical, or natural.

Researchers hypothesize that listening to music causes the brain to release dopamine, a mood elevator, and that studying music enhances ability to learn in fields like mathematics or law. Published work does not always include information on what musical genre produces these results. Experiments suggest that joggers and runners are able to go farther and faster while listening to music. Almost everyone likes some music, but even dedicated aficionados voice their intense dislike of types that differ from their own favorites; one acquaintance quipped that he would rather visit the dentist than attend an opera.

In his reactionary book *The Closing of the American Mind*, classicist Allan Bloom (1930–1992) associated rock music with loss of intellect and went on to say that most young people who "recover" from their affinity for it are nevertheless "deaf," by which I assume he meant they have lost their ability to appreciate what he considered good music. Philosopher Theodore Adorno (1903–1969) also criticized popular music as "standardized" and beneath the intellect of those capable of appreciating true art ("On Popular Music"). My own acquaintance with music-lovers puts the lie to both these assertions: some of the best minds I have known appreciate popular music, and some who grew up listening to rock do not display diminished capacity to think nor to appreciate classical music or any other form of art.

I do not know much about music, but I suspect that knowing how to listen enhances enjoyment. Each generation produces its own distinct popular genre, essential when we are young. As an adolescent, I listened to rock songs as avidly as anyone else but nonetheless favored classical music, my predilections perhaps having evolved from growing up in a religious tradition in which hymns were set to the compositions of Mozart, Bach, Beethoven, Brahms, and Sibelius, among others. Early favorites included Beethoven and Mozart, although now my taste inclines to the Baroque in part because it does *not* create its own mood, especially Bach, Handel, Vivaldi, and Purcell. When driving, however, I sometimes insert my Creedence Clearwater Revival CD into the player and turn up the volume. Since the windows are closed, I burden no one else with my cultural peculiarities.

In "To a Skylark," Percy Bysshe Shelley identifies the irony that "our sweetest songs are those that tell of saddest thought," that art (music or poetry, in this case) enables listeners to achieve greater depth of feeling. Those of us who are very sensitive to sound may have a different reaction. Listening to my favorite composers has not made me a better thinker or enabled me to sympathize or empathize more deeply. I find all music, including my favorites, distracting when I want to concentrate or read. Those times when most attention is required—studying a difficult subject or writing—demand most quiet. Singing is the most detrimental to thought, especially to the creation or reading of poetry, which has its own rhythm and is interrupted by any kind of music external to it. Why proprietors of the few bookstores we have left find it necessary to provide background auditory stimuli—even with classical music—while customers browse their shelves is beyond my comprehension. Nothing in common life impedes intellectual activity like simplistic but mnemonically effective songs, especially advertising jingles designed to assault consciousness with repetitive inanity.

The pervasive soundtrack in grocery and clothing stores reflects the merchants' intention to persuade people to feel good and buy as much unnecessary merchandise as possible. Even managers of hardware stores force this torture on customers. The effect on me is a desire to tear the speakers out of the ceiling, and only the penalties for vandalism and lack of knowledge about electronics prevent my doing so. The result is that I end up buying as little as possible so as to get out of the premises with all possible dispatch.

Storekeepers' motivation, however, cannot explain the omnipresent "mood music" in places where customers and clients are not "shopping": offices, lobbies, filling stations, and examination rooms of physicians, dentists, and veterinarians. We who do not want to listen to someone else's artistic choices believe we should have the right to silence just as others have the right to enjoy what they want to hear. In the days of MP3, headphones, and earbuds—some of the most wonderful inventions of the modern age, along with the television mute button—I do not know why those of us who want silence and those who want music cannot both have our wish.

I am not referring to *amusia,* a condition that prevents people from hearing music the way most do; *misophonia,* sensitivity to certain sounds, such as people chewing or clearing their throats; musical *anhedonia,* which is apathy to music; or *phonophobia,* fear of certain sounds. What I am describing may be called *hyperacusis,* or sensitivity to environmental sounds that most people find "normal." Depending on the study, sounds over 50–70 decibels are considered "loud." Noise between those thresholds for prolonged periods of time can damage hearing; sounds over 120 decibels cause immediate harm. Decibel level, however, is not the only measurement relevant to a study of noise and quality of life: pitch, vibration, intensity, and length of time are all factors in evaluating what is bearable and what is not.

Particularly nerve-racking are the recordings assigned to the telephone connection when one is on some interminable hold and the screaming that must be endured in airport corridors and gate areas; I welcome the internal roar of airline engines after the screeching referred to as "boarding music." When I complain to flight attendants about it, the most frequent answer is that all airlines provide boarding music, and if I don't like it I shouldn't fly. This is a cogent argument, and I travel by air as little as possible.

People who claim they have the right to make as much noise as they want on their own property seem to be unaware that sound, like air and water, respects no boundaries. Twice in the thirty years I have lived in Ashland County, I have had neighbors play loud music outside, one four miles away where the owner installed an auditorium-sized sound system inside an old hen house and one six miles distant where the owner hired a live band to entertain friends at his birthday party. After I reported the first incident to the county sheriff, the music stopped; I later learned that several other neighbors had been disturbed by the noise. When I complained about the second, the birthday man said he was from Elyria and had bought land "where nobody lives" in order to escape the opprobrium of urban neighbors. (As of 2022, Green Township in Ashland County has a population of 3666, but apparently we do not count as residents.) I suggested that he close the doors to the barn occupied by the band; his reply was that the music would not sound right if confined. I explained that in view of the specialness of the day I would not report him that time but would if it ever happened again. It did not.

I wish every problem could be so easily solved.

III. Engines

When we first moved, in 1993, to our farm in northeast Ohio, the county road was four feet narrower than it is today and nearly devoid of traffic. A few cars, trucks, motorcycles, bicycles, and the occasional Amish buggy passed in a day. Vehicles were so infrequent that we sometimes remarked when they went by. In the 1990s, at a meeting of people devoted to farmland preservation, a zoning commissioner stated that in two decades traffic would increase twenty-fold. I do not remember when county officials first widened the road and sometime later widened it again. A few years ago, they installed guardrails along steep embankments and speed limits on curves although there had been only one rollover accident on that road: two men were killed when the driver lost control of his pickup truck as he swerved close to a mailbox that his companion was attempting to smash with a baseball bat. Two decades were not long enough, however, as it turned out. Today, traffic has increased more than the zoning commissioner warned, and since the pandemic restrictions in April 2020, increased still more although the population of the county has not grown commensurately. Sound travels farther in the country than in the city: I can hear big trucks and SUVs a half mile from my place, long before they are visible.

Once every May, a great confluence of motorcycles races southward toward the Mohican Park for their annual rally. I am grateful that they do not come to the park en masse more often, although I cannot understand why bikers want to navigate those steep, twisting roads, engines drowning out the natural sounds everyone else goes there to enjoy; instead, I suggest that they should stage their rallies in the neighborhoods of the CEOs of companies that manufacture motorcycles so that the creators of this ear-splitting din are the ones to endure life with the monster they have made.

Just as traffic noise on our county road has increased geometrically in recent years, so has the incidence of airliners and small planes. For twenty years, I saw but never heard the commercial craft, because their flight patterns took them out of our auditory sphere. Small planes were so few that I forgot they existed. During times when the United States was involved in some military action, once or twice a group of four to five wide-bodied propeller-driven military planes flew in formation, usually from northeast to southwest, low enough so that their grating rumble pervaded the entire environment, and their vibrations could be felt on the ground. Just as with traffic noise, however, the number of airliners flying lower increased in 2020, along with numbers of small planes. When I enquired of officials at Cleveland-Hopkins Airport about the change, I was directed to an office for noise complaints and told by a very sympathetic man that in recent years, the Global Positioning System has enabled pilots to follow the same routes between points, rather than several, as in the days of radar; those who live under these routes will experience more noise. The increase in small planes has to do with utility companies employing larger numbers of them instead of trucks for inspection, state highway patrols for monitoring, private owners for hobby flying, and companies taking people on skydiving excursions. Beyond licensing of pilots, few regulations exist for use of these aircraft.

Agricultural planes fly over my farm infrequently, but when they do, they make twenty or more passes, zooming as low as a hundred feet over my house and barn, engines roaring at over 120 decibels. No longer called "crop dusters," they are now "aerial applicators" because they spread cover-crop seeds and liquid rather than powdered herbicides or insecticides. Aerial seeding and weed control, while more expensive than ground seeding with tractors, avoids issues of soil compaction and allows the process to be completed in less time. These small planes must fly no lower than a thousand feet and "exercise maximum caution over congested areas" but may be operated below five hundred feet over "persons, vessels, vehicles, and structures" in rural areas "if no hazard to people or property is created," according to a blog titled *Aircraft Compare,* and *must* spray at an altitude below five hundred feet in order to avoid contact with vegetation other than that intended for spraying; in order to do so they may go as low as the tops of tall trees in their approach. Over the fields they skim the ground as close as ten feet. The first time I saw one of these "aerial applicators" approaching my land, I ran for cover, as the Great Waldo Pepper appeared to be heading directly for the barn.

Noise is not the only problem with these aircraft: while the National Transportation Safety Board claims that aerial-application pilots are well-trained, it recorded sixty-seven accidents in 2017, involving seven fatalities. The years 2014–17 recorded an average of eleven fatalities annually, not only to pilots but also to people on the ground. Other types of small planes aiming for local airports sometimes crash into buildings. Although no occupants were home in November 2015 when a Hawker 700 struck an apartment building in Akron, four residences were incinerated. The families lost most or all of their possessions, and their neighbors had to live with smoke and debris during the clean-up. Officials of the Florida real estate company that owned the plane issued a statement expressing sympathy for the families of the nine people in the plane who died; they made no apologies to the residents of the building, and they included no assurances that the company would try to prevent any such future occurrence. Near Kidron in Wayne County in January 2019, two pilots died when a seventy-six-year-old DC3 crashed into a front yard, pulling down power lines but missing the house, which was occupied at the time. Not thinking of his own safety, the owner (who later described himself as "blessed") grabbed blankets and ran outside to try to pull any survivors from the burning wreckage. There were none.

In Ashland County's Soil and Water Conservation District's (SWCD) spring newsletter for 2021, the agency advertised cost-sharing incentives for countywide aerial seeding of cover crops, which are important in improving agricultural productivity, soil health, and erosion control. When I contacted the SWCD to ask that the planes not fly directly over my house and barn, the affable receptionist named a company in Knox County that had been hired to do the seeding and assured me that there would be no problem, as their pilots were well trained. I replied that while there was no problem for them, there was for me and asked that I be notified before aerial seeding begins. She responded that the SWCD alerts only the local police, but when I called the Highway Patrol about the noise and danger of aerial applicators, an officer told me he knew nothing about the issue and that I should take down the plane's identification number and contact the company with my complaint, thus creating the "perfect circle" of shifting responsibility: airplane identification numbers are usually not visible from the ground.

All sizes of aircraft ruin the experience for anyone trying to enjoy a hike. If we go deeply enough into the forest we may be able to escape even the roar of traffic, but planes can go anywhere to destroy peace of mind, and their rumble can be heard over forty thousand acres. Hiking in Zaleski Forest in southern Ohio, I once felt as if I were in London in 1941 because a small plane circled the woods for close to an hour. After that, I limited hikes to cloudy days when there were fewer light aircraft flying. Reliance on cloudiness is no longer a solution to the problem, however, as advances in instrumentation enable contemporary pilots to overcome visibility issues.

When I was riding at Malabar Farm recently, the majority of the time the quiet was shattered by the whine of small planes. These aircraft at a thousand feet of altitude produce about seventy decibels of noise to someone on the ground, but the shrillness of the engine is more disturbing than volume. A student of mine once described riding horses with his friends for three days into the heart of Yellowstone National Park only to be plagued by the roar of small planes circling the canyons and forests in order to entertain tourists, even though most of the famous geysers and hot springs that make up the principal attractions of Yellowstone are close to the entrance.

IV. Recitative

Those who are not sensitive to noise deride those who are because they cannot imagine being offended by it, yet most people are very sensitive to unpleasant smells and demand that laws be passed to regulate them. Sound is related to smell in that they are the two senses for which stimuli cannot be controlled. We may look away from something unsightly, refrain from touching something offensive, and refuse to taste what we suspect is unpalatable, but we cannot escape the omnipresence of the auditory or olfactory. Even plugging the ears cannot block out all sound, as vibrations also enter the brain through nasal passages and bones of the skull. No doubt the acute hearing ability of human beings stems from some survival mechanism.

Campaigns to reduce noise can be compared to those waged by nonsmokers against use of tobacco in public. Years in the making, rules and then laws required that it be limited to a few places. In the 1950s, medical panels first articulated the danger of nicotine; it was the decade of the 1970s, however, that saw the first rules against smoking in public places, because of irrefutable data involving the health hazards of secondhand smoke. People now take these rules for granted, but many of us who hated cigarette smoke and lived before antismoking laws were enacted rejoice that they are enforced and most smokers comply. Today, even locations set aside for smoking are restricted, and smokers must be twenty feet or more from the entrances to buildings. If we can recognize the dangers of secondhand smoke, perhaps we can learn to acknowledge the well-documented effects of prolonged noise on health, including increased stress that leads to anxiety, depression, inability to concentrate, high blood pressure, cardiovascular disease, loss of productivity, changes in brain chemistry, drug use, hearing loss, and accidents. "Secondhand noise is really a civil rights issue," says Les Blomberg, executive director of the Noise Pollution Clearinghouse, an anti-noise advocacy group based in Chapel Hill, North Carolina. "Like secondhand smoke, it's put into the environment without people's consent and then has effects on them that they don't have any control over."

Lawmakers have known for a long time that excessive noise is a serious issue. The federal Noise Control Act of 1972 created an Office of Noise Abatement and Control (ONAC). Although the law remained in place, it was defunded in 1982, during the Reagan administration, so that its power was reduced to nothing. In February 1997, Democratic representative Nita Lowey from New York City's Eighteenth District proposed House Bill 536, known as the "Quiet Communities Act," designed to refund ONAC. With forty-five Democratic and ten Republican cosponsors, the bill was referred to the Commerce Committee, which referred it to the Transportation and Infrastructure Committee, which referred it to the Subcommittee on Aviation. The bill never received a vote. The Quiet Skies Caucus, including forty-four Democratic and one Republican member of Congress, and the National Quiet Skies Coalition were subsequently formed to support communities that felt the negative impact of the Federal Aviation Administration's NextGen air traffic modernization plan, begun in 2007, which left many people directly under flight paths of low-flying aircraft.

According to an organization called Noise Free America, the auto and entertainment industries have for a long time employed lobbyists to impede legislation that would protect the public from noise. The National Business Aviation Association and Aircraft Owners and Pilots Association oppose regulation of airline noise, in particular bills creating more local control, such as one proposed in 2020 by Representative Joe Neguse from Colorado and SB 7493A passed by the New York State Assembly on June 3, 2022, that would allow individuals to sue pilots and aviation companies for noise pollution.

The Ohio Environmental Council aided in the effort to convince Republican governor Mike DeWine (no believer in regulation) to eliminate the previous administration's plan (that of Republican governor John Kasich) to allow motorsports on lakes in state parks. Doing so would have effectively destroyed the experience for those who want to enjoy the natural sounds they have a right to expect in parks and preserves.

Small engines as well as large ones contribute to excessive noise. In 2018, the city council of Washington, DC, passed the Leaf Blower Regulation Amendment Act, which prohibited the use of gasoline-powered leaf blowers after January of 2022. Residents and landscaping companies can receive rebates for switching to much quieter electric leaf blowers. The act resulted from community organizing begun in 2015 by James Fallows, a writer for the *Atlantic,* who objected to the incessant roaring from the two-stroke engines that run at about 100 decibels. Like the targets of Xochitl Gonzalez's opprobrium, Fallows received criticism for focusing on a problem affecting only the "privileged," as though he and like-minded community members were not citizens as much as anyone else. Air pollution from these engines affects everyone, however, as well as noise pollution. The California Air Resources Board compiled data that shows that gasoline-powered leaf blowers, generators, and lawn mowers affect air quality more than the state's more than 30 million cars. Consequently, the California state legislature passed a law that ends the sale of these small engines by 2024 and includes $30 million for purchase of zero-emission power tools. While not restricting the use of gasoline-driven small engines, the bill is intended to reduce emissions by retiring 93 percent of them by 2035.

Technology, creator of much excessive noise, can supply the remedy if people possess the will. The Noise Free America website proposes some measures that can be taken to reduce the constant din of traffic, including enforcing laws that prohibit owners from tampering with the exhaust systems of their vehicles, especially motorcycles. While doing so is illegal, violators are seldom cited or fined. Turbofan engines mounted above the wings of airplanes rather than turbojet engines below the wings and a new design called noise-reducing chevrons can be effective, and engineers and civic groups nationwide are working to mitigate engine noise, but it will be a long wait before all airline fleets are replaced with this advanced technology. While newer aircraft are quieter than older ones, overall flight noise is increased because there are more airplanes. Environmentalists suggest that a nationwide system of high-speed electric trains, such as those in Japan and France, would drastically reduce both air and noise pollution. Traffic-free pedestrian zones served by trams and underground transportation improve urban environments. It would be easy to eliminate background noise in shops, offices, airport lobbies, and outdoor locations except for special occasions like holidays or street fairs. Indoor stadiums could be constructed so that motorcyclists, auto racers, and their fans can deafen themselves without driving others to distraction. Urban zones could be designated for outdoor performances or civic celebrations. Even the Harley-Davidson company has recently developed an electric motorcycle. One way to lessen the roar of traffic is to install "quiet" road surfaces, because much of the loud sound is caused not by engines but the rumble of tires on pavement. Four categories currently developed have been tested in Virginia, Arizona, and Washington State: fine-graded rather than dense surfaces; open-graded porous mix; stone-matrix; and rubberized asphalt, which contains fragments of recycled tires.

In *Walking the Flatlands: The Rural Landscape of the Lower Sacramento Valley,* Mike Madison, an orchardist in Yolo County, California, describes the need to listen versus the inescapability of airplane noise, claiming that rural landscapes are not valued and thus not protected. Littering is a misdemeanor, although one that is difficult to enforce; efforts are made, however, to mitigate or clean up the ubiquitous plastic bottles, cigarette butts, aluminum cans, and pizza boxes that line our roadways. The smell of factories or concentrated animal feedlots causes uproar from residential communities, and if people are lucky or wealthy, zoning restricts it. People have even identified light pollution, which keeps us (often against our will) from seeing constellations that were once visible from the earth. Natural sounds, however, are not privileged, because too few people are even capable of hearing them. We cannot really listen to anything because of the incessant groan of industrialism.

Madison demonstrates the importance of considering the auditory environment as much as the visual: "In not hearing what one hears, one chooses to be less than alert, less than fully awake, a little bit dead.... [I]n my twenties I worked on a botanical survey in the remotest parts of the western Amazon. There were no engines to be heard there, or other extraneous noises. Every sound was meaningful, and I learned to be attentive." One way to pay attention is to use all senses as did our remote ancestors, who knew the importance of natural sounds. As temperature, wind direction, rainfall, spring blossoms, and fog sometimes told people the right time for planting or harvesting, sounds also guided and informed. People knew how to judge distances—to water for example—by listening to the song of insects and birds. Some Inuit people knew when to move their dwellings because they recognized the cracking of glacial ice that occurred just before avalanches.

Restricting mechanical noise would make cities more livable and thus partially solve the problem of farmland lost to suburbanization. I have never heard anyone complain about too much peace. We might one day become free enough to demand that the right to quiet is inalienable. We might even become intelligent enough to recognize the right of the auditory biosphere to exist as it was meant to be and find ourselves listening to the sounds of the universal lyre.

Seven

Walking the Trash Line

EVERY FEW MONTHS (or weeks, in the summer) I depart on an expedition to collect trash along the county road that forms the border of the western edge of my land. Initial resentment at the people who throw their rubbish on the ground eventually gave way to curiosity not only about what they discard but also why they feel entitled to deposit their waste on someone else's property. I get to know them through what they leave behind as anthropologists discover facts about ancient civilizations by digging up the detritus of the past—not only material objects and how they were used but what those objects say about attitudes, expectations, and beliefs.

A high school classmate of mine who lived near my early home in Jefferson County used to pick up her family's evening newspaper, the Steubenville *Herald Star,* from a line of receptacles and mailboxes that stood on the other side of US Route 22 from the graveled lane that led to our houses. As we trudged up the hill from the school bus stop, she tore the paper cover off and threw the pieces onto the ground. When I objected and retrieved them, she continued to discard the paper. When I asked her to hand me the pieces, she would not. Why she was unwilling to wait until she arrived at home, a mere five minutes away, to drop the wrapping into a wastebasket or trashcan, I could not understand.

No one likes to be told what to do, but some of us can be convinced by argument or persuasion to change our ways. I was taught that littering was not only wrong but signified lack of character. Only people who had been badly brought up deposited trash on the ground where someone else either has to view the unsightly mess or clean it up. In every other way, my classmate was a person worth knowing—intelligent, generous, and considerate. She had not been badly brought up, but she not only believed she had the right to litter but also felt compelled to do it.

Some people think that no one "owns" the countryside and that where there are few or no houses, no one cares what someone else jettisons. During the 1970s and 1980s, as a contractor transformed the beautiful fields around our house—the original one on a farmstead—into a subdivision, piles of trash began to appear in the woods behind these residences. The forest that created the backdrop to the landscape became to the inhabitants nothing but a dump. The owners belonged to the middle class; no one not in a secure income bracket could have afforded to buy those dwellings, and so they could well have paid to have their refuse hauled away. Evidently they took pride in caring for their places, yet their conscientiousness did not extend to land they did not own, even if it adjoined theirs.

Nonresidents who toss their debris onto other people's lawns must feel extra privileged, as they would not want their own property to be trashed but have nothing against doing so to someone else's. Littering is a misdemeanor that is taken less seriously than other rules, in part because it is so difficult to enforce but more so because it physically harms no one. Yet there is damage to the spirit: it is demeaning, after all, to be subjected to unsightly rubbish. As polluters conceive of the world as a dumping ground, litterers must see it as a giant trash bin. The larger context shows that the unwanted bits and pieces of our daily lives tell the story of a culture not only of waste but also of frivolity, carelessness, and selfishness.

On one of my beautification quests at my farm, I decided to repress resentment and try to adopt a philosophical attitude. Dross is, after all, silent, and so disturbs me much less than irritating noise such as the sound of the internal combustion engine, loud voices, and unwanted "music." I decided to learn to enjoy collecting the oddments of civilization. Much of it consists of cigarette butts, thrown on the ground in eastern states because until recently they posed almost no fire hazard. Westerners tend to know better. I am mystified that people still smoke when the hazards to health have long been known. Perhaps smokers drop cigarette butts because they do not regard such small items as litter, but the most irritating trash consists of diminutive objects, which are more difficult to get hold of than larger ones. Waste can pose a hazard: remnants of cigarettes expand but do not disintegrate, and filters are washed by rainwater down the roadside into ditches that flow into streams and rivers, where the rubbish sometimes ends up in the stomachs of fish and other creatures, which die from the toxic chemicals.

Once when out collecting trash, I witnessed someone throw a beer can from a pickup truck onto my lawn only a few yards in front of me. Had I been quicker, I could have photographed the license plate, but the driver sped away, as cowards do. In Ohio, carrying an open container of alcohol, even an empty one, in a car is illegal, whether the drinker is a passenger or the driver. Since the perpetrator had to have seen me at my task, I conclude that he rejoiced in adding to my labor. This episode reinforced my conviction that many people have no other way of feeling good about themselves than to inconvenience or bully others.

Aluminum cans for libations occupy a large part of my haul, including both soft drinks and alcoholic ones. My finds represent the products of the best-known companies: Seven Up, Coca-Cola, Coors, Stroh's, Budweiser, Pepsi, and Mountain Dew. Plastic water bottles are also a favorite of my donors. Sometimes I think it is better that I receive these containers, since I recycle them; the users would likely never have presence of mind or decency to do so. Having long given up drinking soda pop, I contemplate the effect of sugar on the bloodstream and teeth and its major part in the obesity epidemic, which affects us all by increasing the cost of insurance premiums and healthcare.

Pizza boxes are some of my favorite collectibles, because they are burnable and easy to pick up. Cardboard that has been used for food is not recyclable, but the grease in these boxes makes excellent starter for bonfires. Paperboard coffee cups and plastic drinking cups are also commonly thrown on the ground. Food containers made of Styrofoam must go into the trash, as none of this type of plastic is recyclable. Often, the boxes contain other castoffs, such as plastic eating utensils—also not recyclable—and small containers of condiments, such as ketchup. My donors help to keep me in shape not only because of the exercise I get from collecting but also because their refuse reinforces my extreme distaste for take-out food. I have to rejoice that the plastic bags I pick up are not deposited in lakes and streams, where waterfowl might ingest them. Clean plastic grocery bags are recyclable, or at least the merchants claim they are.

Once I found a list of a discharged inmate's clothing items (from the Mansfield Correctional Institution, I speculate), quite an interesting read, including everything from shirts to underwear. One psychological theory claims that repeat offenders are often those who are incapable of imagining the feelings of others, or at least of people they do not know. Some suffer from narcissistic personality disorder. Littering by anyone is a manifestation of indifference toward others: these people have nothing against inflicting psychological harm or causing unnecessary work. Perhaps they see nothing wrong with defiling their own habitations, but I suspect that many who litter would object to someone else doing so to them—my classmate for example, although she was far from narcissistic and certainly did not harbor criminal thoughts.

Another interesting object I retrieved was a pornographic magazine containing pictures even *Playboy* and *Penthouse* would have rejected as lewd. I regret that I was unable to learn the name of the publication, as its cover had been ripped off. I could have nothing but sympathy for women reduced to lives of posing in very compromising and indecent displays. These beautiful young women could have been successful models. What was their motivation? I also meditate on the need of human beings to waste their time looking at lewd pictures when they could be doing something creative or even remunerative. Then I wondered why someone had thrown it away, if he or she wanted to look at such pictures. This episode taught me more than I had realized about the depravity of *Homo sapiens,* corruption that exists in no other species.

The most fitting penalty for litterers is to make them spend several weekends collecting trash—thus, the punishment would fit the crime, and the perpetrators would contribute to the common benefit. Perhaps with enough experience they might also learn responsibility. Cleanup work as a school assignment might also stimulate thinking about wastefulness, and students' motivation might be enhanced by offering remuneration commensurate with the size of the haul.

One year I found a new groundhog hole near the fence line where a stream crosses the southeastern property boundary. The proprietor had dug out a brown glass jar, very old, to judge by the stains on it and the fact that it flared out at the top and bottom, like a container for applesauce. The labels had long since disintegrated. How much more of our civilization's detritus lies underground, waiting for plows, animals, or the upheaval of freezing and thawing to thrust it into our consciousness not only of our own mortality but also of our complicity in this profligacy? I took it back to the barn and cleaned it out for recycling, one of my favorite discoveries, as it had not been thrown from a vehicle but no doubt originated in the days when the land had been a working farm. Had it been decorated, it might have served as an artifact like a Greek vase, except that it was too common to be noteworthy.

Another discovery might be called "The Lord of the Rings," without Sauron's evil power. Our bonfire site, where we burn brush and paper that cannot be recycled, was the location of a silo that either fell from disrepair or was torn down. The previous owners used it as a dump, and for years we found shards of glass, tops of steel cans, and remnants of fabric thrust to the surface by continuous freezing and thawing. Periodically I rake the ashes, and one day I spied the rim of a little circlet mostly concealed in the soil beneath. I retrieved it to discover my husband's long-lost wedding ring. When cleaning out a desk drawer, he dropped the ring box, which flew open. We searched the room thoroughly, even moving heavy furniture, but never found the ring. Evidently it had landed in the waste basket and been concealed under the flap of a paper bag used as a liner, because even though we emptied the container, we had not found it. As if through benign magic, the earth returned it.

Several times a year, when my pickup truck is parked in some lot, I find trash in its bed. The psychology of people who deposit litter into someone else's vehicle intrigues me: they have presence of mind not to toss their residue on the ground, yet they have no qualms about inconveniencing others with the dross of their selfishness. I redeposit this trash—usually food wrappers or aluminum cans—into bins dispersed in urban locations for that purpose, contented in the knowledge that at least the rubbish was not left on the ground, where it would have to be more painstakingly collected either by a volunteer or paid sanitation worker.

Homo sapiens is the only species that wastes resources. Even remains left by predators after a kill are consumed by scavengers. Insects and birds reliably—and no doubt gratefully—clean up many leftovers. Both retrieving trash and recycling my own remind me about not only the profligacy of our society but also how many of our resources could be put to more creative practices. Charging for throwaway containers would not only encourage people to bring their own but also generate revenue to pay for cleanup. Levying fines on fast-food eating establishments for disposable items that contain their advertising logos would compel them to pass along the costs to customers. Cardboard and hemp are preferable materials, because they are biodegradable. Cutting down on plastic use might lead to shutting down petrochemical plants, which contaminate air and water.

Noting many examples of the same types of containers in the recycling bins reminds me of how much duplication we are willing to pay for when it is not difficult to come up with ways to reuse materials. Buying in bulk would necessitate keeping jars and bottles for refilling. It is less expensive, and just as convenient, to pack single servings into reusable containers than it is to buy the servings already compartmentalized. Many people carry their own canvas totes to the grocery store, along with reusable bags for fruit and vegetables, and some retailers reward customers with a small refund for doing so. Mandating deposits for containers, especially glass—which was a common practice until the 1960s, with the disastrous advent of "nonreturnable bottles"—would motivate people to keep their own or return them for reimbursement. Collecting glass bottles gave children a way to earn spending money. Single-use plastic drinking containers and bags should be discouraged by implementing user fees: in Norway, consumers return plastic bottles for a small refund; in Ireland, customers have to pay a Euro for a plastic or paper sack. The states of California and Hawaii banned single-use plastic bags in retail stores, while Chicago, Los Angeles, and Seattle placed taxes on them. Communities in Ohio, however, which passed laws prohibiting or taxing single-use plastic containers (Bexley, in Franklin County, and Cuyahoga County) were prevented from enforcing their statutes by another law imposed by the gerrymandered Republican state legislature (House Bill 242, passed in 2020), which prohibited any municipality from enacting laws intended to reduce single-use plastic bags and containers. This is the party that claims to support small government, local decision-making, personal responsibility, and self-reliance.

Many people argue that recycling has created more trash and wasted more resources because people assume that if an item is recyclable they can use more of it with a clear conscience; furthermore, some items marked recyclable are not: most plastic numbered three, four, five, and seven and all plastic numbered six (Styrofoam) cannot be recycled, because processing them requires special facilities. Manufacturers' placing the recycling logos on items makes customers feel good about buying them, but even if the empty container is deposited into a recycling bin, it ends up in a landfill. For decades, our local recycling center in Ashland County took all plastic other than Styrofoam, but since 2018 it has accepted only types one and two because recycling facilities in China, which were buying American waste, changed their policies. The Ashland center closed with the pandemic and was replaced by recycling bins in several locations, with no one to oversee what is deposited. While the primary goal is to reduce the amount of waste, we still need to improve reuse and recycling capacity.

In the spring of 2021 I took part in the annual Mohican River Clean-Up Day, when local residents volunteer to collect trash in the state park. Beginning my quest in the horseman's camp, I was amazed at how many items I scoured from among the grass and leaves—plastic bags, aluminum drinking cans, cigarette butts, candy wrappers. Trail riders and equestrians in general tend to be conscientious people who want to take care of the land, but clearly not all. The task took less than an hour, so I followed State Route 97, which runs through the park, from the horseman's camp to Veterans' Memorial Shrine. Although a shorter distance, this part of the endeavor required over an hour. I found not only the requisite plastic bags, aluminum cans, plastic bottles candy wrappers, and cigarette butts but also a car battery; a large piece of corroded steel (the origin of which I never learned); and footwear, including sandals, flip-flops, tennis shoes, and an old boot without a mate. I also retrieved clothing, such as tee shirts and even a pair of jockey shorts—whereupon I contemplated that someone must be running around naked in the woods. Among the leaves I also found a broken baby's bassinette, an empty plastic bottle labeled arthritis medicine, a deflated car tire, several brown glass beer bottles, and two wide-mouth clear glass jars. These were not items likely to have been used at a campsite but were probably dumped because their former possessors did not want to pay to have their trash hauled away—yet they could just as easily have deposited the items into one of many receptacles located near the campgrounds.

Sometimes I volunteer to clean up trash at the Gorge Overlook, the most spectacular vista in the park, where the hillside plunges three hundred feet to the Clear Fork of the Mohican River. Two stone balconies enable visitors to gaze over the valley toward the opposite wooded hillside. On my last visit I collected about twenty gallons of trash, including many cigarette butts, plastic cups complete with covers and drinking straws, newspapers, cardboard cups, cellophane wrapping, an infant-sized plastic shoe, and a cloth muffler. As I climbed through the fence marked "No Visitors Beyond This Point," in order to retrieve more of the refuse, I marveled at the impulse that leads people to throw drinking cups, plastic water bottles, cardboard, and candy wrappers so far down the ravine that they are reachable only with difficulty, yet entirely visible to those who have come to admire the view. On one of my quests, I discovered several articles farther down the slope but decided not to try to retrieve them: the steepness of the incline was too great a challenge. On subsequent expeditions I employed a ten-foot-long limb lopper with a hook.

For several years, I have assisted with repairing trails at Malabar Farm, where I ride often. After the fields near the horseman's camp are mowed, refuse otherwise concealed by sorrel, wild oats, and brome is visible—plastic bags, cigarette butts, drink containers. Quite a stash collects in a location marked "Wildflower Area," which is not mowed. At the campground nearby I once discovered the detritus of a Bacchanal: empty wine bottles, spent condoms, and the ashes of a fire. At that moment I was the only person present. Envisioning a frieze on a Greek vase, I collected and deposited the junk while enjoying birdsong and expecting Dionysus to appear from the woods. At least the revelers had been careful about procreation, if not about driving under the influence—but then again, perhaps the libation bearers had slept off their altered states of consciousness before journeying to their next orgy.

When historians and anthropologists study the kitchen middens of ancient civilizations, they find the remains of baskets, crockery, and sometimes food items—like seeds—that have become fossilized. Items made of steel will rust away in a few years, but plastic can remain for decades or centuries and glass for millennia. Finding these items, the researchers of the future will likely conclude that ours was a very profligate culture although abundant in resources, because only those who possess a great deal—even the poor—can afford to be wasteful. They will also conclude that items were made without attention to craftsmanship or quality, since so much was discarded.

According to the Environmental Protection Agency, Americans produced 292.4 million tons of trash in 2018, a figure that amounts to about 4.9 pounds per person per day. Of this total, 69 million tons were recycled, 35 million tons combusted, 25 million tons composted, and 17 million handled in some other way. This figure leaves 146 million tons, or about 50 percent of total trash, thrown into landfills.

The largest landfill in the world, and the one holding the Guinness record, is Apex Regional, near Las Vegas, 2200 acres in size and accepting 3.28 million tons of trash each year. Size, however, means more than area: the landfill that takes in the most trash per year is Sudokwon near Incheon, South Korea, with 6.9 million tons annually. The second-largest in both area and amount is Bordo Ponicente, near Mexico City, 927 acres in size and taking in 4.4 million tons per year. Annisa Nurul Aziza, of *VICE Indonesia,* claims that Bantargebang landfill near Jakarta is the largest dump in the world, taking in 6500–7000 tons of refuse per day. People make a living from picking out recyclable or reusable items. One of the largest landfills in the world, Puente Hills, over 700 acres in size, was established east of Los Angeles in 1957 and closed in 2013. After turning the site into a preservation area, its administration offers tours. Many municipalities have built energy plants that convert the methane produced by trash into energy. Landfill gas, consisting of 50 percent methane and 50 percent carbon dioxide, contributed about 14.4 percent of methane emissions in the United States in 2022 and is the third-largest source of human-created methane. Martina Igini, editor in chief at the website Earth.org, reports that fast fashion (clothing made cheaply) provides much landfill waste, including 92 million tons worldwide annually. The average US consumer throws away 81.5 pounds of clothing every year. Manufacturers also jettison their own products: in 2018, Burberry—not a company known for cheap goods—burned 90 million pounds sterling of unsold merchandise to keep prices high and products exclusive. I speculate that donating the clothing would not have interfered with their profits, as their well-heeled clientele would never have come into contact with the recipients.

Byers Woods Park in Ashland County, off County Road 655 just north of Hayesville, grew out of a homestead, a farm, and a trash mound. The stone cellar of the original cabin (built in 1825), the barn, and the hand-dug well remain but are inaccessible to visitors. The area was farmed until 1971, when the county acquired some of the acreage for a landfill. A thirteen-acre woodlot that had been used as pasture contained many old trees, including some ancient white oaks. The Ashland–West Holmes Career Center being within walking distance, its resource conservation class received permission from the commissioners to use the woodlot as a lab site. After removing dead elm trees and trimming the oaks, students created trails in the expectation that the area might one day become dedicated to recreation. The commissioners closed the landfill in 2000 and determined that the best use for the area was a park, the first of twenty-two created in 2002 by the newly formed Ashland County Park District, which named it for long-serving county commissioner Marilyn Byers and her husband, former state representative Eugene Byers. Bird nesting areas are off limits to walkers, but many viewing sites allow observation of bluebirds, bobolinks, cardinals, song sparrows, chipping sparrows, woodpeckers, and red-tailed hawks. A stream attracts kingfishers. Thirty additional wooded acres were added in 2020, and in 2023 the commissioners transferred ownership of seventeen acres, including two barns and sheep pasture, to the park. Visitors cannot forget its origin, however: large white PVC pipes sticking up from the ground release methane from the decaying refuse that lies below, out of sight.

Although many landfills have been repurposed for parks and recreation, we could have done better to try to restrict the number and type of items manufactured annually that are intended to be thrown away. Many are biodegradable—clothing and shoes made from natural fibers, for example. A better strategy is to make products that last, as craftsmen once did. Even though the items eventually wear out, creating higher-quality things decreases the need for more and more to be manufactured. Our society promulgates the dogma that the greatest good is consumption. To judge from media, our citizens possess no higher purpose than buying products, and companies that exist only to sell more and more volume are motivated to produce goods with limited durability. According to Sandra Goldmark, the idea of planned obsolescence originated in the 1920s, with light-bulb manufacturers agreeing to limit the usefulness of their products and General Motors chairman (and later philanthropist) Alfred P. Sloan introducing the idea of "dynamic obsolescence" to increase sales.

As Wendell Berry asserts in his essay "Home of the Free," freedom has come to imply liberation from doing our own work; for many it means not only the liberty but also the duty to consume. When, in graduate school, I proudly rode an old single-speed bicycle, an engineering major chided me for my "outmoded" conveyance, as if this constituted some sort of moral lapse. A student of mine once commented during a class discussion about Robinson Jeffers's poem "Shine, Republic" (in which the speaker claims that "freedom is poor and laborious") that the primary reason for working hard is to acquire possessions. At first taken aback, I realized that of course *success* has for too long been synonymous with *ownership* and *convenience,* yet I still marveled at the readiness to affirm acquisitiveness as a founding principle of character. I replied that if I had twice the salary I was earning, I would spend it on solar panels, a geothermal heating system, and longer-lasting products that would enable me to free myself from the fossil fuel industry specifically and corporate control generally—which I regard as a type of totalitarianism. The students stared at me in silence.

Liberation from consumerism entirely is impossible in this age, as is freedom from the propaganda known as advertising. When laws were passed to keep billboards off the near margins of highways, merchants increased their size and moved them into the fields, with printing large enough to read from a quarter mile away and slogans short and snappy enough that motorists could take them in while passing at sixty or seventy miles per hour. Catalogs and internet sites advertise to us constantly. We like to think that we have become savvy to the merchants' ploy that we can buy happiness by acquiring products, but if that were the case, advertisers would have abandoned their barrage and tried some new tactic. I cannot understand the reason we must embrace the throw-away mentality that values only the moment, the most recent invention, the most clannish possession, or whatever will gain membership in the most prestigious clique. Freedom should mean deciding for ourselves about what we value.

A salesperson I knew years ago claimed that the company he worked for, which produced alcoholic drinks, had a product that did not sell well; instead of discontinuing that item, the company undertook a massive marketing strategy to promote it. Advertising thus constitutes not only a nuisance, convincing people that they need things they can do without, but a public menace, convincing people that they desire things they have *decided* to do without. At the same time, participation in society forces us to own items we may or may not want but are compelled to have and into which obsolescence is planned, among them mobile phones and computers. The telephone as a communication device has become a method of harassment; information is no longer widely available in print form—such as newspapers and telephone books (which were recyclable). Economic success is measured in terms of "growth," but seldom do politicians and businesspeople bother to define what they mean by that term, or why, if they argue that free enterprise and business are the answer to all ills, the problems have not yet been solved.

Happily, not all our residue goes to waste. The aircraft carrier *Oriskany*, when it was decommissioned in 2006—forty years after a spectacular fire at sea—was sunk off the coast of Florida, where it became the structure for a coral reef. I have no doubt that more of our trash can be put to environmental use. Raccoons appropriate abandoned farm machinery to establish their homes. Birds build nests in holes that open up in disused fence posts. It is entertaining to watch an old building being taken over by woods and the animals who live there. Chernobyl, unfortunately, makes one of the most notable examples where houses are occupied by foxes, deer, bear, raccoons, and other animals now that people have deserted the area due to radiation levels created by the nuclear accident in 1986, perhaps the most spectacular historic example of carelessness.

Electronic gadgets can be mined for some of the valuable metals found in them, although many parts of the items have to be thrown into landfills. Annually the Ashland County Solid Waste District reserves a collection date when thoughtful people can bring their outdated products for recycling without a fee.

The Center for Regenerative Design and Collaboration (CRDC), founded in 2018 as a nonprofit community outreach program in Costa Rica, recycles all types of plastic (numbered 1–7) into a substance called Resin8, an additive that improves the structural performance of concrete. Partnering with businesses, NGOs, and organizations such as Habitat for Humanity and the Alliance to End Plastic Waste, the CRDC has opened factories in Mexico, Australia, New Zealand, Samoa, the United Kingdom, South Africa, and the United States.

Garage sales may be one manifestation of reuse, as many goods outlast their usefulness to one family—children's clothing, for example. The citizens who lived in the subdivision near my parents' house in the 1980s and dumped their trash in the woods held garage sales every Saturday morning in summer between 9:00 A.M. and noon; nearly every household participated, with card tables and picnic tables laden with goods—mostly clothing but also toys, games, Big Wheels, even sports equipment. The interesting tie between their dumping and their garage sales is the overabundance of material possessions that must somehow be gotten rid of.

A new individualism may involve the freedom *not* to consume—not only willingness but also determination to make things last as long as possible and not to feel compelled to own the latest trend or technology. Henry David Thoreau wrote in the chapter "Where I Lived, and What I Lived For" in *Walden* (1854) that "a man is rich in proportion to the number of things which he can afford to let alone." Perhaps if we abandoned the idea that the best of us are those with the most expensive possessions, we may discover some new meaning to our existence—a new value to life lived for itself and not for the few who decide how the rest will exist. Doing so may constitute a reiteration of the Occupy movement: protesters demonstrated against the misuse of our economy and the abuse of our trust by big financial corporations; current "occupiers" may resist the values that informed the irresponsible transactions that preceded the Great Recession (2008–18).

I come from two families of savers. One reason for this behavior is that the older people lived through the depression of the 1930s, the severest economic downturn in the country's history. While some of their saving became cumbersome—much space is needed for all the towels, quilts, sheets, clothing, even furniture—one valuable lesson is how to make do with what is available. Wasting food was considered not only uneconomic but sinful. Even food that goes bad, however, can be saved, in a sense, by composting, and some municipalities have installed the process into their recycling plans. On average, my cars last twelve years, except the one (my first) annihilated by a large luxury sedan whose driver ran a stop sign. My husband claims that I have clothes left from high school, but he exaggerates. I do, however, own clothes that go back decades. Blue jeans, T-shirts, and boots have much shorter lifespans, as they are required for harder work. Cloth items tattered beyond wearing can be turned into rags. For decades I have kept as a truck mascot a cloth toy donkey purchased at a garage sale for twenty-five cents. I cannot pretend to be as economical as Thoreau, however, as I never retreated entirely from society. Although I was the last person I know to have a cell phone or smartphone, I nevertheless felt compelled to own one as it became impossible to reach people by telephone or mail. The customer is not a king but a slave: businesses dictate conformity in order to ensure their own profits.

Today, due to retirements and downsizing engendered by the pandemic, we have experienced shortages most of us never knew in earlier decades. For a time, cars could not be manufactured fast enough for demand. More people wanted to buy houses than there were places to buy. Perhaps those years can help us to realize the importance of saving and of building structures and manufacturing products to last. One answer to the problem of waste is that individuals can take responsibility for our own choices, buy carefully and conscientiously, use as little as we can, make things last for as long as possible, and donate anything still serviceable. The Netherlands, Sweden, and France all have enacted legislation that promotes product durability. In 2021, the New York State legislature passed a law ensuring that companies produce repairable items; President Biden issued an executive order mandating that the Federal Trade Commission enforce rules that prevent manufacturers from building goods that cannot be fixed.

There are other signs of improvement. In my journeys along the county road, I usually fill at least two fifty-pound bags annually. In the last two years, I recovered considerably less trash than in previous times, enough to fill only half a fifty-pound bag. If refuse-gathering were a business, I would be compelled to declare bankruptcy.

Eight

Dysart Woods

Dysart Woods is a fifty-acre tract of old-growth deciduous trees in Belmont County, Ohio, home to some spectacular white oaks three and four hundred years old, with canopies reaching as high as 140 feet and trunks measuring 20 feet and more in circumference. Seventeen other species include red oak, birch, and tulip poplar. Located in the hilly, unglaciated southeast, the woods reside in one of the most scenic parts of the state and belong to the historic homelands of the Kaskaskia (Osage) and Shawandasse Tula (Shawanwaki/Shawnee) people. Rainfall and temperature provided conditions well-suited for the deciduous trees that once covered much of the eastern United States, of which only .004 percent of the original mesophytic (temperate) forest remains.

The woods were part of a 455-acre farm once owned by pioneer Orin B. Dysart. Upon his death, the property passed to his nieces, Gladys Dysart McGaughy and Margaret Dysart. The rest of the acreage consists of pasture, tilled fields, and new forest. After holding the land for decades, the nieces eventually sold it to the nonprofit Nature Conservancy for a much smaller sum than the lucrative offers they received from lumber and coal companies; in 1967 the property was designated a National Natural Landmark and inducted into the Old Growth Forest Hall of

Fame. Because the Conservancy's goal until 1974 was primarily conservation rather than research, however, it transferred the land to Ohio University in 1968 for use as a laboratory for the study of old-growth forest ecology, and the farmhouse at the entrance to the woods was converted into an interpretive center for visitors and students. Tracts of primeval trees not only allow the public to experience something like the deciduous forest that once covered 95 percent of Ohio; they also constitute the only remaining places where research on this type of ecosystem may occur. Brian McCarthy, professor of forest ecology at Ohio University, studies dendrochronology, the scientific technique of dating events and environmental change by using patterns of annual tree growth. He found that the widely accepted idea that Native Americans regularly burned the woods is misleading: most fires occurred after settlement by Europeans, who cleared and plowed the land and built homesteads. Sedimentary bedrock is mostly sandstone and shale, unfortunately with coal seams occurring both near the surface and hundreds of feet underground. It is that resource that put Dysart Woods in danger.

For decades, mineral companies, especially Ohio Valley Coal, based in St. Clairsville, set their sights on Dysart; their plan was to implement a process of underground extraction called longwall mining, which removes a coal seam band six feet in width about five hundred to six hundred feet below the surface. Given the rarity of the forest, environmentalists and researchers raised objections, citing abundant documentation proving that subsurface activity ignites ripple fractures that precipitate three to six feet of subsidence, resulting in some trees capsizing. Another problem is hydrology: while water running downhill normally percolates into soil, hydrating the trees evenly, horizontal cracks created by mining allow rainwater to seep into the earth much more rapidly, drying the ground on lower slopes and killing trees because water that would have reached them has been absorbed on more elevated terrain. The company proposed an alternative technique known as room-and-pillar mining, in which pedestals of coal are left standing like columns holding up a roof. To this proposal, researchers replied that the soil still fractures and dries; subsidence occurs eventually, because the columns always fail. Room-and-pillar techniques merely delay the severe effects of longwall mining.

The Ohio Valley Coal Company (OVCC), granted a permit in 2001 by the Ohio Division of Mining Resource Management, waged a legal battle. Arguing that it owned the mineral rights to the land, OVCC declared that with its plan, "trees and other surface vegetation will absolutely not be affected by mining," although no data was given to support the claim, and the company's own consultant, Hanjie Chan, testified that there would be at least five inches of subsidence.† OVCC defended its lack of data by citing exemptions previously awarded it by the US Department of Mineral Resources. Conservation organizations, including Buckeye Forest Council (now the Buckeye Environmental Network) and Dysart Defenders as well as Ohio University, disputed the permit for years, claiming that a fifteen-hundred-foot buffer zone would be necessary to ensure protection of the natural water system that sustained the forest. At hearings in 2007, ecologists, geologists, and biologists testified for seven hours that longwall mining would result in ecological damage. As in most such cases, however, tying cause to effect provided the major challenge. OVCC, like many timber and mineral companies that want to mine and log ancient forests, declared that the old trees would have died anyway, regardless of extraction activity. Protracted expert testimony proved ineffective: the courts decided on precedent. After spending $100,000 on litigation, the university would have had to pay $50 million to secure the mineral rights. On March 5, 2007, the Ohio Seventh District Court of Appeals ruled in favor of the OVCC, to allow mining beneath and adjacent to Dysart Woods.

McCarthy, who conducted studies in Dysart before and after mining, found that more than fifty old-growth trees died, or about

---

† I have not been able to learn which owner sold the Dysart mineral rights to OVCC.

25 percent of the forest, essentially of drought. Two decades earlier, the ecosystem had been wetter, as measured by mosses growing on decomposing logs. Impacts on plants with shallower roots were less severe, but changes in the understory indicated that the forest was slowly drying. OVCC argued that not only the age of the trees might have caused mortality but also insect or fungus damage, even though it produced no evidence of either.

The term *split estate* refers to a legal status in which one person, organization, or company may own land while someone else possesses the resources, including water, timber, or grazing. The term *mineral rights* refers to ownership of natural assets below the ground; someone possessing those rights may drill or mine legally so long as the surface, owned by someone else, is not disturbed. The contentious issue involves damage to the surface as a result of extraction activity. In 2010, OVCC mined thousands of acres in Belmont County where many house owners did not possess the mineral rights. Fractures upset the flow of water: following longwall mining, some private water wells dried up. The company first provided large tanks, known colloquially as *water buffaloes,* but then convinced the county to install piped water. Reports circulated that houses in the mined area had shifted on their foundations, but OVCC was never held responsible. Although Ohio law strictly regulates the permitting process, it favors extraction companies with regard to the long-term effects of mining.

Scientists will never know how many years the trees at Dysart might have lived, as research into forest culture is ongoing; nevertheless, tracts of old-growth forest provide the only places where ecologists can study the ancient ecological communities. In addition, these woods are important for climate change mitigation, as they serve as carbon "sinks." Estimates state that as much as 18 percent of atmospheric carbon can be stored by trees, younger ones taking in carbon faster, older trees retaining it for a longer time. The argument that the old-growth trees in Dysart would have died anyway is bankrupt, an attempt to justify exploitation of one resource at the expense of another. The vast majority of biodiversity in the North American continent, moreover, resides in the Appalachian Mountain chain and the Allegheny Plateau, much of it in mature forest ecosystems, and environmentalists argue that what is left is worth saving.

Every eastern state possesses pockets of old-growth forest, sometimes resulting from families preserving the land but often from surveyors' errors. A fifty-acre forest called Gaudineer Scenic Area, near Gaudineer Knob in West Virginia, was preserved for this reason. It represents the virgin red spruce forest that occupied large portions of that part of the Appalachian Mountains. Other species include yellow birch, beech, red maple, sugar maple, and other hardwoods. Individual trees range up to forty inches in diameter and three hundred years of age. While a surveyor's error prevented the woods from being cut down, the foresight of state officials allowed them to be preserved for future generations.

※

Ohio Valley Coal was owned by Robert E. Murray (1940–2020), who created Murray Energy Incorporated, as of 2019 the fourth largest coal company in the United States and the largest still privately owned (not publicly traded). Murray's father's paralysis from a mining accident caused young Robert to go to work to support his family; he began his employment in coal mines at the age of sixteen, having lied about his age, as the legal minimum for such work at the time was seventeen. After earning a degree in mining engineering at Ohio State University, he formed his own company, which by 2020 employed more than seven thousand people worldwide, three thousand in the United States.

Murray's story, however, is not merely that of an industrious, small-town, working-class boy laboring hard and seizing opportunities to rise above adversity. In spite of his family history, during his entire career, Murray fought mine safety regulations. His Crandall Canyon Mine, in Utah, collapsed in August 2007, killing six miners; three more died in the rescue attempt. Cited for sixty-four violations, Murray blamed the collapse on an earthquake, without providing evidence. One year later, his Illinois Galatia Mine garnered thirty-five hundred infractions of rules. On July 24, 2008, the company paid the highest penalty at that time for safety violations, $1.85 million.

In October 2019, OVCC filed for Chapter 11 bankruptcy; Murray stepped down as CEO but stayed on as chairman of the board of a reorganized company, American Consolidated Natural Resources Incorporated (ACNR). OVCC's ill fortune did not impede Murray's financial well-being: according to a *New York Times* article, in 2019 he paid himself $14 million and his successor, Robert D. Moore, a $4 million bonus in addition to his $9 million salary.

Murray fought regulations on power-plant emissions as well as mine safety: he referred to President Obama's Clean Power Plan as "a political power grab of America's power grid to change our country in a diabolical, if not evil, way." He contributed $300,000 to Donald Trump's inauguration ceremony; afterward, Murray's "wish list" for mine deregulation became the administration's "to-do list," and his lobbyist in Washington, Andrew Wheeler, was named to an administrative position in Trump's Environmental Protection Agency. Murray also helped fund climate-change denier organizations Committee for a Constructive Tomorrow, Center for the Study of Carbon Dioxide and Global Change, International Climate Science Coalition, Heartland Institute, and the Competitive Institute. One of his major customers was First Energy Solutions, implicated in the 2019 bribery scheme of Larry Householder, speaker of the Ohio House of Representatives until he was removed from the chamber while under investigation in 2020. Convicted, along with former Ohio Republican Party chairman Matt Borges, of racketeering conspiracy in the biggest public scandal in state history, he is the only House speaker ever expelled from the legislature and convicted in a federal corruption case.

After having fought regulations to prevent black lung disease, in October 2019 Murray filed for federal benefits for black lung disease from the US Department of Labor, although he also claimed that his ailment was idiopathic pulmonary fibrosis. When

Murray retired on October 19, 2020, the ACNR, in its newsletter, praised him for his "tireless efforts on behalf of his employees." Murray died in St. Clairsville, Ohio, on October 25, 2020, one week before his ally Trump was defeated by Joseph R. Biden. On Tuesday, June 8, 2021, Trump endorsed the candidacy of Michael Carey, former vice president of "governmental affairs" at ACNR, in a special election held in August for Ohio's 15th Congressional District and on June 26 attended a rally in Cleveland to support him. Carey won.

*

Dysart Woods Laboratory and National Natural Landmark begins at the intersection of Highway 147 and Dysart Woods Road, a gravel service lane that transects the forest. Two farmhouses stand at the entrance, a large homestead with a wrap-around veranda and a smaller, older structure behind it that appears to be an example of an I house (defined in chapter 3). Through a lower window, one can view a very large stone fireplace. Unfortunately, this second house is being allowed to decay. Visitors may sit at a table in the shade of an old maple tree, although they are encouraged to have their picnics at nearby Barkcamp State Park. The first sound I heard on a visit in mid-June 2021 was the chirping of a least flycatcher. Behind the house, the silo rises, surrounded by heavy brush, near two nonfunctioning outhouses and a low concrete wall, the only section remaining from the original barn.

Three quarters of a mile up the forest road, a level area serves as a parking lot where interpretive signs inform visitors about the kinds of vegetation and birds they may be lucky enough to see or hear. Only two miles long, the red and blue blazed trails begin on either side of the road and loop back to the parking area. The blue trail meanders through newer woods where the forest floor is overgrown with the vegetation familiar to hikers in Ohio: thorny multiflora rose, blackberry vines, May-apple, buttercup, pink lady's thumb, sapling paw-paw, and others. The red trail, a far better option, traverses the section with the largest trees—giant white oaks, birch, maple, and tulip. The forest floor is not a mossy carpet but a leafy layer with maple and oak saplings less than a foot in height. A few metal posts indicating areas of study and several wooden footbridges in advanced stages of decay are the only signs of human interference. In order to let nature take its course, the university allows nothing on the land to be disturbed; fallen trees or limbs are left on the ground to decompose into soil. My companion and I glimpsed several giants fallen years before and two trees more recently capsized, their exposed roots a much lighter color than those of the ancient dwellers. We heard the purring of red-bellied woodpeckers, chipping of least and olive-sided flycatchers, high-pitched shrill of eastern pewee, chirping of rose-breasted grosbeak, rattle of the eastern towhee, and the flutelike music of the wood thrush. Although their song surrounded us, I saw none of them, as the canopy is so high the singers were not visible.

At the edge of the woods, hay- and cornfields stretched over many acres to the end of the working farm. Although not so high as the hillsides in Vinton County's Zaleski Forest, some inclines were steep, especially near the stream: perhaps this quality dissuaded the pioneer farmer from cutting down the trees to make way for cultivation. Thunder threatened, but the storm held off until we had followed both trails back to the terminus. Recent rain had made them muddy, although the streams were not high and we were able to cross easily—fortunately, because the wooden slats of the footbridges had long since rotted through.

Lack of political will enabled the coal company to mine under one of the most precious tracts of land in the state. Some individuals will always resist whatever costs money with no apparent economic utility in the foreseeable future. At the same time, nearly everyone values the national parks and nature preserves, although when they were first designated, people argued against taking the land away from private use. We do know that there is much to be learned from studying old-growth forest ecosystems and the interconnectedness of woodland species. Mycorrhizal networks in the soil enable trees to share nutrients, carbon, and water through small strands of fungi that are more absorptive even than fine root systems; these networks, spanning many acres, can be interrupted even by select cutting.

Resources are used up after a short time. The forest, however, may have continued for centuries as part of what was once a vast, richly diverse ecosystem. If subsidence does not cause further damage, rainfall and a temperate climate may allow more trees to flourish in Dysart Woods, which centuries from now may be "old growth."

Nine

Into the Woods

Hammond Woods

THE VALLEY VIEW SPUR of the Shagbark Woods in Richland County near the small town of Butler is easy to miss, located as it is on an unobtrusive gravel lane that branches off from a township road. I discovered this gem when I was invited to participate in a hike on July 18, 2021, led by conservationist Eric Miller, trustee of the North Central Ohio Land Conservancy (NCOLC). Funded by foundations and individuals, the organization seeks to conserve intact ecosystems. Valley View includes 172 acres of old-growth forest donated by a farmer named Hammond and hence sometimes called Hammond Woods.

 A small gravel lot provided the only parking at the trailhead. We stepped around fish skeletons large and small as well as piles of ash on the gravel, where anglers had cleaned and cooked their catches from Clear Creek, although there was no picnic table or fire ring. Evidently, the stream supports aquatic life. At the entrance to the woods, a sign exhorted hikers to stay on the marked path, because the vegetation was fragile. Nearby, an abandoned nineteenth-century brick schoolhouse loomed in shadows where skinny sapling branches reached through windows. Restored or not, ruins retain a romanticism that no modern building ever achieves. Perhaps the schoolhouse's silence is more eloquent than any historical marker or yellowed record, but I would like to have known something about the people whose children attended that place. The message is clear enough that whatever civilization we are born into will pass away and be replaced by another; even so, we should bear in mind that nothing we do can ever be entirely undone.

We were joined by a naturalist named Branson, a tall, muscular man who wore black elastic hiking pants, long sleeves, and gloves in spite of the heat of midsummer. He did step off the trail, pulling up stems and stuffing some of them into his backpack, while Eric narrated details about the ecosystem. Many of the trees are older than two hundred years and more than eighty feet high; they include red and white oak, red and sugar maple, tulip, shagbark hickory, and other species. Beneath most old-growth forest, the ground is often covered with moss, but the floor of these woods was leaf-strewn with tree seedlings sprouting from the litter along with midsummer-blooming jewelweed, blazing star, and blue vervain (from Latin *verbena,* meaning "sacred plant"). Fallen trees—necessary for official designation as old growth forest by the Ohio Department of Natural Resources Division of Forestry—are not removed but allowed to decay, becoming what are called "nursery logs" where lichens survive along with insects and grubs, which attract birds. Monarch butterflies, which I had previously seen only on wildflowers, clustered around some shrubs I was unable to identify. Spring blossoms had faded into brown petals, but the forest was not the "diminished thing" of Robert Frost's poem of the ovenbird and its summer habitat.

Invasive plants account for more than 40 percent of the decline in populations of threatened and endangered species. Branson scouted for the most intrusive of all—garlic mustard, so-called for the smell produced when its leaves are crushed—which has become particularly destructive in the temperate climates of the Northeast and Midwest. Hikers and gardeners are familiar with

Alliaria petiolata's heart-shaped, dark green, toothed leaves and diminutive but rather attractive white flowers. Brought from Europe in the 1800s for medicinal uses and erosion control, it spreads seeds on the wind. Because it emerges very early in the spring, it crowds out native plants by releasing chemicals that alter the underground network of fungi and ultimately inhibit the growth of some tree species. Although garlic mustard is easy to pull out because of its taproot, getting rid of it entirely sometimes requires years.

A thin-stemmed plant called Tree of Heaven does not transform these woods into paradise. The genus name, *Ailanthus*, comes from an Indonesian language, Ambonese, and means "the tree that reaches for the sky"; the species name, *altissima*, is Latin for "tallest." At one time classified as a sumac because of pinnately compound leaves arranged in pairs across the stem, it can be distinguished from the native sumac, ash, and black walnut by its reddish brown twigs. Sumac leaflets are serrated, whereas the Tree of Heaven's leaves have smooth edges. Unlike other species of *Ailanthus,* the Tree of Heaven thrives not in tropical but in temperate climates and was grown in China as a host for the *ailanthus* silk moth, which produces a sturdier fabric than the silkworm. In the 1740s, merchants and Jesuit missionaries brought the tree, sometimes called the "Chinese sumac," to Europe, where it gained popularity among gardeners because of its rapid growth, shady canopy, and resistance to plant disease.

During the mid-eighteenth century, a style called *chinoiserie* reached its zenith as architects, painters, and designers of clothing, decorative arts, and ceramics imitated East Asian images and patterns. In gardens, the style took the form of *Sharawagdi*—referring to "pleasing irregularity" that followed what was believed to be natural asymmetry. English landscape gardener and horticulturalist Sir William Temple (1628–1699) employed the term in his treatise "Upon the Gardens of Epicurus" (1690), in which he introduced the concept to Europe. In the leisurely style of the seventeenth century, Temple begins his essay with a long disquisition on the custom of gardening and whether *virtue* (defined by the Stoics) or *pleasure* (defined by Epicurus, who is said to have been the first to plant a garden in Athens) brings more happiness to human beings. The word *paradise,* he speculates, comes from Persian; even Xenophon (430–354 BC) uses it. The American Heritage Dictionary (second edition) gives the source as Avestan, a proto-Persian language, and the definition as "walled enclosure"; indeed, Temple's ideal gardens are all surrounded by walls. After naming the great statesmen, poets, and philosophers who examined the topic of virtue versus pleasure, he concludes that gardens produce most contentment because they delight all the senses. He also praises the Chinese way of planting, in which no order is easily observed (although there is planning) but which is far more difficult to master than European symmetrical figures. His descriptions of ideal arrangement prefigured the English country garden, which is designed but does not appear to be: different kinds of flowers and shrubs are placed next to each other with foliage often spilling over the edges of footpaths and borders and something blooming in every season. By contrast, the formal garden—reflecting emphasis on rationalism, balance, and reverence for antiquity—contains symmetrical beds of the same or similar flowers, trimmed hedges and topiary bushes, straight walkways meeting at right angles, and statuary in the Greek style.

Temple does not mention the Tree of Heaven, but it was used in many countries to revegetate areas of acid-mine drainage because it can withstand low pH, low phosphorous, and high salinity and is tolerant of drought and pollution—even sulfur dioxide, cement dust, coal tar fumes, ozone, and mercury. Sometimes referred to as a *ghetto palm,* it colonizes areas of rubble from destroyed buildings, as in Berlin after 1945 and Afghanistan more recently. The plant's notorious hardiness stems in part from its ability to secrete ailanthone, a chemical toxic to surrounding plants, and to produce abundant seeds. Destroying the indigenous plants, it engenders imbalances in the ecosystem, such as creating habitat for the invasive spotted lanternfly—which by 2014 had made its way to Pennsylvania where it caused extensive damage. Betty Smith describes the anomalous nature of the ghetto palm in *A Tree Grows in Brooklyn* (1945):

> There's a tree that grows in Brooklyn. Some people call it the Tree of Heaven. No matter where its seed falls, it makes a tree which struggles to reach the sky. It grows in boarded up lots and out of neglected rubbish heaps. It grows up out of cellar gratings. It is the only tree that grows out of cement. It grows lushly . . . survives without sun, water, and seemingly earth. It would be considered beautiful except that there are too many of it.

The novel tells the story of the hard lives of Irish immigrants who succeeded in bettering their situation through hard work. Today, we might acknowledge that white privilege and opportunity also play a large part in success, but so does environmental justice: the potato blight caused massive emigration from Ireland in the mid-nineteenth century. The Tree of Heaven had its uses, but today it is a curse, crowding out indigenous species much as human colonizers did.

Another invasive that inhibits native species and is named for a cultural myth is the burning bush (*Euonymus alatus*), imported from northeast Asia in 1860 as an ornamental. For about three weeks in the autumn, its flame-red leaves and bright red berries are spectacularly beautiful, but during most of the year it is unattractive, with dark, drab-green leaves and scraggly, gray-brown branches. While it is called a shrub, it can grow to ten feet in height and five or more in width, and so it sometimes becomes unwieldy in gardens and lawns. In forests, its layers of dropped seeds prevent other species from surviving; birds also disseminate seeds. In the myth, God spoke to Moses from a flaming bush that burned and yet lived (Exodus 3:2–6); the message was that he was to lead his people into the promised land of their ancestors. No miracle today, perhaps the burning bush speaks to us of a persistent belief that somewhere there exists a perfect land of our desire, as some of the original colonists hoped when they sailed to what they called "the new world," although it was an old world to those already living here.

In contrast, Jacob's Ladder (*Polemonium van-bruntiae*), also a midsummer flower named for mythological narrative, is indigenous although in some areas considered endangered. A member of the phlox family and a woodland perennial, it grows erect sometimes as high as three feet and has pointed leaves and, in summer, clusters of bell-shaped, bluish-purple flowers that attract pollinators. Paired leaflets are said to resemble the ladder to heaven that appeared in a dream to the patriarch Jacob, son of Isaac and grandson of Abraham (Genesis 28:12). For Christians and Jews, the image represents the connection between earth and heaven, human beings and God; for others it becomes the journey to spiritual perfection or perhaps even Nirvana. Whatever its symbolism, the plant fares best in shady places with organic soils in the Northeast, but once established, it is tolerant both of drought and deer. Horticulturalists are encouraged not to try to transplant the wild species but to choose the garden variety, called *Polemonium caeruleum* (the species name comes from the Latin for "sky" or "heaven"). Jacob's Ladder is sometimes mistaken for another variety from the phlox family, Greek valerian (*Polemonium reptans*), which has blue, bell-shaped flowers growing in clusters but does not grow as tall.

As we hiked, dried grasses lying in the xylem confluence of trees, where small branches attach to the trunks, appeared like birds' nests, except that they were too low to the ground; they turned out to be piles of invasive grasses pulled up and left to dry until the seeds are dead. Volunteers then drop them onto the trail to help prevent soil erosion. Caretakers, Eric explained, must step like Ninjas in a minefield, avoiding indigenous plants while tearing out invasives. Their work was evident: where nonnative species had been eliminated, wild orchids and other colorful woodland flowers grew in abundance. The arboreal confluence used to be called a *crotch:* thus in nomenclature we represent our bodies' relationship to the land, or perhaps our willingness to use the same terms merely reveals a pathetic fallacy.

We climbed a slope where the sky was readily visible and realized from the markers that it was a pipeline access, otherwise known as a highway for invasive species that enter the forest on the tires of the tractors and machines that plowed through the woods, leaving deep ruts in the soil and causing erosion on the slopes. Because the gas company owns the right-of-way, the conservancy cannot prevent the destruction. On both sides of the access lane, stinging nettle grows densely. While it is indigenous and not invasive, stinging nettle usually does not thrive in such profusion.

Pointing out horizontal lines that looked almost like crosscut-saw marks high on the trunks of white oak and tulip trees, Eric explained that they were the work of yellow-bellied sapsuckers, whose pecking allows sticky juice to flow from inner to outer layers of the bark. Insects attracted to the ooze become stuck and make protein-rich meals for the woodpeckers, which also drink the sap. According to Douglas Tallamy in *The Nature of Oaks* (2021), white oaks sustain four thousand species of animals, birds, and insects. By contrast, the burning bush plays host to aphids, black weevils, and spider mites, along with the euonymus caterpillar (*Yponomeuta cagnagella*), which, like its host, is a colonizer.

"Insects, not people, control the world," Eric commented.

Early in the hike, I spied what I guessed were tiny floating pinfeathers from birds, but as I observed them, I realized that they must be living, as they did not fall to the ground but propelled themselves through the air like swimmers. When I pointed them out, other hikers speculated that they must be moths. I had never seen, heard of, or read about a moth so diminutive.

At this point, Eric shared the disappointing fact that illegal "stealth timbering" by one of the heirs to the Hammond land had cut and sold twenty to thirty of the best white oaks and hickory. A family friend discovered the theft and alerted officials, who put a stop to it, but the most blemish-free trees had already been removed. No one seemed to know whether there had been legal consequences.

When Branson stepped away, Eric explained that the men employed to work for the conservancy were drug addicts in rehabilitation and convicted felons who had served their time. The loss rate of these workers was 50 percent, far lower than in most such programs. Eric told us that Branson knew as much about the woods as any formally educated naturalist and had been appointed foreman because he knew how to talk to the others and so could train them and persuade them to come to work on time. Their job was to pull out invasive species from 6:30 A.M. until 3:00 P.M. Branson later told me that his work had helped him to overcome a history of anger and fighting, because nature heals; he declared that he would not trade his current job for one that paid better because he was doing what he loved. Upon discovering three red Canada lilies on the hillside, he shouted and nearly danced. When I asked him for advice about how to motivate students, he answered indirectly. Only experience could teach, he said, and he believed that each day provided a new situation and problem to solve.

We crossed an old farm lane and saw firsthand the result of disturbance: multiflora rose growing profusely, no large trees, no nursery logs. The familiar fencepost with box wire still attached testified that the area had once been pasture. A few meters farther and we were in old growth again, although younger than the previous section of truly ancient inhabitants. There, the dominant older trees were white oak and shagbark hickory; in this section sugar maples dominated, although not nearly as high. Sticks lying horizontal to the slope of the hill, called dry dams, were laid purposely by volunteers to impede soil erosion by preventing the downward flow of water. Sometimes, larger logs were arranged for the same purpose, although volunteers try to disturb as little as possible. In this part of the woods, the slender stalks of common alumroot were now "common" again. Before the systematic removal of invasives, volunteers counted twenty Canada lilies; in

2020, they counted three hundred. Northern maidenhair fern, a threatened indigenous species that grows only in mature forests, spread profusely along the path. One area, nicknamed "Dutchman's bowl," formed a swale, or rounded depression, where Dutchman's breeches, an indigenous plant whose characteristic pantaloon-shaped white flowers bloom only in dense woods during springtime, now thrive. We saw forest flame, or forest candelabra flowers, and we spotted a Luna moth (*Actias luna*), the first I had ever seen in the wild. Its celadon-green wings with purple "fringe" and four "eyes" (colored spots) spread as wide as a person's palm. Although in the same family as the Asiatic silkworm, they are not closely related, and their cocoons do not produce the fine fibers of the Asian moth. They belong to the family called *Saturniidae*—for Saturn, Roman god of time, generation, abundance, and renewal. Usually active at night, they are now endangered, due to pesticide use and habitat loss. Thus, they are not abundant and their renewal today depends not on the will of the gods but on the will of human beings to preserve woodlands.

High in the trees I could hear a willow flycatcher, invisible because of the dense canopy, calling "bi-zyew," perhaps objecting to our intrusion.

Later, I investigated the mystery of the tiny moths and learned they were probably nearly microscopic creatures called *woolly alder aphids* (*Prociphilus tessellatus*), smaller than a half centimeter. Also termed *fairy flies,* they produce fluffy white colonies on tree branches that look like cotton candy and suck phloem from leaves, producing a sticky substance called *honeydew.* A sooty mold fungus then often colonizes the residue and produces a dense black fuzzy mat on leaves. In the fall, this layer becomes spongy and yellow and is sometimes mistaken for arboreal disease, when the only real damage is aesthetic. Woolly alder aphids and maple blight aphids, their relations, cause no harm to overall health of trees but are prey for lacewings, hoverflies, lady beetles, and parasitic wasps that also feed on garden pests such as Japanese beetles, mites, melon aphids, and cabbage worms. Caterpillars of the harvester butterfly are the only strictly carnivorous butterfly larvae in North America, feeding entirely on nutrient-rich aphids. The beautiful yellow and brown butterflies emerge in early spring and frequent wet woodlands and stream banks, continuing to feed on woolly aphids but varying their diet to include mushrooms, sap, and dung, but not the nectar on which most butterflies subsist. Never had I noticed the woolly aphids before in my hikes, perhaps because their tiny white wings, which appear iridescent in the darkness under a high canopy, were invisible in the abundant light in fields and younger woods. I learned to see them in shadows, not in radiance.

These fairylike creatures remind me that although human beings, in our hubris or narcissism, tell ourselves that the world was created for us and we may use it as an unending resource, most of the evidence points in the opposite direction: both the complexity of the biosphere and the unimaginable size of the universe reveal that we are infinitesimally unimportant. The vast majority of the creatures of the earth live their lives taking no notice of us unless we destroy their habitat. We tell ourselves that we are the only creatures who can appreciate beauty, but it may be that other animals do possess this ability, that in going about their own business they know and appreciate it as well. Some Native American groups believed animals were their greatest teachers because nonhuman species know instinctively how to survive, whereas people must be painstakingly taught and are the slowest to mature of all mammals. If one definition of wisdom is humility, then perhaps the greatest lesson we can learn is that we should be glad to be only a tiny part of the infinite beauty, much of which is yet to be known.

Our cultural myth begins with a garden of paradise and the first human being naming all the plants and animals, although we do not know what language he spoke, why he chose the names he did, or which were his favorites. Perhaps he represents an archetype of each tribe or clan that must find names for the creatures they encounter in their environment, as biologists create universal names from languages thought to be "dead" but that survive in contemporary speech. Perhaps we need a new, nature-centered myth or a new understanding of the old myth to provide the foundation for a way of life that might ensure survival of the biosphere as we know and depend on it. It may be that we have already arrived at the Promised Land and failed to recognize it.

Doris Duke Woods

NCOLC and Eric Miller in particular were players in another effort to protect and restore old-growth forests. For twenty years, they worked to convince the state legislature to designate 120 acres of the Doris Duke Woods at Malabar Farm State Park as preserved natural land, unavailable for logging. Heir to a cigarette fortune, their namesake purchased the woods from Louis Bromfield (1896–1956), who had planned to sell them for timbering in order to pay medical bills, although he had earlier criticized farmers for doing the same thing. Doris Duke (1912–1993), who knew Bromfield because of their shared interest in horticulture, donated the forest back to Malabar Farm, obtained by Friends of the Land (1956), who managed it for fourteen years before selling it to the State of Ohio, which designated the farm as a park in 1972.

Doris Duke, as colorful a figure as Louis Bromfield, inherited her fortune from her father, James Buchanan Duke, founder of the American Tobacco Company. She donated much of her money, fittingly, to medical research but also for education of African American children in the US South, restoration and protection of historic buildings, wildlife and ecology, and the performing arts. Her controversial life is well-documented, but as far as Malabar Farm is concerned, she saved the forest to the south of the great house across Bromfield Road, at least until the Ohio Department of Natural Resources (ODNR) became involved.

ODNR officials opposed giving the Doris Duke Woods the status of a protected nature preserve, even though the division had not announced any plans for timbering there, because officials wanted to have the discretion to decide whether a given forest could be made available for logging. NCOLC members invited Mark Romanchuk, Republican state legislator for the district and no environmentalist, to the woods and showed him the difference between conservancy land and ODNR-administered land. Convinced of the need for preservation, he sponsored legislation. On the first of July 2021, Governor Mike DeWine, also no friend to environmentalism or preservation, signed the bill into law, protecting the woods from logging. The Doris Duke Foundation pledged support for maintenance of hiking trails and signs while NCOLC raised $20,000 for removal of invasive species.

While the custom of planting pleasure gardens can be traced at least to ancient Greece, the realization that natural places should be preserved is much more recent. Established by naturalist Charles Waterton in 1821, Walton Hall Estate in West Yorkshire, in northern England, contains a park that may be the first modern nature preserve. Waterton constructed an extensive wall to enclose his park against poachers, encouraged birdlife by planting trees, hollowed out trunks to attract owls, and built artificial nest boxes to house jackdaws and starlings, native species in Great Britain—not reviled there as they are here. He allowed local people access to his estate, realizing that workers during the Industrial Revolution should have the opportunity to experience green space. Waterton was one of the first people who recognized that the natural world "needed protection as humanity made more and more demands on it," according to naturalist and filmmaker David Attenborough (b. 1926).

Not all landowners possessed such civic-mindedness. The various Enclosure Acts (from the twelfth to the nineteenth century), while they resulted in more productive farming practices, benefited mainly large landowners and at the same time drove many smallholders off their farms by prohibiting them from using what had been common land to graze their herds, plant crops, or gather fallen wood for fuel. Trees and forests represented more than landscape; their existence confirmed the power of property ownership, and the older the trees, the more ancient and venerable the family that possessed them. Landowners considered beeches to be patrician, while they associated elms with the working rural countryside.

Species of trees to be planted and choices of garden styles became subjects of serious study. In *The English Garden* (1783), clergyman-poet William Mason (1724–1797) advised planting of oaks, England's most iconic native trees, instead of what he referred to as "exotic" conifers; in *Guide to the Lakes* (1810), Wordsworth compared conifers to the nouveau riche and hardwoods to the aristocracy. English landscape designer William Kent (1685–1749) replaced the eighteenth-century formal garden with more naturalistic compositions. Uvedale Price (1747–1829) argued against Enlightenment symmetry and for asymmetrical nature, with older trees and rutted pathways. England's most famous landscape designer, Lancelot "Capability" Brown (1716–1783), favored groves of trees within extensive grasslands and foregrounded ponds, lakes, or streams.

In the United States, while national parks represent the impulse to protect "wilderness" as we conceive of it, state parks conserve natural areas on a smaller scale. The Butternut Cave trail at Malabar Farm, which begins behind Pugh Cabin and the maple-sugar cabin, and Doris Duke Woods trail, which commences across the road from the site of an old grist mill, both take the hiker into stands of red and white oak, beech, sugar maple, shagbark hickory, aspen, tulip poplar, and a few eastern hemlock. The floor is a leafy expanse with scattered stems of young trees and dark ferns growing around rocky sandstone outcroppings. Students in vocational agriculture programs have constructed benches where hikers and casual walkers can meditate on vistas considered to be particularly aesthetic, all of them on hillsides overlooking valleys or dales. Visiting in late summer, I heard little birdsong but did hear the hammering of woodpeckers, shriek of a red-tailed hawk, and long, shrill notes of the wood peewee. Chipmunks scampered away to perch on fallen logs, where they chattered at me, an intruder into their territory. Orange forget-me-not, pink lady's thumb, yellow wild snapdragons, horseweed, snakeroot, ragweed, coneflowers, primrose, curly dock, Japanese knotweed, white blazing star (also called fairy wand), and bird's-foot trefoil still bloomed, although the beautiful purple blossoms of great lobelia were fading.

Around the margins and near the pathways I saw profusions of American feverfew, tall green stems about two feet high with pointed leaves and clustered, tiny white flowers. As a plant that likes only partial shade, feverfew does not flourish in the dense woods. *Parthenium* obtains its genus name from the Greek *parthenos,* or "virgin"; the Parthenon temple on the Acropolis is dedicated to Athena, goddess of wisdom, revered for her chastity. The species name *integrifolium* comes from Latin and means "uncut." The plant's medicinal properties inspired the common names "feverfew" and "wild quinine": it was once used to cure fever or headaches. Today we rely on manufacturers for healing drugs and have largely forgotten what our ancestors knew of the power of wild plants. I do not suggest that we should give up the miraculous drugs developed over the last century, but only that we should appreciate what quietly grows unbidden around us and not lose the old knowledge.

Sacred trees and forests occupy an important place in legend and myth. Sometimes deep woods are associated in stories with danger, chaos, savagery, lawlessness, or loss of individuality; conversely, they represent safety from corruption, freedom, innocence, and affirmation of personality. The Garden of Eden contained many trees from which its human inhabitants might freely eat, but they were forbidden to taste the fruit of the tree of knowledge, whereby they at last knew themselves. As the story progresses, a tree becomes the cross, although we are not told what kind of wood it was made from. The Greek goddess Artemis, patron of the grove, never allowed herself to be seen by human beings and became emblematic of idealism. Dionysus—god of vegetation, wine, and revelry—who was hanged on a tree, gave his name to primal emotions. In Norse mythology, the ash Yggdrasil stood as the cosmic tree at the center of the world below which flowed springs of destiny, wisdom, and understanding. The god Odin hung from its branches for nine days and nights to acquire its hidden knowledge. The word *tree* in Proto-Indo-European stems from the same root as *true: dreu;* in Anglo-Saxon, the word *trēow* contains both meanings. *Weid* is Proto-Indo-European for "see" or "know"; *deruweid* means "oak-seer" or "oak-knower"; hence, *doire*—Irish for oak tree—becomes "druid," a seer, shaman, priest, or magician. Ancient druids associated oak trees with wisdom and hazel trees with creativity and inspiration.

Interested in horticulture rather than mythology, Doris Duke purchased timbering rights so the forest would not be logged. She lived long enough to see Malabar Farm become a state park, but with the transfer from Friends of the Land to the State of Ohio, the trees were again subject to exploitation, and again, someone who cared about ecological integrity had to become involved before the old-growth woods were protected. Nor can anyone remain content that they always will be: at any point the legislature can repeal the law that NCOLC members worked so hard for, and currently the state legislature is not dominated by people who possess much concern for nature or for preservation.

Ten

Further Reflections on Louis Bromfield and Malabar Farm

FARMERS HAVE LITTLE TIME for writing, but a few have made their names as authors, such as Hector Saint John de Crevecœur (1735–1813), who authored the important memoir *Letters from an American Farmer* (1782). More recent literary agriculturalists include Aldo Leopold (1887–1948), Wendell Berry (b. 1934), and Wes Jackson (b. 1936). One of the most famous American farmers of modern times and the best-known in his day was Louis Bromfield (1896–1956), who earned wealth and fame as a writer of popular novels and screenplays but returned from France at age forty-three to his birthplace in Richland County, Ohio, bought three farms, and engaged in an experiment in sustainable methods of fertilization and cultivation. Like his inspiration Thomas Jefferson (1743–1826), Bromfield possessed resources that enabled him to buy the land, build a mansion, and restore the soil, but while the planter of Virginia inherited his wealth, the Ohioan earned his.

Although he spent much time in New York City, Los Angeles, and Paris, Bromfield declared the best life to be found in farming. While many of his closest friends were famous writers, actors, and socialites, he claimed the best companions were good farmers. One week found him drinking cocktails with influential people at the Algonquin Hotel in Manhattan; the next saw him forking manure from his dairy barn. Bromfield spent much time away from the farm—in Washington, California, and New York—giving speeches on soil conservation, but when he was at home, he worked along with the laborers, harvesting vegetables, weeding the garden, raking hay, fishing with the children of his workers, and walking the land. He believed in self-sufficiency but also in government investment in public works. While placing great faith in education, he criticized academics who relied too much on theory and students who transformed their college experiences into four-year holidays. He found solace in his farm but turned it into an agricultural experiment and welcomed so many guests that eventually he felt it necessary to escape from them. So large was the number of visitors to Malabar Farm that Bromfield inspired the interest of J. Edgar Hoover and the FBI, which kept a file on him.

The thing Bromfield most hated was soil erosion; the thing he loved best was creating rich, fertile humus in which to grow flowers, vegetables, and fruit. He nurtured grasslands, which he called "the great healer" long before most people knew of the power of grass and legumes to sequester carbon. Although part of the expatriate community of Europe during the 1920s, he never lost his optimism. For special criticism he singled out two thinkers who could not have been more opposite: Alexander Hamilton (1755–1804), whose plutocratic values Bromfield believed constituted America's greatest corruption, and Karl Marx (1818–1883), whom the farmer described as "sick and psychopathic." The enemy of a great nation was its unplanned industrial cities, while small, diversified family farms represented salvation. During the war, along with fundraising and political advocacy on the plight of Jews and other refugees in Europe, Bromfield experimented with methods of soil fertility and later stated that after soldiers, farmers were the heroes of the conflict because they created food surpluses that sustained the military effort. Fittingly, at Malabar they celebrated VE Day (May 8, 1945) by plowing.

The *Dictionary of Literary Biography: Twentieth-Century American Nature Prose Writers* (2003), *American Nature Writers* (1996), and the *Norton Anthology of Nature Writing* (1990) include not only authors famous for their environmentalism, such as Edward Abbey, Rick Bass, Gretel Ehrlich, and Wallace Stegner, but even some who are not primarily nature writers, such as Ursula Le Guin and John Steinbeck; yet they leave out Louis Bromfield, who early on shared an interest in sustainability with his own contemporary, the influential conservationist Aldo Leopold, as well as his most famous predecessor, Henry David Thoreau (1817–1862). Perhaps editors omit Bromfield because they consider his writing too restricted to one region—although the same objection could be raised about Abbey's and Stegner's works—and both his fiction and nonfiction prose reveal universality of concern. Sustainable agriculturalists today recognize the importance of his contribution, among them farmer, poet, and essayist Wendell Berry, who testifies in his essay "For the Love of Farming" that Bromfield was "not one of those bad pastoral writers whose love for farming is distant, sentimental, and condescending"; his love of the land was not a "quaint souvenir of an outdated past" but an "economic necessity." Agricultural experience as well as prose style should earn Bromfield a place in anthologies of nature writing, but he also deserves to be numbered among the philosophers of environmentalism, such as Leopold and John Muir (1838–1914).

The recent biography by historian Stephen Heyman, *The Planter of Modern Life: Louis Bromfield and the Seeds of a Food Revolution* (2020), narrates a fascinating story, although one beset by personal tribulations, including restlessness, infidelity, alcoholism, and chain-smoking. Heyman gives the credit for restoration of the soil at Malabar to Max Drake, Bromfield's first farm manager, and describes Drake's chagrin when his boss exaggerated claims of how quickly and economically soil could be restored;

others praised Bromfield for inspiring excitement about sustainability, however overstated the details may have been. The biographer relates the story of Louis as a boy learning his first lessons on his grandfather's farm, which was eventually lost; the young man in Europe driving an ambulance during the Great War; Bromfield in his twenties working as a journalist in New York City; the family living in a country house near Senlis, in France, and entertaining some of the most interesting people in the literary world at the time, including Gertrude Stein and Edith Wharton; their return to Ohio and Bromfield's experiments in soil restoration; and finally the middle-aged man's crusade to bring the message of conservation to the country at large. In *Malabar Farm: Louis Bromfield, Friends of the Land, and the Rise of Sustainable Agriculture* (2021) Anneliese Abbott explains that the farm's legacy is diminished today because "the soil conservation movement that made the farm famous was almost completely left out of agricultural history books published during the Cold War." In addition, Bromfield's later politics alienate many contemporary ecologists.

※

Telling his mother, "It is better to be killed than to miss the greatest experience of your generation," Bromfield left his studies in journalism at Columbia to volunteer for the American Field Service, becoming an ambulance driver in France during the spring of 1917, as so many other literary figures of the time did, including Ernest Hemingway, Malcom Cowley, John Dos Passos, and E. E. Cummings. In a narrative that reads like a novel, Heyman describes in a few pages the harrowing experiences of the ambulance drivers—who were under fire much of the time, seeing and handling the mangled wounded and dead—and quotes from one of Bromfield's letters: "It is a terrible responsibility that at times I think I shall go mad." At the same time, the young midwesterner was charmed and inspired by the landscape of France, including carefully tended gardens and "blue evening light" among the trees.

After the war, Bromfield spent six years in New York City working for *Time, Musical America,* G. P. Putnam, and the *Bookman* as a journalist, critic, editor, publicity director, and columnist, during which time he was described as having "boundless vigor," "astonishing vitality," and an "inexhaustible fund of native energy" but also as being nervous, volatile, and periodically almost insolent. Charming while also sometimes awkwardly shy, he spent hours in coffeehouses and bars and yet also wrote and published his well-received first novel, *The Green Bay Tree* (1924), and a five-hundred-page sequel, *Possession* (1925).

From Heyman's description and some of Bromfield's journal entries, such as one in *Malabar Farm* in which he describes talking with friends until 3:30 A.M. before a fifteen-mile drive home and working the next morning on articles about state natural resources, I conclude that Bromfield was among those people who need little sleep in order to function. Although the quality of his work was uneven, he wrote at a stunning rate, delivered lectures all over the country, gave and attended parties, and labored diligently on his farm. It may be, however, that his great early success interfered with his ability to improve his talent and become a really good novelist rather than a popular storyteller, as current critics describe him.

Those six years in New York convinced Louis and his wife, Mary Appleton Wood, that they needed an adventure. Paris offered them a new life, as it had so many American expatriates, including Zelda and Scott Fitzgerald, Ernest and Hadley Hemingway, Gertrude Stein, Edith Wharton, and Edna Ferber, among others. Bromfield's literary reputation first blossomed with nearly instant popular success, critical acclaim, and a Pulitzer Prize for *Early Autumn* (1926). While America suffered from the effects of the 1929 stock market crash, Bromfield earned a good living with his bestselling short story collection *Awake and Rehearse* (1929) and a lucrative five-year contract from *Cosmopolitan* to serialize his new novels. In the *New York Herald Tribune,* columnist Lucius

Beebe described Bromfield as "one of the most glittering and opulent of the Paris–Manhattan commuters."

By the 1930s, when these glitterati were either returning home or leaving the city for the suburbs, Bromfield did the latter, leasing and renovating the eighteenth-century Presbytère de Saint-Étienne. Possessing knowledge of cultivation from his work on his grandfather's farm, he increased his horticultural talents with help from his peasant gardener, Victor Picquet, and the working-man gardener, Bosquet, whom Bromfield describes in *Pleasant Valley* (1945) as a person who made himself entirely self-sufficient on his own two acres where he grew or raised nearly everything his family ate. (Heyman cautions, however, that Bromfield's romantic vision of the French laborers' independence should be tempered by an understanding of the poverty many of them experienced.) The Paris society set visited the family in Senlis, including writers Stein, Wharton, Ferber, and Rebecca West; actors Douglas Fairbanks, Myrna Loy, and Leslie Howard; aristocrats Lady Juliet Duff and the Maharani of the Indian state of Cooch Behar; and others, such as designers Elsa Schiaparelli and Van Day Truex. In France, where the land was "sacred," gardens were creations; an artist friend of Stein's named Francis Rose even compared Bromfield's flower beds with Monet's.

Although Bromfield lived in France during the Depression and Dust Bowl of the 1930s, those events helped to change his thinking. While receiving acclaim for his bestsellers, which resembled many nineteenth-century novels of manners, he decided to produce a new work of a very different type. The result, a heavily embroidered family history called *The Farm*, was a 350-page saga of four generations, beginning with the nineteenth-century colonel who moves his family from Maryland to the frontier country of Ohio after serving in the War of 1812 and begins life as an agriculturalist, much as Bromfield's great-grandfather (a captain, not a colonel) had done. "The Town" and "the County" in the novel sound much like Mansfield and Richland County. The farmer called "Old Jamie" resembles Bromfield's maternal grandfather, and his grandson Johnny, who leaves the farm to become urbane and successful, is probably a stand-in for the author. Praising *The Farm* as a reversal of the pioneer archetype like James Fennimore Cooper's heroes, Gertrude Stein claimed Bromfield was the first to describe the "now frontierless and uprooted" descendants of settlers. While *The Farm* suffers from confusing shifts in focus and overreliance on straight description rather than development, it was a bestseller, as was Stein's own autobiography, published in 1933.

Five years later, as all Europe beheld with horror the increasing power of Fascism in Spain, Germany, and Italy, Bromfield took charge of the Emergency Committee for the American Wounded, which aided more than a thousand men of the Lincoln Brigadiers, who had fought against the Fascists in the Spanish Civil War—for which he eventually received the French Legion of Honor. In September 1938, Mary and their three daughters returned to the United States while Bromfield stayed on to continue his relief work. During a visit to a park in Ermenonville in November, where Jean-Jacques Rousseau (1712–1778) spent his final days, Bromfield met with a good friend, the literary critic and art historian Louis Gillet, who persuaded him to return home, where he could be of greater help to France: according to Bromfield, Gillet "sent me back to the country where I was born, to Pleasant Valley and the richest life I have ever known."

The narrative of *Pleasant Valley* describes Bromfield's process of creating and running his famous experimental farm. In 1939, he first purchased 246 acres from Clement Herring, whose land included what Bromfield refers to as the Ferguson Place because it was originally settled by William Ferguson, a pioneer fur-trader from Pennsylvania. Shortly afterward, Bromfield bought from Frederick Beck about 110 acres (now the working farm) that had been owned by people named Berry and before that by Charles Schrack, a year later adding about seventy low-lying acres, which at Malabar became a pleasure garden called The Jungle. Finally, in 1942, Bromfield acquired about 150 acres, which included the red-brick house built by David Schrack and which is now the

Malabar Farm Inn and the hillside known then as Poverty Knob and now as Mount Jeez. He named his estate for the Malabar Coast of India, the setting for his novel *The Rains Came* (1937) and the movie of the same name (1939), acknowledging that the money from that novel and screenplay rights paid for the farm.

Bromfield employed pseudonyms for the places he purchased, ostensibly to avoid offending the previous owners or perhaps to avoid law suits, as he severely criticizes their farming practices. He refers to the Herring farm as the Anson place, the Schrack/Berry/Beck farm as the Fleming place, and the Schrack/Niman farm as the Bailey place. The Ferguson land remains with its original name, as Bromfield was fond of the story of the pioneer farmer. He criticizes the Berry house caustically, calling it a mail-order structure; yet it is a large, white, rather elegant frame residence built in 1910 with many rooms and a view of Switzer Creek. After the farm became a state park, the Berry house was used for offices; later it served as a youth hostel and is now headquarters for the Fiber Arts Guild.

In his nonfiction, Bromfield explored theories about agricultural best practices, social order, and personal philosophy. Stephen Heyman describes *Pleasant Valley* as a "drippy memoir," yet it contains some of Bromfield's most lyrical passages. A national bestseller, it was nevertheless satirized by Nobel laureate Sinclair Lewis (1885–1951) in an *Esquire* essay titled "The Boxers of M. Voltaire" (Bromfield kept several boxers), in which Lewis wrote that the farmer botched his attempt to create an enduring book. Perhaps the best of Bromfield's nonfiction works are *Malabar Farm* (1947), which comes close to being a twentieth-century *Walden* (1847), and *From My Experience* (1955), which includes some of his most philosophical essays.

In the short preface to *Pleasant Valley*, Bromfield wrote that farming was the key to America's economy and that the "wealth, welfare, prosperity and even the future freedom of this nation are based upon the soil," and he warned that Americans would pay dearly for the destruction of the soil and wilderness because of greed. Agriculture was the backbone of civilization, and when agriculture failed, society did as well, because a nation unable to feed itself could never achieve independence. Soil erosion constituted moral failure. "Man himself cannot escape from Nature," he wrote; "neither can he ever subdue her or attempt to exploit her endlessly without becoming himself the victim." This statement appears unusually prescient in a time when climate change, caused by the burning of fossil fuels, constitutes the greatest threat to survival. In the same book, Bromfield articulates his theory about the need for a new race of pioneer farmers concerned primarily with the land. Soil and forests were "eternally renewable and productive" if treated sustainably. Here again, Bromfield suggests his literary debt to Thoreau, who muses in *Walden*, "Ancient poetry and mythology suggest, at least, that husbandry was once a sacred art; but it is pursued with irreverent haste and heedlessness by us, our object being to have large farms and large crops merely." Considering the soil as mere property, Thoreau continued, degraded husbandry to the extent that the farmer led "the meanest of lives."

Always searching for practical solutions, Bromfield articulated in *From My Experience* his conviction that research should begin through observation in the field followed by controlled experimentation. To restore the land, he and Max Drake employed low tillage, a method in which some crop residue is left on the surface. No-till management, advocated by Edward H. Faulkner (1886–1964) in *Plowman's Folly* (1943), leaves most or all crop residue after harvest in order to hold the soil when rain would otherwise carry it downhill and into ditches or waterways. Bromfield also praised Sir Albert Howard (1873–1947), who in *Soil and Health* (1945) and *An Agricultural Testament* (1940) emphasized soil's living nature. Now widely employed, low tillage increases biological diversity, provides fertilization, reduces release of carbon dioxide, decreases compaction, retains moisture, moderates temperature, and controls erosion. From his garden in Senlis, Bromfield had learned that fungi attach to roots and feed the plants in a symbiotic relationship. To correct imbalances between minerals and organic material in the soil, the manager at Malabar Farm employed barnyard manure, legumes in rotation, lime, and some commercial fertilizer to restore humus and create inches of topsoil rapidly; by contrast, nature required a thousand years to create one inch of fertile soil. Crop rotation cut down on insect damage. Seventeen years before the publication of Rachel Carson's *Silent Spring* (1962), Bromfield warned against the indiscriminate use of DDT; it eventually created insects resistant to the insecticide and killed birds and fish.

Given the similarity of their interests, it is strange that Bromfield never met Aldo Leopold, who restored his acreage in Wisconsin mostly at the same time as the Malabar experiment. Posthumously published, *A Sand County Almanac and Sketches Here and There* (1949) contains essays that share Bromfield's anecdotal style and articulate the conviction that "progress" defined in material terms presented diminishing returns. The collection concludes with four essays on the ethics of a conservation movement, making the case for considering nature to have basic rights as human beings do: "That land is a community is the basic concept of ecology, but that land is to be loved and respected is an extension of ethics. That land yields a cultural harvest is a fact long known, but latterly often forgotten."

While Leopold focused on wilderness and wildlife, Bromfield's major concern was soil. Arguing that monocropping led to erosion, Bromfield singled out for special criticism corn, cotton, and tobacco—"commodity" crops, in contemporary argot. He wrote that General Sherman's 1864 "scorched earth" campaign paled in comparison to what Georgians did to their own land by overplanting cash crops and employing chemical fertilizers exclusively. He even encouraged young farmers to "Go South, Young Man!" because there were more opportunities there to correct bad practices.

Soil was his first concern, but Bromfield also loved animals and interspersed his chapters on restoration with anecdotes about best practices in husbandry. First published in *Animals and Other Peo-*

ple (1955) and later in *From My Experience* (1955), an essay called "A Hymn to Hawgs" bluntly rejected the idea that all animals are alike. Pigs and goats are "gifted with great powers of logic, reflection, judgment, deduction and mockery," traits associated with witchcraft. Allowing hens to feed where steers had been pastured—a technique organic farmers now widely practice—improved the birds' health because they received vitamin B12 from cattle manure. He cautions against the common practice of clipping their beaks to reduce cannibalism because feeding them properly will create the desired result. Free-range chickens were happier and produced better, as they acquired protein from worms, insects, and legumes.

One of Bromfield's ideas that turned out to be disastrous was the importation of multiflora rose from Europe to serve as natural hedgerows. Planted along existing fence lines, the thicket became impenetrable to cows or sheep and created "ideal wildlife conditions," such as bird habitat, especially for thrushes, which are voracious insect-eaters. Bromfield did not live to see his ideal fencerow become an invasive weed, crowding out indigenous vegetation. It does create habitat, however, much favored by deer, groundhogs, and birds, and bees and other pollinators frequent the voluminous white spring flowers.

Desiring self-sufficiency and a sense of permanence, Bromfield originally envisioned his operation as an old-fashioned general farm, on which he grew every type of vegetable and fruit the resident families used—as well as cattle, hens, hogs, goats, and sheep. The gradual disappearance of the diversified family farm and its replacement with mechanized factory cultivation were the reasons for the sickness of American agriculture: regimentation, centralization, mechanization, and industrialism did not represent progress. The origins of good farming lay not in pioneer sod-busting or in large-scale production but in European methods, customs that only the Amish and Mennonite farmers still kept. He soon realized, however, that economic realities would not allow his model to be profitable; in the current age, specialization was necessary, so he turned to grass farming while continuing to raise bees for honey, apple trees for cider, and maple trees for syrup.

Bromfield also weighed in on the necessity of water conservation. Draining the swamps of Minnesota by the Works Progress Administration revealed the soil's unsuitability for agriculture. The WPA then restored the swamps (what we call wetlands today) by reintroducing beavers, which built ponds, and by constructing artificial lakes—as they did in Belgium, France, Denmark, and Holland—to control floods aggravated by deforestation. Because of devastation caused by the Great Flood of 1913, Ohio's greatest "natural" disaster, the state authorized watershed administrations, among them the Muskingum Watershed Conservancy District. Rainfall in 1947 proved to be as heavy as in 1913, but no widespread property damage resulted. One body of water the conservancy district created was Pleasant Hill Lake, which Bromfield could see from the hills of Malabar Farm. Praising the conservancy, he declares that it belongs to the people and creates wealth through tourism, flood control, and improved agriculture, without spending tax revenue. He pointed out the superiority of such projects over socialism while neglecting to acknowledge that government projects do require tax revenue and are intended to benefit all the people. Bromfield also warned against the dangers of dams as indiscriminate flood control while ignoring "erosion, bare earth, siltation, rainfall, and *actual* value of marshes." One example was the levees built on the lower Mississippi when the solution, he claimed, lay in the headwaters. At the same time, Bromfield praised the "knowledgeable engineers" who designed the Tennessee Valley Authority—criticized today by some environmentalists for its near-monopolistic control of water resources.

A century after the appearance of Thoreau's *Walden*, Bromfield published his own version of moral and naturalist philosophy in *Malabar Farm*. Like Thoreau's chapter "The Ponds," Bromfield began "The Cycle of a Farm Pond" by calling the body of water "a symbol of life itself" and "a whole universe." The pond contains everything in the seasons from the "frozen, silent sleep of winter" to the "fierce breeding life of early summer. . . . And like the fishponds of the abbeys and castles of medieval Europe . . . they provide not only food for the table but peace for the soul and an understanding of man's relationship to the universe." Thoreau described Walden Pond as "green at one time and blue at another, even from the same point of view. Lying between the earth and the heavens, it partakes of the color of both." A lake or pond was beautiful and expressive: "It is earth's eye; looking into which the beholder measures the depth of his own nature." White Pond and Walden were "great crystals on the surface of the earth, Lakes of Light." As Bromfield was to do later, Thoreau also named the pond's inhabitants—the fish, ducks, skaters, and water bugs—as neighbors and friends.

While Thoreau wrote that "a town is saved by the woods and swamps that surround it," Bromfield reserved his greatest criticism for industry and big cities that he termed "the curse of the nation, perhaps of the whole world" because they brought "bad health and morals and insecurity and misery," which were not worth the gains from the machinery created in big factories: "A growing urban proletariat without economic security can wreck everything that America has been in the past and darken the whole of her future." Comparing postwar America with the Roman Empire, he stated that the United States had reached a peak in its civilization and would descend through exhaustion and "moral decadence" into anarchy and primitive existence.

Bromfield's social essays reveal stridently classist and regionalist assumptions, particularly with regard to those whom he calls "the southern hill people," claiming that northern farmhands possessed initiative and energy born of rich soil. With some empathy, Bromfield declared that economic problems of impoverished whites were not their own fault but were caused by poor "soil, diet, and education in that order." While blaming degrading Jim Crow laws for keeping southern Negroes (Bromfield's term) from economic advancement, he describes them as "scarcely above the level of an African savage . . . some of them considerably below the level of many an African native with a background of native tradition and primitive civilization." In spite of his regrettable vocabulary and implicit racism, Bromfield here identified the problem not as something endemic to a racial or ethnic group but to inferior economic conditions and loss of indigenous culture. As the cure for bad farming was to end soil erosion by building up humus from organic material, the cure for social ills and racial differences was equal economic opportunity, education, ethics, healthier diet, enriched soil, and "the annihilation of ideas about the superiority of one race over another." Returning to his overarching theme, Bromfield declared that human beings who worked in harmony with the earth achieved prosperity and happiness; fighting it left them impoverished, defeated, miserable, and eventually destroyed.

Unlike many of the writers of his generation, Bromfield apparently believed in the possibility of improvement of human beings and civilization. The world needed another Rousseau, who influenced the Romantic writers with his notion of a classless society living in a state of nature, uncorrupted by commerce and property ownership. He emphasized that true "progress" and better living conditions were not synonymous with materialism. Human beings, Bromfield asserted, did not live by things alone—not machines or guaranteed wages—if nature and the spirit are ignored: "Mankind can do without plumbing but not without Saint Francis of Assisi." The faith of a good farmer transcends religion grounded in church-going, fear, or superstition because he observes daily the laws of the universe, which are "essentially beyond understanding."

Like *Walden*, *Malabar Farm* contains chapters describing specific places important to an understanding of local ecology. As did Thoreau, Bromfield advocates close observation in order to understand the natural world; for example, tree frogs' singing prophesized rain. "The Story of Kemper's Run" narrates the history of a beautiful, abundant creek surrounded by marshes, but overfarming and cutting of willows (I assume swamp willows, which thrive on stream banks) have caused flooding and siltation. Thinking they would improve the stream, people straightened and deepened it, but soil erosion continued. The problem lay with bad practices, not with the creek.

Bromfield began his 1955 memoir *From My Experience: The Pleasures and Miseries of Life on a Farm* with a lyrical chapter titled "Fifteen Years After (By Way of Introduction)," in which he describes what he hoped to find: "I knew the country in the marrow of my bones. . . . I knew the marshes and the hills, the thick, hardwood forests, the wide fields and the beautiful hills behind which lay one lovely small valley after another," each a new, rich, mysterious self-contained world. Approaching the owners of one of the farms, he was "knocking at the door of my long-gone boyhood." Neither the chapter nor the book is a sentimental sojourn down memory lane, however; in a footnote Bromfield indicates that although he sought escape from "the troubles, the follies and the squabbles of Europe," he found no relief from political turmoil in the United States, nor could he take pride in its "meddling in the affairs of other nations . . . saber rattling . . . attempts to dominate the world and dictate the policies of other nations." As Thoreau wrote in "Life Without Principle," "Even if we grant that the American has freed himself from a political tyrant, he is still the slave of an economical and moral tyrant," Bromfield denied notions of American superiority, wisdom, or vision; neither citizens nor politicians understood much about other countries.

After a long and successful career, Bromfield confessed his realization that the "mysteries of the human mind" were less interesting than the "cosmic mysteries which take place within a cubic foot of rich productive soil." Again sounding like Aldo Leopold and Henry David Thoreau, he stated, "One of the great errors of our time . . . is the attribution of an overweening and disproportionate importance to man and his mind . . . his ego and self-importance . . . are given a distorted, decadent and tragicomic importance. . . . Man is merely a part of the universe, and not a very great part." Mere learnedness was insignificant without understanding. Bromfield believed his real contribution was not to literature but to agriculture, the only profession that made use of all science and philosophy. He had not found a return to the past but a new, more useful way of life.

In his nonfiction, Bromfield's tone alternated between lyrical and hortatory, his discourse between pastoral and harangue. Americans resembled reckless sons who inherit too much money and whose get-rich-quick philosophies led them to want something for nothing and to equate a better life with automobiles, cinemas, refrigerators, and plumbing. The true meaning of civilization involved education, spirit, and sense of humanity: "Mechanized progress is a matter of comfort and convenience which can have the result of blocking the growth of civilization, distorting it and perhaps destroying it." The industrial revolution had not created better thinkers or statesmen; Bromfield concluded that real simplicity was born of intelligence, vitality, and elimination of nonessentials, even as he lived in a large house and enjoyed many modern conveniences.

"Of Green Hills and Valleys," one of the most lyrical chapters in *Pleasant Valley,* articulates the naturalist's philosophy of the interrelatedness of all beings. Beginning with the colorful Mr. Jarvis, the county bee inspector, the farmer stated that bees change the look of the valley by increasing fertility. Watching the rabbits in his garden gave Bromfield a "vague and curious sense of participating in the mystery of Nature itself, of being not a specimen of dauntless, clever, all-powerful mankind, but of being only an integral and humble part of something very great and very beautiful," like the Jains of India who hold that what is sacred is the principle of life itself.

In the same essay, Bromfield describes the land slowly restoring itself until it seemed like a new world. With more advanced contour farming, water percolated more deeply into the ground. Where bare soil once eroded during winter, there was now orchard grass, and among the hundred-year-old apple trees grew peach, pear, and plum trees and grapes, raspberries, and blueberries. Natural springs reappeared: "As year passed into year the flow of the old springs increased and new ones appeared.... What we had done was a simple thing; simply to restore the balance of Nature, to keep the water where it belonged, on our land rather than turning it loose down the long course of the rivers finally to reach the Gulf of Mexico." The most famous spring on his farm, at the Bailey place, was "one of the largest in all Ohio, where a whole brook gushes out of the sandstone outcrop behind the old house. It flows through an ancient springhouse with great troughs hewn from single blocks of the native stone. In the troughs filled with icy water stand cans of milk, crocks of cream and butter."

The farmer declared his favorite place at Malabar to be the pond created near the working farm. Bluegrass and white clover in the pasture around it grew "like an extravagant lawn, the kind of lawn an English gardener dreams of." Domesticated ducks and geese shared their home with wild ducks, fish, frogs, turtles, and muskrats. Red-winged blackbirds and song sparrows lived in the willows, dogwood, and sycamore that grew around the border. The little world contained sad stories like an ancient snapping turtle killing baby ducks and comic ones such a goose biting a sow's ear. He concluded with the theme of his collection, that when he visited the pond he began to "understand exactly where man fits in"—not at the apex looking over his kingdom, but part of the biosphere.

"The White Room" in *From My Experience* may rank as the most philosophical essay in all of Bromfield's nonfiction. Although the meditation mostly concerns his life at Malabar Farm and in France, the narration begins in his study at his daughter's farm in Brazil. Workers came from many countries, including Italy, Portugal, Japan, Spain, France, Germany, and the United States, as well as Brazil. The place provided an escape from Malabar Farm, which had become so busy with visitors that there could be no peace but only "the driving turmoil that affects nearly all Americans, and prevents us at times from really living at all, permitting us merely to go through life in one long and somewhat noisy procession, always animated but at times empty," like Thoreau's conviction that most men lead lives of "quiet desperation."

In a life of great activity, Bromfield found it necessary to reexamine his ambitions and conclude with an "accounting." Thinking of himself as Deist and animist, Bromfield finally found what he sought in Albert Schweitzer's *Out of My Life and Thought*. Schweitzer (1875–1965) represented the complete man—not a specialist, but a musician, scientist, and philosopher who sought to make a lasting contribution. He was also a theologian and physician. Bromfield particularly admired Schweitzer's "Reverence for Life," which brought together the elements of the material with the ethical and spiritual, something the Church had not been able to do but which contained "the shadow of the glory of the Greeks." Agriculture, furthermore, enabled man to deal constantly with all the laws of the universe: "Every good farmer practices, even though he may not understand clearly, the principle of Reverence for Life, and in this he is among the most fortunate of men, for he lives close enough to Life to hear the very pulsations of the heart, which are concealed from those whose lives are concentrated upon the unbalanced shabbiness of the completely material." Only the ignorant and bigoted thought that they alone knew the path toward heaven and compelled others by persecution.

Bromfield articulated his economic and psychological theories clearly but also stridently in *A Few Brass Tacks* (1946), a series of four essays on social philosophy. In "Real Wealth Versus Money," he defines wealth not as currency but resources, and asserts that its only effective use is investment such as in construction (dams and highways), reforestation, and soil conservation. Agricultural land constituted the greatest wealth in the United States. While many New Deal programs squandered money rather than invested it, industrialists and bankers similarly destroyed both the natural and created US wealth at a rate unparalleled in world history.

Acknowledging that political ideologies followed crises and were born of bad economic conditions, Bromfield, from the vantage point of nearly a century, declared Karl Marx, "Germany's first totalitarian thinker," yet he also claimed that no one is a greater victim of the illusion that money equaled wealth than the industrial worker constantly struggling for higher wages; economic stability was instead based on agriculture or more specifically the soil. What Bromfield does not acknowledge is that, however incorrect his theories of dialectical materialism proved to be, Karl Marx nevertheless understood that the growth of industrial cities led to economic insecurity for workers, and he envisioned not totalitarianism but freedom for the individual "wage slave," a sentiment with which Bromfield would have concurred. Marx's ideal life included the annihilation of dehumanizing routine, which the Ohioan criticized severely.

Bromfield claimed in "Agriculture in Relation to Our National Economy" that few city-dwellers had any idea of how the mismanagement of the soil affected their lives, health, and even social and political liberties. Americans should realize—and I have read this detail nowhere else—that the record food production which helped to win the war was not the result of advanced agricultural practices but of four years of "almost ideal" weather. To continue the same level in postwar years, producers needed to adopt better and more sustainable techniques. He advanced the theory that the United States needed less acreage in agriculture and greater efficiency on the order of Denmark, Holland, Belgium, and France, where each acre produced the maximum without loss of fertility. He did not live to see the current situation—in which farmland, forest, and grassland are being lost at an unprecedented rate to suburbanization.

In "Thomas Jefferson Versus Karl Marx," Bromfield described his hero Jefferson as a "complete" man whose vision consisted of a nation of "yeoman farmers." No specialist, he was a writer, thinker, farmer, horticulturalist, and statesman. The nation's problems, Bromfield maintained, resulted from large urban areas that created a "homeless, dispossessed migratory population of workers"; he terms cities the "cancers of every nation, carrying in themselves the seeds of the eventual destruction of society itself." Interestingly, Bromfield identified the greatest destruction as having taken place when he lived mostly abroad, during the two decades between 1926 and 1946. He singled out Detroit and Pittsburgh for special abuse as "great monstrosities" and monuments to superficiality and the failure to understand that a decent place to live is essential to freedom. In small towns and rural communities outside "the darker regions of the Deep South" one found fewer racial and social problems:

> Race rioting, anti-semitism, bitter class hatreds are essentially the products of our great cities here as in Europe. In our great industrial cities man leads an evil and abnormal life, hag-ridden with prejudice, perpetually seeking a scapegoat for his own failures, worries and maladjustments. . . . The real cause [of social problems and malaise] is the modern industrial city, as evil an institution as the worst slums of the Middle Ages and to man's mind and nerves and self-respect infinitely more destructive.

Bromfield neglected to mention that the publishing houses which made him rich were located in New York City and that large urban centers are likelier than small towns to be able to offer social, cultural, and professional opportunities.

The ambitious essay "The Nature of Man" contains the warning that human beings were in danger of becoming the victims of the "great mechanical-industrial structure" they created: "Man's advance upward is not determined by the number or the ingenuity of the machines he invents nor even by the number of discoveries he makes concerning the universe and natural law but the use to which he puts these inventions and this knowledge. Here it is that morality, ethics and even religious values and mysticism become of first importance." Western-style democracy, "the luxury of rich nations," required "a high degree of information, literacy and at least a moderately experienced intelligence" in most people; otherwise, it degenerates into dictatorship and decline. In a reversal of his earlier stance, he stated that a form of Marxist communism could result in more literacy and the development of real wealth as the first step in the movement toward democracy.

Large-scale manufacturing meant more products but decreased fulfillment for the laborer. There could be no spiritual or physical satisfaction for the assembly-line operative as there had been for the craftsman of a century earlier. Sounding very much like Marx, Bromfield stated that industry made the worker a slave "scarcely above the level of an animal chained to a treadmill." No Luddite seeking a return to preindustrial times, Bromfield declared that machines should be servants, not masters of civilization; mechanization should increase efficiency and decrease drudgery so that human beings had more time for leisure and learning:

> If I wished to find a well-developed, intelligent, balanced civilized specimen of mankind in our times, I should have to seek him among the farmers, among the foresters and the engineers engaged in building government dams and canals or in terracing, worn-out eroded land. . . . I should certainly not find him among the industrialists and bankers of our great cities, nor among the desiccated specialists of our universities, nor among the sterile, arrogant, materialistic philosophers of the school of Bertrand Russell.

This ideal person was to be found among "great and civilized men of the Renaissance, a part of nature and of the universe itself, among the people who still remain both humble and possessed of a profound and true sense of human and civilized values."

Much has changed since Bromfield published those words. The magnificent barn across from the great house burned down in 1993 due to faulty wiring in an incubator and was replaced with a replica designed by members of the Timber-Framers Guild and constructed by Amish laborers. The environs of Pleasant Hill

Lake, which Bromfield compared to the Lakeland of England, now contain a marina, and motorized craft roar among canoes and rowboats.

The Victory Garden, identified by a large white sign, was once located down the slope from the Olivetti cemetery, so that visitors to the graves of Louis and Mary Bromfield were sure to see it. Volunteers planted and cultivated beans, melons, corn, tomatoes, peppers, and peas. More than a decade ago, the garden was abandoned. No sign now reminds anyone of the importance of individual effort in helping to win the war.

The devastating derecho storm of June 2022 uprooted many of the big trees in the woods above Malabar Farm and forced the closing of two of the most beautiful sections of the bridle trail. One of them, on the Ferguson place, wound through forest at the crest of a hill to traverse a meadow surrounded by red and white oak, sugar maple, and sweet gum, which produced magnificent displays of color in autumn. It then led through the maple grove and pine plantation. The trail from the horseman's staging area, which is still open, takes the rider across Hastings Road, circles a large field, emerges from woods just above the great house, and follows the edge of a large hay field. Unfortunately, that trail runs parallel to much of the storm devastation, with large trees lying on the ground, their dead root systems exposed.

Most egregious of all, a fracking well was drilled on the corner of State Routes 95 and 603 on private land not a thousand feet from Malabar Farm's eastern border, the fence line of one of the pastures where Bromfield experimented with cell (rotational) grazing. About a half mile away are the Malabar Inn, the spring that sustained the farm market, and the pond that was the subject of one of his chapters in *Malabar Farm*. Since the fracking well was eventually abandoned, locals assume it did not produce, but the site, now used for storage, is quite visible from State Route 95.

Agricultural problems that Bromfield identified have continued to get worse. Stephen Heyman points out that most of his recommendations have been ignored. He advocated for humane treatment of animals, but today the majority of farm animals remain "caged, crowded, and drugged in an industrial system that produces a superabundance of meat whose cheap price does not factor in its enormous nutritional and ecological costs." Farm subsidies in the United States, most of which support "commodity crops," exceed $20 billion a year. Bromfield identified corn as one of the most destructive as measured in fertilizer, energy, and wasted soil fertility, yet corn and soybeans dominate our agriculture, taking up between one half and two thirds of cropland, while fruits and vegetables take up 2 to 3 percent. He warned against exclusive reliance on chemical fertilizer, yet growers use more each year, and chemicals run off into waterways, where they create algae blooms and dead zones. One in 2019 measured seven thousand square miles in the Gulf of Mexico. Ohioans heard much about the toxic algae bloom in the western end of Lake Erie, which for a time poisoned the water for residents of Toledo—until the city built a new filtration plant.

Many schoolchildren file through the interpretive center at Malabar Farm every year, however, to learn that one of Ohio's largest exports is eroded soil blown on wind or washed downstream, and they discover that sound farming practices prevent the damage. Two antique barns survive, one dated 1832. Visitors tour the working farm, although the wagons are pulled not by teams of draft horses but by tractors. While the dairy is no longer used, beef cattle graze the pastures. A full-time farm manager oversees the planting and harvesting of fields. The sawmill stands, and some of the best maple syrup in the area is processed in late winter, although the sap is collected from maple trees by plastic tubing that descends the hillside rather than in metal cans carried in horse-drawn wagons. Engaged members of the Malabar Farm Foundation continue historical research. The summit of Mount Jeez, the highest elevation, still inspires visitors with a view of nearly the entire farm—big house, barns, ponds, fields, and forests—which remains a monument to one person's energy and commitment.

Eleven

Modern Pioneers

"NO RACE CAN PROSPER TILL it learns there is as much dignity in tilling a field as in writing a poem," declared Booker T. Washington in his controversial speech to the Cotton States and International Exposition in Atlanta in 1895. Other equally famous people testify not only to the seminal place farmers occupy in society but the sacredness of their calling, including Hesiod (eighth century BC) and Xenophon (430–355 BC). Thomas Jefferson in "Notes on the State of Virginia" (1785) termed yeoman (independent) farmers the "chosen people." Wendell Berry begins his poem "Horses" (1977) by stating that in his youth "a teamster / was thought an accomplished man, / his art an essential discipline" and concludes: "This work of love rhymes / living and dead. A dance / is what this plodding is. / A song, whatever is said." In *Pleasant Valley*, Louis Bromfield defines a good farmer as one who had "a passion for the soil" and an "understanding and sympathy with animals." He cannot sleep if his animals are not well fed, and "he respects the animals that are linked into the chain of life which explains and justifies the whole of his activity." In the same book, Bromfield articulates his theory about how to improve American agriculture: "What we need is a new courage and a new race of pioneers, as sturdy as the original pioneers, but wiser than they—a race of pioneers concerned with the physical, economic and social paradise which this country could be." The good life for any nation is founded on soil, water, and forests.

Human beings began to cultivate soil and breed animals about twelve thousand years ago. When part of the population grew most of the food, more people could be involved in other pursuits—such as art and science. Attitudes toward farming in particular and the rural way of life in general, however, have been contradictory, from veneration and romanticization to ridicule and oppression. Farmers and herders are by turns noble, independent, hard-working, thrifty, and honest or vulgar, narrow, hard-bitten, parsimonious, and crafty. The rural way of life is described as bucolic but also stifling, essential yet taken for granted. The term *rustic* can mean country dweller or buffoon, natural or unsophisticated, simple or coarse. Prejudice mostly works in two ways, however, and some farmers hurl derision against city people, whom they regard as frivolous and corrupt. I do not subscribe to the idea that the rural way of life is more "virtuous" or builds stronger ethics than the urban; on the contrary, it often exacerbates patriarchalism and parochialism. The supposed independence of farmers is limited by much greater dependence on markets than urban dwellers and in some cases on price supports; nor do I accept the idea that city dwellers are necessarily more sophisticated and tolerant.

Estimates of the number of people engaged in farming today range from one to four percent of the total US population. In 1790, nearly 90 percent of Americans were famers; by 1850 that statistic was 64 percent; by 1900 it was 41 percent, and by 1930, 21 percent. In 1950, farmers comprised about 15 percent of the population. Those who celebrate this trend ignore the fact that economic realities force many would-be farmers off their land and transform agriculture into a profession that only people who inherit land or are already wealthy can practice. They also ignore the fact that specialization among a shrinking group means that essential expertise will be increasingly unavailable.

Major threats to farming as a way of life include the high cost of land and consequent loss of farmland to what is euphemistically referred to as "development." In the half century between 1950 and 2000, Ohio lost 6.9 million acres, or one-third of its available agricultural land, mostly to urban or residential use, according to the state office of farmland preservation. One 2022 report from the US Department of Agriculture estimates total farmland in 2021 as 895 million acres, with 1.3 million acres lost to development during 2020. Ohio has some of the richest soil in the country, but between 2020 and 2021 it lost more than three hundred thousand acres of farmland, of which 60 percent included some of the best (or "prime") cropland, according to a recent newsletter of the Ohio Ecological Food and Farm Association (OEFFA). Along county and township roads, more farms are being auctioned off in several parcels, a practice that means tillable land will be lost due to suburbanization.

Large-scale or factory farming also threatens small family farms through unfair competition and perpetuates unsustainable practices such as monoculture, waterway pollution due to over-fertilizing and manure runoff, soil erosion, and emissions from machinery. Some of these large farms, especially concentrated animal feeding operations, contain as much pavement as grassland.

Another casualty caused by factory farms is the loss of rural vistas. A current neologism for this phenomenon is the "endangered landscape." Ralph Waldo Emerson (1803–1882) in "Nature" wrote happily that while individual farmers owned their own land, "none of them owns the landscape. There is a property in the horizon which no man has but he whose eye can integrate all the parts, that is, the poet." Today the landscape *is* owned, and people are forced to endure the ugliness of billboards, factories, and enormous windowless boxes owned by the purveyors of consumerism.

I. Modern Pioneer

Forty miles northeast of Columbus, Knox County is a land of rolling green hills and woods, family farms, villages, and one small city, Mount Vernon, which has maintained its quaint town center and many elegant nineteenth-century houses. One of the most scenic and rural counties in the state, it is a place where many people still know their neighbors and live near extended families. For five years, between 1946 and 1951, when other farmers were already using tractors, George Shalter did things the hard way. He had worked as a boy and teenager on a friend's family farm and had learned the techniques from that experience. I met him through his daughter who owned a horse farm with a Connemara standing at stud, one of only two in Ohio in those years.

"I helped to make the hay and harvest crops for a dollar a day and board," George related to me when I met him in 1994. George's mentor helped him choose the machinery and livestock for his own farm. Aware that pioneer farming would be risky, George's father, a professor of religion at Kenyon College in Gambier, approved of his son's adventurous spirit when he left Kenyon after two years to go to The Ohio State University to study agriculture.

In 1942, however, military service put his plans on hold, as the Great War (1914–18) had done with Louis Bromfield. George spent four years in the Merchant Marine Corps and traveled to England, the Mediterranean, Russia, South America, and Guam. Returning from the war, George would let nothing stop him from pursuing his dream. His father lent him the money to buy his land, livestock, and machinery. The farm's 160 acres were located in the northeast corner of Knox County, near his birthplace in Gambier and a burg named Artanna for its founders, named Art and Anna. Formerly rented out, the land had been neglected and abused with overplanting. George describes it as a typical family farm with a six-room frame house, two barns, henhouse, wagon shed, and a granary / corn crib. One half of it was cropland, the rest pasture.

George bought six purebred Guernsey cows cheaply because each was blemished in some way. Today, the preferred breed is Holstein, which produces a larger quantity of milk, although the Guernsey product is richer. Milking took one hour every morning and evening; there was one ten-gallon can every day for the Carnation truck. The check that came every two weeks paid all the household expenses.

Annually, the cows were artificially inseminated by a professional who came to the farm. "You always hoped for a heifer to build your herd," George said. Farmers sold bull calves for slaughter in Mount Vernon or butchered them at home. First they were shot and skinned; the hide was pulled and the fat cut off. People canned meat in glass jars in those days, he explained, adding, "It was really tender." Butchers not only cut up the beef but provided lockers for freezing; people rented them and took meat out as they needed it.

Along with the cattle, George kept thirty head of sheep, including one buck that was pastured with the cows when the ewes were not in season. "You always kept ewes that bore twin lambs, since they were more valuable," George said. Buck lambs were sold for slaughter in Mount Vernon, as were ewes that were periodically culled from the herd. Orphaned lambs could be smeared with the afterbirth of one which had died in order to persuade its mother to accept the orphan; the technique worked about half the time. If the ewe wouldn't cooperate, the farmer could feed the orphan on a bottle. "We named lambs for the type of bottle they'd been raised on," George told me, "and so we had lambs named Hires and Vesscola." The best sheep pasture was hilly and well-drained; swampy ground caused livestock to become infested with parasites. The pasture had to be rested periodically, because sheep graze it so closely. Wool provided a cash crop; either a hired professional or the farmer sheared in the spring. George remarked, "I was a pioneer and did my own."

Swine were primarily raised for home use, most farmers keeping one to two hogs and butchering them after the first frost of the autumn, which killed flies that could have spoiled the meat. They shot the hog, cut its throat, dunked it using a block and tackle into a large kettle of boiling water, and finally scraped off the hair. Farm women, not men, cured the meat, using all parts of the hog. They pasted the outside of the hams with salt and hung them up to smoke over hickory wood. The women rendered the lard in a kettle over an open fire. Neighbors helped in the work and in the evenings played music, sang songs, and shared a picnic.

George and his wife also kept chickens—primarily for home use, although they did sell some eggs. They kept one rooster to every five to ten hens. Young roosters that weren't needed, and hens past their laying time were decapitated with a hatchet, immersed in boiling water, plucked, singed in order to get rid of pin feathers, and cut up. Usually the chickens were fried in lard in a heavy skillet.

"We had a vegetable garden and orchard, but we didn't have much time for them," George said. "Only city people have time to keep a garden perfectly weeded."

Calendars were less useful than the changing seasons for telling time. "When the dogwoods were in bloom," George said, "I knew it was time to plant the corn."

He also planted wheat, oats, timothy, and alfalfa. Wheat, harvested in late summer with a thresher and sold as a cash crop, depletes soil fertility and so had to be rotated. Oats and corn became livestock feed; any surplus was sold. Hay, however, could not be harvested until two years after planting, but it invested nitrogen into the soil, improving tilth and preventing erosion. Today one cannot drive the rural roads of Ohio without seeing soybean fields, dark green in summer and rusty brown in autumn, but in the forties soybean cultivation was less common.

"We didn't have fertilizer and lime in those days, so the land was less productive," George explained. "Extension agents tried to get farmers to use lime, but they were reluctant to try anything new, so the agents secretly spread lime on a corner of their fields and then the next summer showed them how much bigger the crops were in that patch. Only then were the farmers convinced." Apparently no one thought of suing the agents for trespassing.

George plowed with teams of two or three horses. For a walking plow the farmer needed two horses, while a sulky plow, on which the farmer rode, required three. George's horses were a type he called *chunks;* they were fifteen to sixteen hands high and weighed twelve to sixteen hundred pounds, smaller than Percheron or Belgian draft horses but larger than the Haflingers that are raised today as harness horses. "You plowed with the reins over your shoulder and around your waist," George explained. With a good team of horses, a farmer could plow two to three acres a day or cultivate about seven.

Defined by English law as early as 1275, the term *acre* (43,560 square feet) once referred to the amount of previously uncultivated land that could be turned over in one day with a team of oxen pulling a wooden plow. The word descends from Middle English *aker,* "tilled land," from Anglo-Saxon *aecer,* or "open land." The metric unit is hectare, or 10,000 square meters. A furlong (contraction of "furrow-long") measures 660 feet in length, or one eighth of a mile; today used to measure distances in horse racing, in Anglo-Saxon times it referred to the length of a furrow in a ten-acre field.

Unsentimental about cattle, sheep, pigs, and chickens, George described his horses and shepherd dog as coworkers and friends. The dog followed George's commands exactly, including bringing in each cow when he referred to it by name. The horses had to know what the farmer wanted them to do and respond to voice commands, to step right or left ("gee" or "haw") when the farmer called to them. They also had to be well matched in size and strength, since working in harness required that they step in cadence in order to achieve a straight row.

After plowing, the land was disked, with three horses pulling hard at angles so that the blade cut up the sod. Two horses were sufficient to drag the spike-toothed harrow that made the seed beds and also the cultivator that kept the crop rows free of weeds until the corn was high. Haying time came after the crops had all been planted. Two horses pulled the mowing machine. After cutting, the hay was left to lie on the ground for one day, as is still the practice, before being raked into windrows. Then the farmer drove the horses, harnessed to a loader, along the windrows to pick the hay up and toss it onto a wagon. Well-trained horses that obeyed voice commands proved invaluable. "Sometimes when I was making hay, my wife called me into the house," George said, "and I'd leave those two horses standing out in the field. I'd come back, and they'd still be where I left them. They were always willing to go back to work."

Transferring the hay to the loft took much time. The farmer could use a rope tied to a horse to lift and toss the hay or do it manually with a three-tined fork. Either way, it was a difficult job to do right. "I could do five loads a day working by myself," George said. "Those were good horses. Betty and Pet. And later I got Dolly. You needed good horses. Farmers took care of their animals because they worked with them every day. I groomed mine carefully. It's important to make sure that you clean under their harness collars," he continued, "because if it gets dirty, it can chafe. I combed out their tails and tied them up in the winter in order to keep them clean. I took pride in keeping those horses looking good."

In the spring, the first job a farmer had to do was to haul manure from the barn. The horses had to step close to the side for the farmer to be able to fork the manure into the spreader. Again, the horses had to respond immediately to voice commands. Hauling and spreading the manure helped to get them into shape for plowing, disking, harrowing, planting, and cultivating, which toughened them up for the most difficult job of mowing the hay. "Pulling the mowing machine was hardest of all on horses because of the vibrations. 'Course, you don't mow all day," George said. "You do plow all day, though."

The horses were also necessary for transportation even though the family owned a car. "We'd even start that old car with the horses," George laughed. "I'd harness them to the bumper and they'd pull it downhill until the engine turned over. We drove that thing to church every Sunday, then to my father's for dinner in Gambier. That was our day off." There was never a day off, however, from taking care of the animals.

"We had a strict division of labor, Annie and me," he said of his wife, who at the time was no longer living. He described their separation of duties—she took care of everything inside the house, while he did all the outside work—as a partnership, not a hierarchy, as the work of the housewife on a homestead was essential to the survival of the family. "Annie was a meticulous housekeeper. She'd been the oldest of nine children in a family where they canned and cured all their own food. Her father farmed with horses. So she was willing to help me in my experiment.

"She did the washing on Mondays. We had a gas-driven Maytag washer in our summer kitchen that had a foot treadle and an exhaust pipe. I carried water in buckets from the springhouse on Mondays to do the washing. We had galvanized rinse tubs and a wringing machine, and she hung the clothes on a line. She heated the iron on the stove. Then she baked, because the stove was so hot from heating the wash water. At first we burned wood in the stove; later we used gas. Finally, we got a water pump and years later a bathroom. There was no refrigerator. We cooled milk in the spring house. For light, we used kerosene lamps. Annie cured and canned all the meat and canned vegetables and fruit. She was the right one for the job, but it was intolerable to expect a woman to raise children under those primitive conditions," he said pensively. "After four years we got electricity."

Like most rural people, George held strong opinions about politics. "FDR was highly respected by farmers," he said. "He was an educated, cultivated gentleman and did exactly what was needed. The programs he started were the greatest things to happen in this country for one hundred years. All the high schools in Knox County were built by the Works Progress Administration. They closed down the one-room schoolhouses. The Civilian

Conservation Corps created all the state parks and some of the national parks and planted trees. There were hardly any trees in Ohio in those years, and look at it now." George gestured toward the window, which faced a thickly wooded ravine.

"Old-time farmers wouldn't pay much attention to Louis Bromfield," George said of the Malabar Farm founder. "They used to say anybody could be a success at farming with the money he made from his books and movies. The good thing was that he got people to start thinking about conservation. One of Bromfield's ideas that I adopted turns out to have been the wrong one, though," he admitted. "My fences weren't the best, and my cows kept getting out, so I was the first one in Harrison Township to plant multiflora rose as a natural hedgerow. The old-timers warned against it." He chuckled. "They were right."

George didn't regret his decision to try his hand at pioneer farming. "I've lived in lots of places, and there's nowhere like Knox County," George said. "I was glad for the chance to live that independent life, though it was foolhardy even to try. I couldn't make a go of it and had to quit and get into something else after five years. I became a machine technician. We lived on the farm for ten more years, and I leased out the fields. I kept those horses until they died.

"I'm glad I got out of it when I did, though. Farming was always competitive, but now it's nothing but a rat race," he said. "Dairy farms are food factories. You have to do it that way now just in order to stay in business. Where's the joy in that? Where's the meaning if it's all economic and nothing else?

"I loved working on the farm, working as hard as I could every day. I used to get up at 5:00 A.M. and fire up the stove and put the coffee on. Then I'd go out to milk. My daughter came out to watch me, and I'd sing to her every song I knew. I worked until dark and came in tired and slept well. My ambition was always to farm with horses, and I did. I still keep two trail horses, and I'll ride them as long as I can."

II. The New Breed

In the summer of 2019, before the COVID-19 pandemic, in the annual farm tour sponsored by the local Farm Bureau, my husband and I visited one of the largest farms in Ashland County. With more than 350 dairy cows, the place deserves the title *food factory*. We were ferried from site to site on a tractor-drawn wagon while guides using loudspeakers explained the routine. The dairyman himself was not present, but not because he is a "gentleman farmer" or absentee owner. He works with his computer in an office inside a trailer like those found at large construction sites, while hired technicians perform the labor. These men are no longer called *hands*, as they are not the same as the workers of previous years who actually handled the animals and got to know them. Instead, they keep the cows moving, assembly-line fashion, into the parlor, where milking by machine begins as early as 4:00 A.M. and continues to 6:00 or 7:00 P.M. The cows spend the rest of their day in long sheds, fed on hay and ensilage, not pasture.

A large tanker truck sat near the parlor waiting for thousands of gallons of milk that are shipped every day. Most of the farm's six hundred acres are planted in hay and corn to feed the cattle. Although the owner inherited his land, and his ancestors had lived in the county for over a century, there is no antique barn or house; the cowshed and milking parlor, close to fourteen hundred feet long, are constructed of sheet metal. To cap the experience, visitors could purchase what was termed ice cream but turned out to be nothing involving dairy products. Described as "soft-serve," the substance is actually made of guar gum and carrageenan, a type of seaweed, using polysorbate 80 as an emulsifier and artificial flavoring.[†] The mass is whipped with air to increase volume.

The vast amount of manure is cycled into two ponds, or "lagoons," which attract swarms of flies. According to Eric Schaef-

---

[†] Polysorbate 80 is a nonionic surfactant, emulsifier, and excipient approved by the Food and Drug Administration.

fer of the Environmental Integrity Project, "agriculture runoff is really the leading cause of water pollution in the US today." The major sources are fertilizer from cropland and manure from factory farms, leading to waterways polluted with pesticides, phosphorous, nitrogen, and fecal bacteria. Many people suspicious of regulations describe them as overreach by government, but US water quality has improved in the fifty-plus years since bipartisan majorities in both the House of Representatives and Senate overrode President Richard Nixon's veto and created the Clean Water Act in 1972. Unfortunately, the recent decision by the Supreme Court in Sackett vs EPA (May 2023) severely curtails protections for wetlands, which are critical to ensuring good water quality.

Some entrepreneurs, however, dedicate themselves to reversing this trend toward farming as assembly-line production. A new curriculum established in 2022 at The Ohio State University focuses on sustainable agriculture. OEFFA, formed in 1979, joined other conservation groups to promote legislation called the Ohio Soil Health Initiative, which sponsored best practices in soil management to increase fertility, decrease erosion, and sequester carbon. The annual OEFFA convention, usually held in Granville over a three-day weekend during February, attracts over a thousand organic farmers, urban gardeners, and environmentalists, mostly from Ohio but also the surrounding states, concerned about the effect of modern farming techniques on the biosphere and international food supply. They come to hear keynote speeches from award-winning sustainable farmers and gardeners, agricultural consultants, agronomists, entomologists, botanists, and horticulturalists and attend the breakout sessions on many subjects such as growing practices, animal feeds, food preservation, fertilization, weed control, agricultural business management, attraction of wild birds, solar array construction, and other topics. The book fair and exhibits grow larger every year. Attendants sharing their different expertise and passionate interest in sustainability create an exhilarating atmosphere. Until the pandemic, participants danced on Saturday evenings to the music of the Back Porch Swing Band. The conference continued virtually in 2020 and 2021; in 2022 it returned with both in-person and virtual sessions.

OEFFA sponsors tours every year that demonstrate trends toward a new era in niche and organic farming. The first I ever attended, in 1998, took place in Knox County, where two brothers and a nephew combined their lands and started an organic soybean and beef operation, because, as one of them said, "we were tired of handling chemicals." Our tour guide explained that much of their business came from Japan, where organic soybeans sold at a premium. Visitors rode in a hay wagon to see fields of organic alfalfa and corn as well as pastures where healthy cattle grazed. He pointed out rows of trees between fields that serve as windbreaks, which not only control soil erosion but also provide habitat for beneficial insects such as wasps, some of which spend the winter under bark. The mature trees had grown from saplings that sprouted beneath old fence lines where mowing was impossible. In Ohio, windbreaks often began this way, and so walkers (and equestrians) often encounter broken wire hidden among leaves.

A 2023 tour in Holmes County demonstrated the opposite type of dairy farming from the factory operation. Milking fifty smaller cows, the farmer and two sons kept them on pasture most of the year, rotating them among several cells, or areas fenced off with electrical wire every two days. The farmer earns extra income by raising hens for egg production. He knew every type of plant in his fields including alfalfa, brome, and orchard grass. About twenty of his ninety acres are in woods, which allow shade and minimize erosion. Massive birdhouses and hollowed gourds provide nesting space for purple martins and tree swallows, which control crop-eating insects such as beetles, aphids, and cabbage moths. When the group hiked out to the pasture where the cows grazed, the animals walked up to meet us and studied with curious, friendly eyes, not the harassed expression of animals in factory operations.

In Athens County, a farmer raises organic hogs and pastures them in wooded ravines while guests at his solar-powered bed-and-breakfast admire the blue Appalachian vista from a balcony. The year I visited, he was in the process of putting up a new building because his current one could not hold all the people who requested rooms.

During a tour in northern Ashland County, an agronomist from The Ohio State University explained the use of cover crops such as rye and buckwheat planted in one year and plowed under the next to inhibit weeds. Other methods of weed control include partial tillage, which leaves large chunks of earth between rows of crops for weed control, and spreading crushed walnut shells, which are rich in the compound juglone, an allelopathic, or natural, weed suppressant.

One of the most ingenious examples of the new agriculture is a group of five young people, two married couples and a friend, who raise organic rabbits, hens, and hogs on a farm that a grandmother still owns in the deep countryside of Knox County. Even with GPS, I was unable to find the place and stopped at a crossroads surrounded by cornfields until one of them came searching for me. The wives are teachers who work on the farm during summers, and the friend is a potter who sells her clay vases and statuettes at shows and fairs. Their business, they told visitors, "grew out of a conversation around a table."

Many OEFFA members specialize in vegetables and fruit because less land is required than for raising animals and grain. In Wayne County, two brothers and their wives grow melons, radishes, summer and winter squash, peas, beans, and spinach in long beds and tend rows of raspberries, broccoli, and tomatoes. They also design farm implements intended for use by the new generation of organic farmers, who work fewer acres than their predecessors. Some small farmers make their land affordable by crop-sharing with others who lend large, expensive combines and balers to harvest corn, soybeans, and hay; leasing land; and co-purchasing equipment with multiple small growers. The Green Field Dairy, a farmer-owned cooperative also in Wayne County, sells organic white and chocolate milk, cream, and skimmed milk. Its plan was to begin selling ice cream at a later date. A quarterly newsletter, *Fruechte des Feldes,* or "Fruit of the Fields," notifies customers about new products.

During the back-to-the-land days of the 1970s, a quarter century after George Shalter began his experiment in pioneer farming, Mick Luber returned to his home county of Harrison after ten years of teaching history in Chicago high schools and bought sixty-five sloping acres that had been logged. After reclaiming it from extensive soil erosion, he founded Bluebird Farm, an organic egg and produce operation, using hand tools, greenhouses he built himself, natural fertilizer (mostly compost and poultry manure), and ecological pest control: contour rows and crop rotation inhibit damaging insects. He also makes use of ecological predator control in the form of two diligent Saint Bernard–Labrador crosses, which protect the gardens from groundhogs and deer. He was so successful selling his produce at organic farm markets in Pittsburgh and Wheeling that he was able to hire local workers. He needs no tractor, combine, or other large equipment, as planting, cultivating, and harvesting are all done with hand tools. Large sections of his farm are now shaded with second-growth woods, which help to decrease soil erosion and water loss and provide habitat for sparrows, quail, and thrushes that feed on crop-damaging insects.

In September 2021, with some pandemic restrictions relaxed, I visited a farm inside the Cuyahoga Valley National Park, in Cuyahoga and Summit Counties. September is usually one of the best months in Ohio, with the deciduous trees beginning to turn red and gold and the weather dry and warm. The twelve-acre farm is located on a hillside above the village of Stowe where the old railway station has been converted into an interpretive center and the track bed into a bicycle trail. Ten working farms exist within the park, restored with money from the National Park Service. Agencies like the National Resources Conservation Service (NRCS) and Sustainable Agricultural Research Education (SARE) provide grants to enable first-time farmers to pursue organic agriculture. Prospective gardeners applied for tenancies; the process proved to be very competitive, with many people applying for a few places and those not chosen requesting that their names be kept on waiting lists for future years. To the argument that the farms should have been allowed to return to nature, Park Service officials replied that they wanted to preserve the antique houses and barns and encourage organic farming. In addition, tenants pull invasive plant species from the pastures, thus saving the Park Service money it would have spent hiring workers to do the job.

Because she could lease the land, the tenant farmer, a woman who comes not from an agricultural background but from community development, needed no down payment to start her project. Her husband works full-time away from the farm. More young women today become farmers specializing in crops such as vegetables, fruit, and honey, which do not require expensive machinery.

The proprietor, whose goal is permaculture—a type of planting in which something is growing at all times except winter—maintains bee hives and orchards, cultivates organic mushrooms, and raises pork. Similar to the Amish farmer and writer David Klein, she says that size often proves crucial for success and that larger amounts of acreage will not necessarily ensure prosperity. Instead, the farm mimics the forest it came from. In the orchard, horseradish, mint, chives, and asparagus are planted beneath pear and apple trees. Wood chips or recycled cardboard provide mulch between rows; wide walkways are grass-covered. Mulch can also be hairy vetch, red clover, straw, or cover crops. Comfrey increases soil fertility, while mint helps to inhibit poison ivy. Monarch butterflies and honeybees delved into the petals on the wildflowers left to grow as pollinator rows.

During spring, summer, and fall, the farmer rotates the pigs every few days inside moveable electrical fences; in winter they occupy sheds. Pigs repel predators and keep down weeds, but they also root into the ground, creating holes that can be challenging for walkers, as the visitors learned. Hens follow in moveable houses and pens, digging through the manure for grain and fertilizing the land in the process. They also eat slugs that feed on garden plants. The pond, created for fire insurance when the farm was built, was overgrown and covered with algae when the present family moved in. Now the perimeter has been mown, a windmill set up to aerate the pond, and a pump installed to provide water for the animals. Ducks consume mosquitoes and other insects. The farmer removes algae with a long-handled tool called a *pond rake*.

Near the water, an extensive high tunnel is lined with cut logs on which organic mushrooms mature: the farmer confides that they are easy to grow, cheap to produce, light to carry, and guaranteed to provide a profit. Last year she ran a farm market; this year a store opened in the town of Peninsula where the park's farmers sell organic vegetables, fruit, and meat as well as cut flowers. None of them feared a lack of customers, as more than 2 million people visit the park annually.

Extensive groundcover prevents upper slopes from drying. Moving the pigs several times per week conserves the root systems that hold the soil and keep the grass down, so no mowing is necessary. In earlier decades, removing the forest cover to make way for crops caused deep gashes in the field. Now the practice of planting in contour rows prevents erosion by allowing water to percolate through the soil, eliminating the necessity of irrigation; gardens and orchards are planted on lower slopes because rainwater carries minerals.

A family-run operation in Ashland County that has been in business for three decades consists of thirty acres of intensive organic farming specializing in honey, maple syrup, apples, peaches, berries, and various vegetables. A grist mill produces flour and pancake mixes. The pharmacist-turned-farmer began by raising grain and cattle before turning to smaller vegetables, fruit, and honey. The family operation involves the owner and his wife, sons, daughter, and grandchildren. As part of a recent Farm Bureau tour, he explained that he constructs the hives himself and bottles the honey for sale at farm markets, local organic food outlets, and his own retail store. Honeybees forage among rows of wildflowers and hops that are grown not for beer but tea; the hops also contain lupulones, naturally occurring weak organic acids that kill the Varroa mites which prey on the blood of worker bees and cause colony collapse. The compounds have had no effect on bee mortality. A model owl keeps the birds away from blueberry and raspberry bushes—at least so far. Apple trees yield the raw material for unpasteurized cider, but the operation turned out to be so successful that the farmer must purchase additional apples.

In 2019, a conference of the Association for the Study of Literature and Environment at the University of California, Davis included visits to local organic orchards. On thirty acres, a husband and wife grew pomegranates, olives, plums, dates, apples, oranges, lemons, persimmons, apricots, grapes, and peaches. Most of the planting, pruning, and harvesting was done by hand, much of it with help from Mexican workers. Almond trees need bees to pollinate them, but the almonds bloom for only a few weeks, so farmers keep rows of flowers and permaculture such as mustard and clover to keep the bees and other pollinators resident throughout the summer. Polyculture thus creates a sustainable ecosystem.

On the second farm, only twenty acres in size, the orchardist grew several varieties of fruit but specialized in apricots. Take whatever you want, he told us, because he cannot harvest the fruit fast enough and loses half his crop every year to spoilage. Working alone, he nevertheless made a go of his operation, in part selling what he called "value-added" products such as homemade jam. Dislike of academic politics drove him to leave a position as professor of biology at an eastern university and return home to become a farmer.

For several years as a graduate student, I rented a garden plot from The Ohio State University on a broad expanse of level land near the Olentangy River. Since there was no fence around the plot, vandalism was a problem, and each year I lost several heads of broccoli. A Nigerian graduate student related his method of discouraging theft by planting okra and kale that "Americans are not familiar with" next to the pathway. Vegetables such as beans that require more effort to harvest usually went untouched or were minimally reduced. Tomatoes and peppers produce so abundantly that if some were stolen I did not notice. Perennials such as strawberries could not be planted, as the land was plowed every year.

Public gardens provide one solution to the scarcity of fresh produce in inner-city areas, but they should be located near the people who use them, as bus routes seldom extend to outlying areas. Together We Grow Gardens, an organization begun in 2012, promotes urban gardening in Newark, Ohio, in Licking County, where public middle schools have greenhouses, and most public elementary schools possess areas where students learn growing skills. Jeff Gordon Community Garden, begun by people from the nearby Church of the Nazarene, contains plots for individuals to rent for $10.00 per year, a cost that includes seeds and plant starts. The organizer lives in the high-crime community she serves. The easy-to-tend raised rows are on land donated by a private individual after a derelict house had been demolished. The J. Evans Foundation also leases land and provides funds, and Licking County Land Bank makes lots available when dilapidated houses are pulled down after designation as fire hazards. Some public schools require students to do twenty hours of service per year, and teenagers on probation can work off some of their community service hours in the gardens.

One of seven community gardens in Newark, Everett Park produced four thousand pounds of food in 2012, sixty-five hundred in 2020, and ten thousand in 2021. Originally, the administrators sold produce at farmers' markets, but now they donate it to food pantries, and some individuals participate in harvesting the vegetables they receive. Although its location requires a six-foot chain-link fence to prevent vandalism, the director claimed that the other gardens, which are not fenced off, have had little damage or theft. When I visited in June 2021, the peas were already two feet high. Steel arches supported pumpkin vines tied with repurposed pantyhose. Lowe's and Tractor Supply Company donated garden materials such as plastic mulch and tarp for high tunnels, where plants are grown under cover. A fan blowing air between the two layers adds the insulation that allows for starting plants early in the season. Adults with disabilities grow medicinal plants at the solar-powered Heritage School greenhouse, which includes an area for flowers designed to attract monarch butterflies. Volunteers perform other jobs that are more physically taxing, while various foundations provide funding.

Many high schools, Granville and Ashland among them, have greenhouses in which students raise vegetables, fruit, flowers, and trees and sell produce and plants; the money earned supports the programs. Students learn what is involved in growing food sustainably. Some of the best experiences for children are field trips to parks, riparian ecosystems, and old-growth forests and for older students, co-ops and agricultural internships.

The Agraria Center for Regenerative Practice in Greene County, also a community organization, includes a 138-acre farm where people of all ages can learn to grow food and acquire other skills, like making tools. Funded by organizations and donations, Agraria works toward bioregional regeneration in the Little Miami River watershed and together with the Nature Conservancy helped to restore Jacoby Creek.

Near Johnstown, Ohio, a landowner leases forty acres that for years had been exclusively in corn and soybeans, crops known to deplete soil. Ten cultivated acres are divided into three microfarms, which have been in production since 2017. The $1000 annual rent includes electricity and water. The USDA extends tax credits for these farms, which must follow a ten-year commitment. Other costs were borne by a SARE grant. The farmer's husband is a beekeeper, while she grows melons, cucumbers, tomatoes, and berries. A journalist by training, she managed a six-acre farm at

Mid-Ohio Food Bank; later she earned a master of science in horticulture. A double electric fence had been successful so far in keeping out deer. Tomatoes, cucumbers, and melons are started in tunnels in March and transplanted by the first of June. A combination of buckwheat, sorghum, and sunn hemp provides cover crop for pollinators and also fertilizes soil with nitrogen; buckwheat suppresses weeds; sorghum also builds soil. The farmer first mows the cover, then tarps it, and plants beets in August. Winter planting must be finished by September. Tomatoes earn profits, she told visitors, but require more work; she double-crops them with basil. Shallots grow next to Brussels sprouts. Crops grown on raised rows, created with a combination of compost and mulch, proved easier to tend than those on flat ground. Beetles can be controlled by installing insect netting, planting sunn hemp, and encouraging bindweed. Bumblebees kept inside the tunnels do the work of pollinating. Per week, the farmer produces an average of five hundred melons in six rows 140 feet long during a four-week harvest. Melons and raspberries sell out at every market.

For one three-acre farm, a grant from NRCS covered 75 percent of the cost of high tunnels, which require metal ribs covered with tarp. Propane provides heat during winter, but many growers who use high tunnels also run fans, which increase air circulation, prevent freezing, and lengthen the growing season. The new science called *agro-meteorology* studies in part the effects of wind on plant growth. North of Interstate 70, tunnels should be assembled along a southwest to northeast axis, the direction of most weather systems, because airflow dynamics can result in uprooting; seed displacement; and disruption of photosynthesis, insect communication, and plant motion. Atmospheric turbulence raises the supply of carbon dioxide, which increases the rate of photosynthesis and decreases insect activity in both beneficial and destructive species. The so-called lake effect refers to northerly and westerly winds traveling over large bodies of water and picking up moisture, which, when sent into the upper atmosphere during winter, freezes and returns to earth as snow. Northern

Ohio receives this phenomenon from Lake Erie, where the airflow is west to east, while southern Ohio sometimes experiences a Lake Effect from Michigan when wind travels north to south.

One of the most ambitious experimental farms I have visited, the Strasburg Ecological Center in Delaware County, includes 230 acres, with 65 used for farming. Having inherited the woods from her father, Gale Warner, Louise Warner donated them to the center, which has been incorporated for thirty-four years, its primary purpose being to teach children how to grow food. The key issues are grassland agriculture (grazing and haymaking), biodiversity, and sustainability. Five full-time staff members are paid through grants; volunteers donate sixteen hundred hours annually.

Visitors can hike on trails through restored woodland—although, as the director pointed out, not the deep woods that covered the area before settlement. Making use of federal programs, volunteers planted more than thirteen hundred trees, including many sugar maples. While oak trees mature slowly, cam plants grow more rapidly. Trees more than fifty years old sequester the most carbon, while their roots provide nutrients to younger trees.

The modern visitors center is heated by a geothermal system, while passive solar energy heats the high tunnels. A fifty-six-kilowatt-hour solar rooftop system on the west side of the barn produces enough electricity to power the entire farm. The operation is, however, tied to the grid of American Electric Power which, according to the Strasburg director, does not allow institutions to use only their own produced electricity. The annual bill is now a fraction of the amount it was before solar panels were installed. Rain collected in cisterns provides water for one of the smaller gardens. A black tank produces enough energy from sunlight to keep water from freezing, although pipes must be heated.

Colorful chickens of many varieties forage beneath apple trees in a symbiotic arrangement: trees provide shade and cover from hawks while the poultry consume unsaleable dropped fruit and insects that would attack the better apples. Chickens' scratching in the grass is believed to increase the amount of nutrients available to tree roots. Animals in feedlots produce constant noise, but the clucking of foraging flocks sounds pleasant. Children, visitors were told, love to see chickens. The petting farm includes sheep, goats, and llamas. (Chickens are not fond of petting.) Cattle graze farther away, fed entirely on grass, a practice that helps to reduce parasites, while poultry and hogs are fed grain. An eight-year crop rotation reduces incidence of disease, damage from insects, and need for fertilizer. When the manager at Stratford first began to make hay, the land produced nine hundred bales in a year; in 2022 it had produced eighteen hundred by July, with at least one more crop expected that summer.

Record heat and rain in 2022 nevertheless had negative effects. An incremental shift in temperature decreases nutrients in the soil. The quality of animal health is lower with increases in temperature, because mosquitoes are more voracious and flies more numerous.

At a seminar provided by Ashland County Soil and Water Conservation District, speakers explained that farmers can earn income from solar leases and carbon contracts, which companies pay for to be able to advertise their businesses as "carbon neutral." Although the installation of solar panels may preclude some crop production, solar leases may exceed $1000 per acre per year. The *Farmland Owner's Guide to Solar Leasing,* developed by Peggy Kirk-Hall, associate professor at The Ohio State University, contains information for farmers considering leasing land. Far less lucrative are carbon contracts between businesses and farmers, which pay about $20 per acre and require a change in practices that increase sustainability. Ways of obtaining carbon contracts include riparian improvements, converting tillable fields to grassland, diverting part of their operations to organic farming, or adopting any sustainable practices. Carbon contracts can then underwrite part of the cost of whatever improvement the farmer makes in sustainability, and businesses advertise themselves as "sustainable."

Grass farming (using land for grazing and hay) aids in the effort to reduce effects of climate change, as grasslands have proven to be more reliable carbon sinks than trees, although both are important, according to research by Pawlok Dass, Benjamin Z. Houlton, Yingping Wang, and David Warlind published in *Environmental Research Letters* in July 2018. An acre of grass takes in four to seventeen metric tons of carbon annually, depending on the type of grass and length of roots. Studies by Joseph Veldman, ecologist at Texas A&M, and Rattan Lal, agronomist at The Ohio State University, verify that trees are not the only important carbon sinks. The Climate Trust published research indicating that grassland soil carbon is a critical piece of natural climate solutions, that the top meter of grassland stores forty-nine tons of carbon per acre. In the same article, the researcher stated that between 2012 and 2015, the United States lost 2.4 million acres of grassland to housing, energy exploration, and cultivation in corn and soybeans.

Unfortunately, small famers still face challenges in land acquisition. The US Department of Agriculture found that just 13 percent of farms control 75 percent of croplands nationwide, and when land is sold, the larger farmers are the only ones able to place competitive bids, thus preventing smaller farmers from increasing their acreage. OEFFA lobbied to advance the Land Access and Soil Health Bills in the Ohio legislature such as the Family Farm ReGeneration Act (2019) written to enable beginning farmers to acquire affordable farmland through tax incentives to landowners who sell or lease land. After passing unanimously through the House Agriculture Committee, it foundered in the legislature. Representatives Susan Manchester (R-84) and Mary Lightbody (D-19) reintroduced House Bill 95 in the 134th legislative session (2021), where it passed the newly formed House Agriculture and Conservation Committee unanimously a second time. The Current Agriculture Use Value rule helps people to continue farming by taxing the land at lower than market value if at least ten acres are devoted to commercial agriculture or if the farm produces an average yearly gross income of $2500 or more.

To return to Booker T. Washington, in his speech at the 1895 Cotton States and International Exposition he asserted that people would prosper if they could learn to "dignify and glorify" common labor. "It is at the bottom of life we must begin," he said, "and not at the top. Nor should we permit our grievances to overshadow our opportunities." Perhaps we do not need to "glorify" common labor but merely to respect it. Today, those who engage in farming do not need to be provincial; they may be as well-read as any urban dweller. Government-sponsored programs that attract a young, educated generation—a new race of pioneers—to the profession of farming may ensure that agriculture thrives and skills are not lost.

Twelve

Sacrifice Zone

A PERVASIVE IMAGE FROM my early years includes the steel mills and coal-burning power plants along the Ohio River with white vapor pouring from high smokestacks that young kids called "cloud makers." We did not know that what billowed from these vertical pipes was toxic and that the pipes existed for the purpose of spreading pollutants farther from town, over the surrounding hills. After learning the truth, whenever I questioned parents and others about why the air, water, and soil must be polluted to allow for temporary "prosperity," they answered with some combination of anguish, impatience, disgust, or hostility that I was ungrateful and thought people should go hungry. In the 1960s, steel mills in Weirton and Wheeling did afford their workers a good living, because of high demand and strong labor unions. Employment in the industry began to decline in 1977, however, due not only to cheaper imports but also to greater efficiency and productivity on the part of workers. In effect, they had put themselves out of a job.

Scrubbers—a term that describes several flue gas treatment processes—were invented in the 1930s to neutralize toxic gases from coal-burning power plants and reduce particulate material spread from smokestacks, but it was 1967 before they were commonly used in Ohio.† According to an October 22, 2018, article that Joseph Cotruvo published on *Water Technology*, wet and dry scrubbers, adsorbents, and mercury removal processes "chemically convert volatile elemental mercury in the hot flue gas into solid water soluble salts" that are then collected. Variants include electrostatic precipitators and desulfurizing processes. When I first heard about them, I thought the problem of air pollution from the mills could and would surely be solved.

In the country, with relatively clean air, the pervasive image is that of strip mines—large areas denuded of trees and other vegetation by machines called "shovels," which were big as houses with buckets large as rooms that dug coal from seams near the surface. Strip mines look like giant pits with terraced sides. After completion of mining, the machines push the earth back into place; without groundcover, extensive erosion follows. One could travel many back roads that wound among farms, pastures, or woods and suddenly come upon these desecrated moonscapes. Strip-mined land, however, began to restore itself with broom sedge and poverty grass. Hawthorn followed, and trees adapted for survival on acidic soil, like wild cherry and big-tooth aspen. In 1972, the State of Ohio passed rules requiring planning, environmental impact assessment, and reclamation of strip-mined land, said to be some of the strictest in the nation, and in 1977, Congress passed the Surface Mining Control and Reclamation Act. Due to abundant rainfall and reseeding, extensive areas of stripped land recovered. Crown vetch, a legume developed in England and widely sown in Ohio's eastern counties, helped to replace topsoil. Other trees hardy enough to grow on reclaimed land include black alder, cottonwood, white ash, white pine, tulip, red maple, elm, and sweet gum. Restored strip mines do not look like the original steep hills: they are sculpted into gently rising mounds, often fenced for grazing cattle and sheep. Locals can

---

† According to Cotruvo's *Water Technology* article, both liquid- and solid-type gas treatment processes are used depending on the physical and chemical properties of whatever contaminant is being removed.

always tell the difference. Still, reclamation is preferable to abandonment. Assuming that the population had recognized the need for environmental protection, I believed we had turned the corner on industrial pollution and that regulations would protect air, water, and soil from that time on. I was wrong.

In 1993, I moved to Ashland County, a place not plagued with strip mines or power plants; most vertical natural gas wells had been drilled, and many were played out. Agriculture, especially dairy farming, was thriving, yet the biggest danger to the land was development, at least for the first twenty years. In 2010, a letter in the local paper alerted residents to the fact that a new form of drilling—horizontal hydraulic fracturing, or fracking—could compromise water and air quality, seriously affect health, and destroy property values; furthermore, the companies that engaged in the practice were exempt from environmental impact assessments. The writer was a woman who had seen the devastation caused by fracking in Pennsylvania. In 2011, a group calling itself Frack-Free Ohio contacted members of the Buckeye Forest Council, now the Buckeye Environmental Network, about a film titled *Gasland* that was being shown in Columbus. The producer and narrator, Josh Fox, described what happened in areas of Maryland where fracking occurred, including fish kills and contamination of wells with methane to the extent that residents were able to set their water on fire.

While gas-company spokespersons are quick to point out that rock fracturing is a proven technology first used in the 1940s, at that time the process involved vertical drilling. Widespread use of horizontal fracturing—far more devastating for the environment than vertical fracturing—gained momentum in 2005 with the Bush administration's passing of the Energy Policy Act. For that reason, I usually refer to the process with its three-word nomenclature (horizontal hydraulic fracturing), as people connected with the industry will claim the process is infallible, having been tested over decades. They neglect to mention that the Energy Policy Act, which received bipartisan support, exempted horizontal fracturing from seven environmental laws precisely because it was a new, experimental technology that the drilling companies were investing in, and they requested that Congress relax the regulations in order to recover costs.‡

In Ohio, as oil and natural gas have replaced coal as the state's most valuable fossil fuels, horizontal hydraulic fracturing poses the largest threat to water, air, and soil quality. Drilling companies pump millions of gallons of water mixed with hundreds of thousands of gallons of toxic chemicals into the ground at high pressure to fracture the shale and release oil and gas. Toxic chemicals from fracking wells can leak into neighboring water-wells, and about 20 percent of the contaminated effluent flows back to the surface along with volatile organic compounds and radioactive drill cuttings, which are stored in waste pits until they can be transported by tanker trucks and injected into old vertical gas wells—mostly in Ohio. Accidents from fracking sites that resulted in contaminated air, water, and soil are well documented in Pennsylvania, Maryland, New York, North Dakota, Colorado, Texas, and other states.

Speakers at a forum on fracking held at the Mansfield Public Library alerted local residents that toxic waste produced in eastern states and counties was being transported by tanker truck to Ohio and deposited into played-out gas wells, with little or no regulation or oversight by the Ohio Department of Natural Re-

---

‡ The Energy Policy Act of 2005 exempts horizontal hydraulic fracturing from the provisions of the Clean Air Act (1963), National Environmental Policy Act (1970), Clean Water Act (1972), Safe Drinking Water Act (1974), Resource Conservation and Recovery Act (1976), Comprehensive Environmental Response, Compensation, and Liability Act (also known as Superfund, 1980), and Emergency Planning and Community Right-to-Know Act (1986), the last being the law that requires polluting companies to inform states and local governments about the manufacture, storage, use, and accidental release of toxic chemicals. It was inspired by the 1984 disaster in Bhopal, India, involving the leak of methylisocyanate by a Union Carbide Corporation affiliate. More than five hundred thousand people were exposed to the gas; more than two thousand died immediately; another eight thousand died in the two weeks that followed; and approximately eight thousand died later of diseases related to the accident.

sources Division of Oil and Gas—the state agency that handles such matters. Local attorney Eric Miller, of the Nature Conservancy, was leading the effort to investigate the laws; a community organizer from Mansfield moderated the panel, which included Republican state representative David Hall, who favored fracking and sat grinning throughout the entire discussion as if it were a performance.

For many months, the Loudonville Public Library served as the location of meetings of local citizens concerned about fracking. We discussed drilling permits issued by the state and organized action campaigns that included passing out informational leaflets at canoe liveries, festivals, and village street fairs. Unfortunately, dissention among the members put an end to those strategy meetings. Monthly gatherings in the Methodist church in Jelloway in Knox County involved films by Anthony Ingraffea, professor of engineering at Cornell, once an industry insider, who warned against the dangers of fracking in particular and fossil fuel extraction more generally. Other films featured pharmacist and zoologist Theo Colborne, who testified before Congress that water contamination from fracking contains endocrine disruptors. Still, fracking was mostly being conducted in the eastern part of the state in counties over the Marcellus Shale. Hilly areas that had been coal country were now natural gas country; they were among the poorest, where people were so desperate for investment (the steel mills having shut down or cut back their operations) that they welcomed polluting industries in spite of evidence of serious toxic spills.

Frack-Free Ohio subsequently sponsored a showing of an Emmy Award–winning documentary film, *Split Estate* (2009), in the Loudonville Theater. In one scene, then Colorado governor Ken Salazar arrives in a private jet to talk with people who suffered serious health effects—including neurological and endocrinal damage—from water wells contaminated by horizontal fracturing. Later, serving as President Obama's secretary of the Interior (2009–13), in a blatant example of political expediency, Salazar publicly expressed his support for fracking, while knowing the consequences for landowners and residents. President Obama himself, for whom I voted twice, supported what he called "an all-of-the-above" energy policy, shorthand for oil and gas development. When I wrote to Obama asking him to oppose fracking, I received a letter bearing his signature (although of course he never saw either my letter or the answer), declaring that fracking would provide the country with energy for a hundred years. The formulaic answer made no mention of my concerns about water quality or climate disruption.

Since the middle of the nineteenth century, fracturing processes have been employed to release oil and gas from rock layers. In the late 1940s, the Department of Energy helped to subsidize research into new technologies involving well performance and pressure, especially by Floyd Farris and Joseph B. Clark, engineers at Stanolind Oil & Gas Company. The fossil fuel industry had known of the presence of natural gas in shale deposits since the early 1970s, and President Richard Nixon claimed that exploiting these resources would release the United States from reliance on "foreign energy sources." In a November 6, 1973, television address, he cited the Rock Mountains as a prime location for drilling because of their oil shale. By 1981, geologist George Mitchell employed hydraulic fracturing to drill for oil and gas in the Barnett Shale in Texas, and by 1997 he showed that horizontal fracturing could be commercially viable.

The first well in Ashland County was drilled more than twenty miles northwest of my farm. When I drove to the site in February, the daytime temperature hovered near zero degrees Fahrenheit, and strong wind drove snow over the level fields surrounding the wellhead. Farms bordered all sides of the site, including an organic dairy operation not more than 250 feet away. A friendly police officer, who monitored incoming traffic at the head of the entrance lane from a portable office heated by a gasoline generator, advised me to return the next day "when the safety officer would be here." A black tarp surrounding the site prevented curious onlookers from viewing the machinery and tankers, although the drilling rig was visible, rising about 125 feet. I talked with a young Amish farmer whose land lay just across the one-lane township road and the inhabitants of a house on the corner of the township and county roads who verified that trucks carrying water and chemicals rolled all day and night for weeks, the drilling site was noisy, and lights left on all night made sleeping difficult.

When I returned the next day, there was no safety officer present, but I was able to talk to technicians who gave me brochures. They knew I was not merely curious: they answered my questions briefly and guardedly. One man admitted that they did not like to go to the local grocery stores or restaurants because their Texas accents betrayed the fact that workers from outside the state were filling most of the jobs associated with fracking. His unease stemmed from the fact that drilling companies seeking variances on ordinances or rights-of-way claim that they create jobs for local people.

After several wells failed to produce, environmentalists celebrated, believing we were safe, especially when Devon and Chesapeake pulled their equipment out of Ashland, Wayne, and Knox Counties. The euphoria was short-lived. In October 2017, vibroseis trucks, massive vehicles nicknamed "thumpers," slowly traversed the county and township roads, using sonar waves to detect the presence of mineral resources. The companies that authorize these seismic surveys claim that sonar waves do not harm land or animals, although no reliable data exist concerning the effect on animals; locals reported feeling their houses shake, and sonar waves have been known to crack the grout casing around well pipes. One man who lived west of Perrysville and suffered from epilepsy stated that he thought he was having a seizure when the thumpers drove past his land. No laws exist to regulate their use. Cabot Oil & Gas—the corporation whose poor construction caused massive contamination of water wells in Dimock Township in northeastern Pennsylvania, one of the most notorious examples of environmental damage caused by fracking—contacted local landowners about buying leases to fracture the Clinton and Knox Dolomite Shale Layers horizontally. The Clinton layer is much closer to the surface than either the Utica or Marcellus, while the Knox Dolomite is much deeper, eight thousand feet in much of Ashland County.

More recent innovations in the drilling process allow companies to extend their operations far beyond their 2012 capability: whereas the horizontal pipes called *arms* in those days reached a mile, by 2012 they could travel four miles. When the process was first used, each frack required 3 million gallons of water; later, each one required as many as 40 million, with similar increases in toxic flowback. The Muskingum Watershed Conservancy District—the agency charged with oversight of water supply and flood control—sold millions of gallons of water from the Black Fork River. In addition to the large, well-publicized transmission pipelines, drilling for gas and oil requires construction of smaller gathering lines, or shallow conduits that transport the resources locally. As of 2018, no regulations existed in their construction or operation. Landowners who do not own the mineral rights to their property have no voice in whether oil and gas companies can drill beneath their land but are subject to the decisions of those who do possess and control the rights and who may or may not live nearby. A 2015 Ohio Supreme Court ruling upheld the state's exclusive power to regulate oil and gas exploration, denying local municipalities the right to ban, restrict, or regulate extraction activities. Played-out gas wells may be sold to domestic or foreign companies for disposal of toxic fracking waste, creating increased risks of residential water-well contamination by owners who often live far away from drilling sites.

In 2018, a new well site in Green Township received a permit, four miles from my land. A group of about thirty people met at Malabar Farm in the evening of May 21 to plan a demonstration. The community organizer instructed us on how to behave; this was no time for belligerence or illegal trespassing. The best approach was rational. He was right, of course; even if the oil company executives would not listen, we might influence public opinion. Every house we drove past on the seven-mile route to the site had an antidrilling sign in its yard. The landowner, a man from an old Green Township family, had sold the mineral rights in hopes of being able to pay medical bills. His farm lay on a narrow, east–west township road, unpaved until Cabot covered it with asphalt. Bordered by fields and woods, the lane passes a stone farmhouse over a hundred years old in a dell that reminded me of wooded places I had seen in England and Wales. Across from the drilling site, a hobby farm with a large new house and barn was home to horses, cattle, sheep, and goats. When we arrived, the owner of that house came out on his four-wheeler and stated that he was not happy about the drilling. The young security guard said he knew nothing about the plans for the well. He called the public relations director, George Stark, a man perhaps in his forties, who assured us that he was concerned about the environment, since he had a young son. Initially he told us he was from Pennsylvania, but he later he admitted that he was originally from Texas. He demonstrated his responsibility to the area, he claimed, by walking the road picking up trash. The community organizer tried to explain that local residents were concerned about water and air quality. Stark, known for his ability to reduce complex issues to simple slogans, made the usual ploy about how risk is "relative": getting into your car involves taking a risk, he declared. When I mentioned the accidents in Pennsylvania, he replied, "There are risks." At that point, I lost my patience and began to shout at him that I chose not to take the risk and that he should take it. I stated that the cost of water testing put it beyond the reach of many people, and that landowners who possessed mineral rights might make money, but those who did not own the rights would receive no benefit but only the threat to their water and rural way of life. Others in the group finally led me away. The community organizer never spoke to me again and later moved to Pennsylvania. Another community organizer retired to West Virginia, from where she sent pictures of the devastation caused by mountain-top mining.

The company never publicized the results of the drilling, but Cabot pulled its equipment out of the state, so neighbors concluded that the well had not produced and the landowner had not made the profit he sought.

A group calling itself the Ohio Oil and Gas Energy Educational Project maintains an office in the historic village of Granville and sends its representative Rhonda Reeda far and wide, "educating" the public on the safety of fracking. I went to hear her speak in the high school in the village of Butler and tried to stay silent—until she included the caveat that although fracking was safe, people living near fracking sites needed to have their water tested. I shouted from the bleachers that she should tell people that those tests cost about $1000 and should be repeated several times per year. When neighbors organize, they can bring a water testing agent for $500 per well if houses are close together. Those prices, I stated, were not in the budget for many households. No one led me out of the auditorium, but people on both sides began shouting at each other, and the principal later stated that he would never allow another forum to take place in his school.

The threat of fracking remains. During the 2018 election, my enthusiasm was diminished for Senator Sherrod Brown, a Democrat for whom I had voted in 2006 and in 2012, because he expressed support for fracking in an interview published in the quarterly Farm Bureau magazine, *Harvest*. I expected the Republican senator, Rob Portman, to support fracking, as he supported all business interests over sustainability and preservation, but I was also disappointed in the Democratic candidate for governor, Richard Cordray, director of President Obama's Consumer Finance Protection Bureau—and so, I thought naively, would favor protection for people against predatory industry—who expressed his support for fracking in the same article. I voted for the Green Party gubernatorial ticket, Constance Gadell-Newton and Brett Joseph, although my vote did not matter: Mike DeWine, a Republican and staunch supporter of fracking and fossil fuel mining and drilling, won by six percentage points.

Taking my case before the Ashland County Commissioners, I showed them a PowerPoint presentation about the dangers of toxic waste produced in fracking. I asked them to consider that many people in Ashland County valued the rural character of the place, that fracking threatened not only water and air but also their way of life, and that true energy independence meant investing in renewables. None of the county commissioners had visited any fracking site or knew the details about fracking accidents. One of them, Kim Edwards, whose husband worked for an electric company, asked rhetorically, "Who wants to look at solar panels?"

The only state representative who agreed to talk to me, Republican Margaret Ruhl of the Sixty-Eighth District, told me she had visited fracking sights and declared she had not seen or smelled "anything objectionable." A member of the House Agriculture and Natural Resources Committee in 2013, she heard testimony concerning House Bills 41 and 42. The first would have returned authority to municipalities to regulate drilling and health and safety standards, while the second would have revised language in the state code requiring transparency and disclosure of chemicals used in drilling operations. A member of the party that claims to support local government, she voted against both bills, which were defeated.

While companies are legally required to clean up and "plug" oil and gas wells after production, observers report that few companies have plans to do so; furthermore, bankruptcy laws allow failing oil and gas companies to renege on their obligations to communities they have polluted while rewarding the executives who oversee the process. The result is that cleanup costs fall to states and local communities. Private individuals may sue oil and gas companies, and sometimes even win, but collecting from a company that has declared bankruptcy is difficult or impossible.

Since 2010, more than eighty thousand wells have been drilled in Ohio, mostly in Belmont, Carroll, Guernsey, Harrison, Jefferson, Monroe, and Noble Counties, those with the lowest economic growth and greatest poverty, according to Beth Berger, *Columbus*

Dispatch reporter. During a 2019 drive to Martins Ferry, from Route 9 in Belmont County, I was able to see clearly the flare-off from a distant drilling site. Fracking had been taking place in Belmont County for at least ten years at that point, yet it had not translated to better conditions in Martins Ferry or the other towns in the area. A 2021 report, "Appalachia's Natural Gas Counties: Contributing More to the U.S. Economy and Getting Less in Return," by Sean O'Leary of the Ohio River Valley Institute (ORVI), an organization that reports on oil and gas drilling, delivered a scathing rebuke to companies which predicted that the natural gas boom in the Marcellus and Utica shale regions would create prosperity in places that had suffered economic downturn with the decline of the coal and steel industries. Twenty-two counties in Ohio, Pennsylvania, and West Virginia produce more than 90 percent of the region's natural gas. Oil and gas companies predicted that over 450,000 jobs would be created, yet data from the US Bureau of Economic Analysis showed that jobs in those counties grew during 2010–20 by only 1.7 percent, in contrast to the nationwide increase of 10 percent. Although economic output from those counties grew by 60 percent, personal income fell by 6.3 percent, numbers of jobs fell by 7.5 percent, and population declined 9.6 percent. Clearly, employment in the oil and gas sector had gone to people from out of state.

Sacrifice zone is a term the US Department of Energy first used in the 1950s to describe locations downwind from atomic detonations—notably islands in the Kwajalein Atoll. Later, the department employed the term to designate areas that had been radioactively contaminated by uranium mining. In a 1973 article from the National Academy of Sciences, the writer identified regions affected by coal mining as sacrifice zones. Used in 1987 in connection with pollution by petrochemical industries in Louisiana, the phrase became a rallying cry for people who live in places with elevated risks of cancer due to mining, industry, or dumping; it is the title of a 2010 book by Steve Lerner published by MIT Press, in which he interviewed residents of areas across the country where residents successfully opposed polluting industries. That the agency which regulates energy production should find it "acceptable" for some people to inhabit such places or for other locations to be abandoned rather than reclaimed reveals fundamental indifference to responsibility.

What is clear is that neither business nor government under either major party possessed the will to protect inhabitants from toxic chemicals released in the process of drilling for or processing of natural gas until President Biden introduced the Inflation Reduction Act of 2022. Ohio's land and water are being exploited by energy companies from out of state and by its own politicians. Many residents reveal remarkable complacency about the danger posed by fracking, believing either that it will bring prosperity to the region—in spite of evidence to the contrary—or that they can do nothing about it.

Henry David Thoreau famously wrote that "a town is saved by the woods and swamps that surround it," but today I must reverse this statement and declare that the salvation of the woods, wetlands, and biosphere need the protection of the people of the cities—their numbers and political will are the only things that will save the rural and natural environments from becoming sacrifice zones.

Thirteen

Home, or Where I'm From

WHEN T. S. ELIOT WROTE in "Little Gidding" that we "know the place for the first time" upon returning to a familiar location or state of being after long absence or quest, he referred to a perspective changed by experience (that of the questor), but he may also have been alluding to the persistence of memory. We are all protagonists in our own stories, and although we cannot relive events, we can mentally rewrite the narrative, and it is a commonplace that how we remember as well as what we remember affects our understanding. The word *nostalgia* derives from *nostos*, Greek for "home"; *sentimentality*, however, derives from *sentire*, Latin for "to feel," and although it stems from the same root as the term *sense*, *sentimentality* often refers to shallow longing for some imagined ideal, while *nostalgia* merits more respect, containing the idea that what has been lost is of value, although with memory altered by emotion.

The word *home* contains many meanings: once a noun and modifier, now it is colloquially used as a verb. Some people define home as a person's current residence. Others believe it is the place where one is born and raised. For me, it refers to the physical surroundings and cultural influences that have formed a person's character. When I am out of state and someone asks where I am from, I say "Ohio," but if instate, I reply "Jefferson County" or "east, on the river." The house, built in the 1940s, was in the country, small by today's standards, not the large, rambling, multigenerational place associated with farmsteads. Two symmetrical picture windows framing an inverted V-shaped roof over the front porch gave it a Christmas-card-house charm. Large, square-cut stones across the back lawn near a stream indicate the site where a springhouse stood. For decades, an old pump rose from the slope above that rivulet, and, higher up the hill, a pile of stones remained from the original barn. Over the years, those stones were pilfered for other uses. Mature locust trees lined the edge of the lawn to the west. Although now in an advanced state of decay, the surviving barn—which did not belong to us—across the lane in front of the house was much more recent, a one-story sheep cote with a gabled roof, open to the east with a large area in back for hay. A nearby metal Quonset hut, obscured from the lane by white pine trees, housed machinery. Hayfields stretched to the north, south, and west, while pastures extended eastward to the tree line, where the land sloped steeply toward Cross Creek. Beyond those treetops, wooded hills rose, blue on paler blue, in the distance.

Every morning in summer, I woke early and walked in those fields and woods. At the north end of the pasture, a large old white oak held the decaying wooden platform of a tree house, and a stile allowed a walker to cross the barbed-wire fence line. Drops of dew sparkled like jewels on the strands of the orb weavers' enormous octagonal webs strung between long stems of wild oats and Queen Anne's lace. Rabbits bounded away into the brush, and cardinals called from the branches of hickory trees. A small copse of young maple and locust became my Eden, the space between them the "rooms" of an outdoor "sanctuary." Like Thoreau, I found solitude to be my most companionable companion.

I was not alone, however. My dog always accompanied me, a stray mixed-breed beagle I called Duke, after a grandfather's deceased boxer dog. I had not found him; he found me and remained my companion for eight years, until I went to college. After that, he was a family pet until he died. My other walking partner was my cat, a tabby male called Tuffy.

For one halcyon summer, in exchange for riding privileges, I took care of horses boarded in that barn—a chestnut Thoroughbred racing mare, stocky piebald hunter, large black-and-white Welsh pony, and smaller brown-and-white Shetland—but later the landowner ejected his tenant in order to raise Hereford cattle. The rural township had many working farms, owned mostly by German and Serbian immigrants who kept very much to themselves, but no one would board horses, so I could not have my own. A cousin and I worked for a local farmer—famous countywide for parsimoniousness—who raised grain, hens, and Ayrshire cows. We cleaned stalls, collected ears of corn left lying on the ground after harvest, forked the manure out of chicken coops, and raked hay in exchange for riding the farmer's ponies, a bay Welsh gelding and a tricolored pinto of mysterious breeding.

Although I took care of horses, girls were not thought capable of driving a tractor, handling tools, or repairing fence line; and requests to be taught were met not only with refusal but also derision. I was an adult before I learned how to drive a tractor, pull a brush hog, leverage heavy loads, dig postholes, repair wire, and clear overgrown fence lines. I still have never plowed with a tractor or driven a team.

Before they built their own house, that horsey cousin's family rented a place we called "the farm." The nineteenth-century house on a homestead of about eighty acres boasted six capacious rooms, a screened back porch, and a front veranda looking over about an acre of lawn. At the entrance to the homestead, a large old sycamore tree stood sentinel. A long arbor shaded a walkway and produced table grapes in September. In front of a pine windbreak, a henhouse occupied the west side, at last taken over by vines and shrubs. The owners had sold the mineral rights to a company that strip-mined the rest of the acreage. Eventually, my aunt and uncle bought a pony for my cousin, and we used to ride on that desecrated land, which we called "the strips," because no one cared what we did. We could gallop fairly long distances unimpeded by fences. Erosion wore rivulets in the earth, but watching the soil partially restoring itself gave me confidence in the power of nature. "The farm," however transformed, was an ideal place for children to play. The house, barn, garage, and henhouse were demolished in the late 1960s when the remainder of the land was strip-mined. Later, the entire farm was sold as an industrial park.

Girls frequently lose interest in horses as soon as they discover boys; I did not. The fourth year after we moved to the country, a new neighbor bought the farm on the other side of the hill, about a quarter of a mile away, renovated an old shed, and brought in horses. In exchange for taking care of them, I was allowed to board my own, a chestnut American Saddlebred gelding purchased from the same man who had stabled his horses near our house years before. I rode every day in summer and weekends and evenings during the school year. Not only did Duke follow me on my daily trek to the barn, but so did five or six other neighborhood dogs. When I rode in that pasture of about eighty acres, half of which was wooded, they strung out before me like foxhounds.

With friends, I used to ride down over the eastern hillside through undergrowth and trees to a place called Reeds Mill. We swam the horses across the creek and climbed the other side where it was rumored that in the nineteenth century a stagecoach trail had crossed those hills. Sometimes we followed a gravel lane locally nicknamed Possum Hollow and emerged at the top of a slope onto a large, gently rolling plain that had been strip-mined. We trotted and galloped all over the land, not knowing or caring who owned it, and were never stopped. If we got lost, we let the horses find their way home.

I joined 4-H but was the only person in the club who rode in an English saddle. The single club in the county that included English riders, all of whom owned Arabian horses, maintained an exclusive membership. While the county-fair horse show offered multiple classes for western riders, it offered only one for those who rode English. Unable to fit in with the crowd, I left 4-H after a year.

The cattleman owner of most of the land around our house was a contractor who had bought the entire farm (about six hundred acres) for development. Throughout my adolescence, I watched those fields sectioned off in lots of one-eighth to one-quarter of an acre of grass; he built single-story brick houses that all looked alike except for a few doors and windows changed around, the type people were buying during that time: three bedrooms, kitchen-dinette, living room, one or two bathrooms, two-car garage. The new residents planted tree saplings, ornamental shrubs, flowers along walkways, and vegetable gardens in back; built fish ponds and barbecue pits; hung feeders for wild birds; and surrounded their yards with chain-link or post-and-rail fences. In a few years, the five loops of the subdivision were nearly indistinguishable from each other, landscaped housing developments against the backdrop of bucolic woods. One very foggy morning when I sought a friend's house, I was unable to tell which loop I was on, because the houses were so similar. Later, more affluent people built much larger houses, a few with the pitched roofs and half-timbering of Tudor revival or southern-style white pillars on the front and swimming pools or tennis courts in back. When I expressed disappointment at seeing the landscape ruined—as I thought—one friend regaled me with her philosophy: "That's the only way they're going to make any money off of it," she declared, "not with *cattle*." She referred to the woods on her own place—the farm where I was boarding my horse—as "a heap of dirt."

The extensive acreage east of our house and the woods on the hillside remained undisturbed, however. The owner sometimes grazed his cattle there, while at other times the pasture lay fallow, the grass reaching as high as my waist while birds sang from oak and hickory trees.

※

Aside from humorous anecdotes, the few stories shared on either side of my family primarily involved loss. Although six great-grandparents were still alive when I was born, I met only three great-grandmothers but never got to know them. Two lived in Texas and one in Logan County, Ohio, about two hundred miles away. None left me with any wisdom.

When the members of my father's immediate family resided in Steubenville, they owned a large lot of about an acre with mature trees, two barns, garden, and orchard surrounded by a high fence. The house probably had been a multigenerational farmhouse at one time, as it was very old and had five bedrooms upstairs and four rooms down—kitchen, dining room, living room, and what was called the parlor, which contained a piano and fireplace that was never used and was separated from the front vestibule by old-fashioned pull-doors. A staircase from the dining room led to an attic; another in the vestibule with a carved, curving balustrade allowed access to the second floor. A wide front porch, which nobody ever used, faced the front, while a screened porch–mud room led to the back, where everyone entered. A roofed veranda that spanned the length of the house on the east side looked out over a dell in a historic cemetery. The house, barns, and garden were razed in the early 1960s to build a clover-leaf interchange on Market Street (US Route 22), the main road through town to the river.

My paternal grandmother, who had grown up on a farm, was good at mathematics and kept the books for her husband's various businesses. After he died in 1972, she worked as a church treasurer and operated a florist business from her own house. Working was nothing new to the women in that family. Her own mother, having grown up on a farm near Belle Center in Logan County, married a farmer who died in the influenza epidemic of 1918. Forced to sell their land, she supported herself as a seamstress and church janitor. Somehow, she was able to send two daughters to Miami University for their certifications as elementary school teachers. Both eventually completed their four-year degrees. I inherited my great-grandfather's watch but no story to go with it.

My father's paternal aunt, a doctor's wife and avid genealogical researcher, discovered that her mother's family had emigrated from England to Massachusetts in the early eighteenth century and by the early nineteenth had settled in what was then the Northwest Territories. Unable to make his farm profitable, her father operated a dairy but lost it in the Great Depression of the 1930s. The embodiment of contradictions, my great-aunt bragged about her ancestors even though none had accomplished anything noteworthy. While heavily invested in automotive companies, she reminisced about the days when people drove wagons into town to sell their products. She never kept livestock and lived most of her life in town but loved animals; knew the breeds of dogs, sheep, goats, and dairy cattle; and subscribed to the *Farm Quarterly*—a large, illustrated magazine that featured articles by Louis Bromfield—and the *Eastern Breeder: The Magazine of Horse and Livestock Breeders*. Although she seldom rode horses and never owned one, she hung on a wall a framed photograph of herself dressed in saddle-seat jodhpurs on a gaited horse. As she seldom rose before eight, I could not imagine her getting up at six in the morning in January to break the ice in water buckets or clean stalls. Although her attitudes and prejudices belonged to an earlier era, her influence on me was larger than I wanted to admit: I admired her antique furniture and landscape paintings of English country houses and shared her concern about pollution from pesticides and overuse of chemical fertilizers. In spite of her interest in conservation, however, she sold her farm for strip-mining, the very one where my cousin and I used to ride horses. My great-aunt, who had lost her family homestead, gained another only to give it up willingly.

One fuzzy brown-and-white photograph now in my possession shows her brother, my paternal grandfather, as a boy standing in a hay wagon in a field on the family farm near Mount Pleasant. An entrepreneur at heart, as a young man he worked in his father's dairy and at the same time became one of the first flyers in the county. He delivered mail until he lost his plane during the Depression. He owned a feed store for many years, but when it was no longer profitable, he bought a hatchery, a business in which he purchased fertilized eggs from poultry farmers, hatched them in an incubator, and sold the chicks back to the farmers. This increased the number of chickens a farmer could raise, by ensuring that a higher percentage of fertilized eggs would hatch. The business began to suffer in the late 1950s with the advent of factory-style poultry operations, when owners of sizable flocks (six hundred to a thousand birds) either bought or leased their own incubators and large companies bought up the feed mills and hatcheries in order to control production. My grandfather sold his business and operated a taxicab company in St. Clairsville until he died.

My mother's parents represented a very different history. They were born in Bell County, in eastern Texas, their ancestors part of the migration from Northern Ireland to Virginia at the beginning of the eighteenth century that moved south and westward. My grandfather grew up on a ranch, where his father raised angora goats, my grandmother on a cotton and sugarcane farm. A very generous, self-effacing, and patient person, she told few stories about her youth other than one about her mother's strictness and another about returning home from a dance with a boy who, trying to show off, drove the horse at a hard gallop and eventually overturned the buggy. She and my grandfather left for Ohio in the 1920s, when factory jobs paid better than anything they could have found in the South. One photograph shows them looking prosperous and standing next to their first car. They lost their entire savings in the stock market crash of 1929, and nearly every visit included a narrative about how bad things were during the depression. Not once did I hear her say anything about how she felt about women's suffrage or the Great War; on World War II she said nothing except to comment on the food rationing. Nostalgic about her close-knit family and the virtues of farm life, she refused ever again to live that life.

My great-grandmother had been born near Marietta, and legend has it that she traveled on a raft down the Ohio and Mississippi Rivers and in a wagon across Arkansas to Texas. My mother often repeated what she said about her courtship: "The minute I saw him, I knowed he was the one." Her parents disallowed the marriage, however, so she eloped with her intended and lost a shoe when they ran across a plowed field. The first thing he did when they reached the town was buy her a pair of shoes. At her fiftieth wedding anniversary, in 1950, each grandchild received a tiny yellow porcelain shoe; my mother kept hers all her life. I turned it over to read "made in Japan" stamped on the bottom. When I inherited the paperwork from the ranch, I learned that every year throughout the 1940s my great-grandfather increased the size of his holdings, even as the market made ranching increasingly difficult. That pile of bank transactions and deeds, along with a few photographs, was all that remained of the homestead, sold after he died in 1950. One second cousin who visited the land after decades had passed related that the barn my great-grandfather built had subsequently burned down.

Two miles west of Wintersville, a bridge crosses a stream called Reeds Mill Creek, named for two brothers who built several grist mills in the early 1800s. Unincorporated, with only three houses, the area looms large enough in the local consciousness to merit a highway sign at an exit ramp. At one point in the twentieth century, someone established a dealership there, the Steubenville Motor Company, which sold Model T Fords. In 1929, a woman named Mrs. Chalfant purchased the building and opened a restaurant called the Reeds Mill Inn, a one-story, square white building, which included a filling station, dance hall, slot machine, and, years later, a parrot that had been taught to curse. Before he became famous, singer Dean Martin (Dino Paul Crocetti, who grew up in Steubenville) performed there several times with a group called the Night Owls, who heralded from the nearby village of Unionport. Passes were sold at the restaurant to allow swimming in a widened section of the creek, although it is not clear what right the proprietor had to do so, as she did not own the waterway. The advertisement on the side of the building reads

Reeds Mills Service Station
Dancing, Swimming, Free Picnic Tables, Lunches
Beer, Pretzels
24 hr. service, Atlantic White Flash Gas and Oil
Stonebraker & Chalfant—Props., nine miles west of Steubenville,
Ohio, on Route 22.

The name over the door read "Reeds Mill Inn, Round and Square Dancing," beneath a larger sign advertising Coca-Cola, sandwiches, and cigarettes. In the early 1950s, a truck demolished the building when the driver apparently lost control on one of the steep, winding curves on either side of the bridge. While the driver was killed, the parrot survived and was found by rescuers, who could hear him cursing.

An event that persists in my memory is stopping on a gravel lane when out driving with my parents and seeing a shack surrounded by the detritus of a life: broken toys, a rocking horse, the blade of an axe buried in a tree stump, a rusted well hydrant, dolls, brooms, pitchforks, pieces of wooden furniture, a derelict washing machine, laminated bowls, a rusting 1950s car mounted on cement blocks, and other things, all surrounded by chicken wire. When my mother asked who lived there, my father answered that an old widowed man used to occupy the place but now lived with his daughter in Mingo. She lamented that the old man had not been able to take with him all the things he saved—things that appeared like junk to me had been to him what remained of his life.

Another local story tells of a woman who carried on a long-standing affair with her married boss, the owner of an insurance agency. When he died of a heart attack, his children barred her from the funeral, and they managed to keep her from receiving the money he had left her. She finished her days living in the woods in a small house, little more than a cabin, inherited from her parents, and always kept many German shepherd dogs on the property. Hardly anyone visited her, although she had relatives in the area. One day she disappeared without a trace.

Further back in history, in the early nineteenth century, John Chapman, known as Johnny Appleseed, visited the territory and planted orchards before migrating northwestward. An Indian fighter named George Carpenter is said to have leaped during a bad dream into a vat of boiling sugar water. He died screaming about savages twisting and leaping around a fire. Frontiersman Joseph Ross refused to leave his property until the government could issue a title for the land he had cleared. It was said that he, his wife, and child survived by sheltering in a hollow sycamore. Three years later, in possession of the title, he died when a limb fell on him from a tree he was trying to cut down. Two ministers, named Intrepid Morse and Lorenzo Dow, crossed the river to preach the Gospel to settlers. One of them died after a month. The other, so the story goes, was driven crazy by loneliness or perhaps the vastness of wilderness.

During a visit in 2017, I drove to the old school in Bloomingdale, which I attended from fifth to twelfth grades. Mine was the last class (1968) to graduate from there before the district consolidated with two others, Wintersville and Mingo Junction. The building had been closed down and the doors padlocked. Playground and football field were grown in grass high enough to bale. Swings, bleachers, and scoreboard had been removed, and weeds grew up in the cracks of the parking lot. Almost fifty years since I last walked those hallways, I peered through the windows, wondering at the smallness of a place that loomed so large in memory, one I had resolved to escape not only in distance but in spirit. "To regret one's own experiences is to arrest one's own development," wrote Oscar Wilde in a letter later titled "De Profundis." He should know, but an author writing a story can create unity and meaning out of events that have neither, at least when they occur.

In 2019, I revisited some old haunts after the memorial service of my oldest cousin, the last member of a once-sizable extended family to live in Jefferson County. Most of them had belonged for half a century to a Presbyterian church that had been forced to close in 1989 because of decreasing membership. The old building, its cornerstone dated 1895, was made of dark-gray local sandstone with a rectangular bell tower. The new owners, an evangelical group, replaced the choir loft and organ pipes with a pool for baptism by immersion. For many years, a large Victorian mansion, the original manse, had been operated as a funeral parlor, but that was finally razed to make room for a parking lot.

I drove up the hillside to the house where I spent my first ten years, conscious of people watching from their porch swings as I parked my truck and climbed the steps from the street. The neighborhood had increased its racial diversity. The duplex where we had lived and the one next to it, where my maternal grandparents had lived, were both derelict, the windows boarded up. The yard where I played was so small I could not imagine how there had been room for games with neighborhood children. A small, grassy field across the street looked the same; beyond it the wooded hillside sloped all the way to railroad tracks downtown. It took only five minutes to walk the two blocks to the elementary school, which had seemed a journey in those days. The red-brick building bore a sign identifying it as a nursing home, but even that had been closed and the windows boarded up; the playground remained, however, with swings and slide. The small general store across the street had been torn down and replaced by a parking lot, but the fire house still stood on the corner.

None of these visits inspired any feeling of having belonged.

Driving the road out of town that ran parallel to the Ohio River, I desired to catch a glimpse, so I pulled my truck onto a small gravel lot and strode up a grassy incline. There, beyond a few struggling saplings, some brush, and large rocks, the dark, gray-green water folded over on itself like muscle tissue. Sheer rock and wooded hills rose on the West Virginia side. I heard no birdsong nor saw any wildlife, but I could hear the rush of the deep water that had flowed all the way from the Monongahela and Allegheny Rivers and would roll on to the Mississippi and eventually the Gulf of Mexico. "I've known rivers," Langston Hughes wrote in his famous poem "The Negro Speaks of Rivers," in which some of the greatest waterways of the world became emblems of the history of civilizations. "Nothing is trite along a river," James Wright declared in his prose poem "Honey." Born and raised in Martins Ferry in Belmont County, he knew a great deal about the derelict neighborhoods along its banks and stories about people who had drowned in the undertow. I had been fascinated by the river cities, with their polluting steel mills and tarnished reputations as places that people could not wait to get out of. I loved the countryside, even with its strip mines and shacks. I had, however, always felt like a foreigner. Not only did I not know the place, I had never known it. Even so, I had no other source. I could leave home, but it would not leave me. Fifty years were not long enough to make the escape. Memory persisted, embodied in what remained as well as what had gone.

As I watched the flowing current, I heard a vehicle drive up and stop nearby. I paid it no attention until some minutes passed without voices or slamming of car doors. Glancing in its direction, I saw a red pickup with two people in the cab watching me. Restless under their gaze, I cut short my meditations and walked back to my truck, pulled out onto the road, and headed for home.

Only later, as I drove westward onto Route 22, did I realize that those people in the red truck were probably part of some sort of rescue squad waiting to see whether I would jump.

Fourteen

Progress, Economy, and Preservation

"How many a man has dated a new era in his life from the reading of a book!" Thoreau exclaimed in his "Reading" chapter in *Walden*. A new era began for me at fifteen when I read that book with its lyrical message of communion with the life of the woods and its philosophy of solitude and contemplation. It was the 1960s, and I was also excited by the idea that a person could question the norms of society, create his own values, and live life his own way. The woods were not a metaphor: the forests and fields around Concord were still ancient, while the village was the newcomer. When he narrates the story of individuals who lived before him, he shows that however transient the human residents were, the natural world endured. While Thoreau's declaration that during his stay at Walden (1845–47) he lived "a mile from any neighbor" may not seem remarkable at the same time the Donner Party was struggling to survive in the Sierra Nevada (1846–47), perhaps his statement is not so much a claim as an explanation. For part of Thoreau's life (1817–1862) he was contemporary with John Chapman ("Johnny Appleseed," 1774–1845), who also felt at home in the woods, although Thoreau spent most of his years in Massachusetts and sought contemplation while Chapman wandered ever westward. Thoreau wrote extensively about the natural world and

· 195 ·

its relation to moral philosophy; Chapman left no record of his adventures other than the orchards he planted. Thoreau's transcendentalist philosophy would have nevertheless resonated with Chapman, whose Swedenborgian religion included belief in the eternal as inseparable from the temporal.

Many writers agree with the preacher of Ecclesiastes, chapter 1, verse 9, that there is nothing new under the sun and that all new wisdom is old wisdom written down differently. In the same chapter, Thoreau asserts that the adventurous student will always study the classics because the "symbol of an ancient man's thought becomes a modern man's speech," and ancient languages do reveal much about the evolution of contemporary belief. The term *pagan* refers to followers of pantheistic religions—those who identify the deity with nature rather than separate from it. The Latin *paganus* means "country dweller," and what we refer to as *paganism* began with belief in earth gods. *Heathen* also refers to country dwellers—literally, dwellers on the heath, an area of low-growing shrubs such as heather—only this time, the word comes from Anglo-Saxon *haethen*. Belief in nature gods was thus associated with those who lived in the country and were dependent on the soil. While both terms acquired a pejorative connotation, perhaps today we can appreciate the idea that people once believed the divine and the natural were inseparable. When Thoreau wrote that he wished to live "deliberately," he may have meant that he desired to find otherworldly immanence or at least permanence in the temporal world. John Muir described a similar conviction in *My First Summer in the Sierra* (1911), based on his journals kept while he was sheepherding near the headwaters of the Merced and Tuolumne Rivers (1869), when he declared his desire to "learn to live like the wild animals, gleaning nourishment here and there from seeds, berries, etc., sauntering and climbing in joyful independence of money or baggage."

For the existentialist, what we do is what we are. For the Buddhist, what we think is what we are. For the Christian, what we believe is what we are. Perhaps the truly "complete" person—like Chapman,

Thoreau, and Muir—knows that everything we do, think, and believe is holy; every moment and action counts, even the mundane, not as if every day were the last but rather as if it were the first.

Thoreau's affirmation of simplicity in *Walden* constitutes a declaration of independence. He questions the need for modern inventions like the telegraph and railroad, speculating that much news received from the telegraph was not worth knowing (as much on our Internet is not worth reading). The railroad, he declared, "rides upon us," referring to the fact that modern inventions have a way of taking over the lives they are supposed to improve. Today we celebrate that information is immediately available, but much of it is inaccurate and useless; high-speed travel allows us to visit wonderful places, but it also creates pollution, noise, traffic jams, and accidents. Inventions bring dependence as well as freedom, unless we make them work for ourselves rather than the companies which receive the profits. *Progress* should mean more than products and possessions. Politicians speak of making "a better life" for people but seldom define that phrase: existence based solely on acquisition ignores the need for reflection, possibility of inspiration, and capacity for transcendence.

Dependence on energy, furthermore, enslaves us to forces outside our control, whether human or weather-related. In September 2022, a third of the people of Ukraine were without electricity because their power stations had been bombed. Destruction of the Zaporizhzhia plant made clear the inherent danger of nuclear plants: even if they can be made "safe" in peacetime, their very existence creates insecurity and instability.

A robust economy, we are told, must grow, yet cycles of recession and depression reveal the flaw in the machinery of endless production and consumption. The word *economy* stems from the Greek *oikos* (house) and *nemein* (manage); *oikonomia* means "household management." Xenophon's (430–354 BC) essay "Economy" (after 362 BC) discusses, among other topics, duty and cultivation of land: "Husbandry is an art so gentle, so humane, that mistress-like she [the earth] makes all those who look on her or listen to her voice intelligent of herself at once." *Ecology* derives from *oikos* and *logia* (study); thus, ecology is the study of the earth, the only home we have. We need a new way of life and revolutionary concept of economy not predicated on continuous acquisition but on sustainability and preservation. As I write, a new computer-chip factory is being built in Licking County, on prime farmland. It is said that the factory will make in one year what it would take the farmer a lifetime to earn, but we should learn to differentiate between price and value. A real estate company is buying up houses and farmland for development, driving up prices and taxes for everyone and creating dissention between long-term residents who want to stay and those who hope to sell out at inflated prices. Human beings can live without computer chips or fossil fuel, but they cannot live without food, water, and air.

While we cannot eliminate material needs, we can find ways of making ourselves more resilient. Strength and independence result from sustainability: growing more of our own food locally, doing more of our own physical work insofar as possible, producing sustainable energy, conserving rather than exploiting resources, making greater use of mass transit (including high-speed electric trains), designing cities around walkable areas, creating more parks (especially urban ones), building near existing towns and villages rather than destroying farmland, and preserving grassland, forests, and wilderness. Above all, we need to hold our unelected leaders—lobbyists and influential business people—accountable as well as elected lawmakers. It will be a great day, furthermore, when clothing is once again manufactured in this country, as a nation that does not make its own clothes possesses a deeply flawed character.

We congratulate ourselves on the fact that we are the most intelligent animals, yet in some ways we are the least intelligent. Every single-celled creature, insect, bird, amphibian, and mammal knows how to survive in its habitat or learns because the adults teach the young. Our parents and society instruct us about competition for things, the majority of which are extraneous to survival. Most of us cannot build our own houses, make our own clothes, or grow our own food. We even consult experts for advice on rearing young. Animals carry their history within themselves in the form of instinct, while we must learn from history, and what it tells us is that "progress" is not linear or inevitable; we are continuously solving the same problems dressed up in new raiment. Technology has not made us better thinkers.

If greed is the progenitor of destruction, carelessness is the other parent. Imagination inspires the desire for more, but lack of imagination enables people to destroy without conscience. Writers from Thoreau and John Muir to Rachel Carson, Wendell Berry, and Wes Jackson have stated that ecosystems have integrity and the right to endure. Aldo Leopold perhaps makes the strongest case for a land ethic, the right of the natural world to exist just as human beings claim to possess rights. While we need the biosphere, it does not need us.

As I drove south on the county road one evening after dark, I passed a doe sprawled on the pavement. Both hind legs had been broken, no doubt by a collision with a car, and she struggled to drag herself into the woods, but she was unable to grip the surface with her front hooves. The accident clearly had happened only minutes earlier, as I was the first of several drivers to stop. One woman alerted her husband, a hunter who skinned and butchered his own meat. Minutes later he arrived and advised me to leave. He was right, but I stayed and watched as the hunter removed his knife from its sheath and grabbed her neck. Mute until then, she cried out a roar of despair as moving as any human being's when all hope is lost. He cut her throat quickly, and all was silent. Although I had heard deer chuff in alarm, I had never before heard one wail. He did the right thing; she could not have been saved, but I was more than ever convinced that regardless of whether a creature has a sense of the future or of self-consciousness, it possesses feelings and a desire to live. The limp body nevertheless held a kind of dignity and even superiority: we were mere killers; she had passed into that other realm which most of us exist in fear of.

One day as we were loading hay, a neighbor farmer remarked that he had trapped a number of groundhogs. They often help themselves to garden produce and dig beneath structures to make their dens, causing problems for the foundations. He continued, "They are a nuisance. Completely useless."

Who, I wondered, has the right to designate a creature as useless? Early pioneers ate groundhogs, including Thoreau's Canadian woodchopper, mentioned affectionately in *Walden*.† The only species that is completely unnecessary to the biosphere, however, and also the most invasive, is *Homo sapiens*. Unable to master the language of our own species for several years, we take many more to mature into usefulness. The noisiest of all animals, we are not particularly good to look at with our nearly hairless, rather awkward bodies. Only a few large predators think we make good eating, and most prefer other fare. We force our progeny to pay for our profligacy, wreak destruction, frequently do not account for our actions, overpopulate, and appropriate the homes of other creatures. We are destructive and opportunistic colonizers, the only species that destroys its habitat with full knowledge of the consequences. When we do answer for ourselves, we claim a right based on our own self-justification, a circular argument, yet we pride ourselves on our ability to reason. We are proud of what we create yet have never produced anything as beautiful as a sunset, magnificent as the aurora borealis, or pleasing as birdsong. We think we are in control even as drought, floods, storms, and earthquakes show us we are not masters of our fate. We do resemble nearly every other mammal, however, in that we are born helpless, naked, ungainly, and ignorant. It is certain that one day we will have to answer for ourselves, and that day looms not terribly far in the future.

† Thoreau described the Canadian named Alek Therien in the *Journals* (July 14, 1845) as a "boor," "post maker," and "Paphlagonian man" who nevertheless had heard of Homer and avidly read books on rainy days.

We are nevertheless very good at solving problems and capable of introspection and rectifying our wrongs. Many times people have chosen to do so, and their descendants dated new eras from their ancestors' resolutions not to repeat the mistakes of the past and to preserve what experience told them should be venerated. We have the capacity to marvel at the intricacies of the world we did not create but which we have inherited through no virtue of our own. We can even revere it—and learn to live deliberately.

Bibliography

Works Cited

Abbott, Anneliese. *Malabar Farm: Louis Bromfield, Friends of the Land, and the Rise of Sustainable Agriculture*. Kent, OH: Kent State Univ. Press, 2021.

Abhat, Divya. "Inside the Heads of People Who Don't Like Music." *Atlantic*, Mar. 10, 2017, https://www.theatlantic.com/health/archive/2017/03/please-dont-stop-the-music-or-do-stop-the-music-i-dont-really-mind/519099/.

Adorno, Theodor. "On Popular Music." *Studies in Philosophy and Social Science* 9, no. 1 (1941): 17–48.

Aziza, Annisa Nurul. "The 'World's Largest Dump' Is in Indonesia, and It's a Ticking Time Bomb." *VICE Indonesia*, Oct. 14, 2019, https://www.vice.com/en/article/the-worlds-largest-dump-is-in-indonesia-and-its-a-ticking-time-bomb/.

Baldwin, James. "Sonny's Blues." In *Going to Meet the Man*, 101–41. New York: Dial, 1965.

Berger, Beth, "Fracking Boom Never Translated to Jobs and Growth." *Columbus Dispatch*, Feb. 20, 2021.

Berry, Wendell. *Collected Poems, 1957–1982*. New York: North Point Press, 1984.

———. "For the Love of Farming." *Farming*, Summer 2009, 8.

Black, John Baxter. *A History of the Family of Mr. and Mrs. Frank Blymyer Black of Mansfield, Ohio*. Vols. 1 and 2. Baltimore, MD: Gateway Press, 1995.

Bloom, Allan. *The Closing of the American Mind: How Higher Education Has Failed Democracy and Impoverished the Souls of Today's Students*. New York: Simon & Schuster, 1987.

Bromfield, Louis. *Animals and Other People.* New York: Harper & Brothers, 1955.
———. *Awake and Rehearse.* New York: Frederick A. Stokes Co., 1928.
———. *Early Autumn.* New York: Frederick A. Stokes Co., 1920.
———. *Pleasant Valley.* New York: Harper & Brothers, 1945.
———. *The Farm.* New York: Grosset & Dunlap, 1933.
———. *A Few Brass Tacks.* New York: Harper & Brothers, 1946.
———. *From My Experience: The Pleasures and Miseries of Life on a Farm.* 1955. Reprint, Kent, OH: Kent State Univ. Press, 2023.
———. *The Green Bay Tree.* New York: Grosset & Dunlap, 1924.
———. *Malabar Farm.* New York: Harper & Brothers, 1948.
———. *Possession.* New York: Grosset & Dunlap, 1925.
Burns, Jim. "Rare Ohio Plants Associated with the Teays River." *On the Fringe: The Journal of the Ohio Nature Plant Society* 6 (Sept.–Oct. 1988): 11–12.
Caldwell, J. A. *Ashland County Atlas.* Condit, OH: J. A. Caldwell, 1874.
Careless, James. "Turning the Volume Down: Reducing Road Noise with Pavement Design." *Asphalt: The Magazine of the Asphalt Institute* 30 (Apr. 1, 2015): 7–12.
Carter, Robert A., and Michael C. Cullen. *Water-Powered Mills of Richland County.* Corpus Christi, TX: Turas, 2016.
Chepesiuk, Ron. "Decibel Hell: The Effects of Living in a Noisy World." *Environmental Health Perspectives* 113, no. 11 (2005): A34–41.
"Collaborative Study Finds Noise from Oil and Gas Operations Stresses Birds and Hinders Their Reproduction." *Cal Poly News,* Jan. 5, 2018, https://www.calpoly.edu/news/collaborative-study-finds-noise-oil-and-gas-operations-stresses-birds-and-hinders-their.
Cosgrove, Denis, and Stephen Daniels, eds. *The Iconography of Landscape: Essays on the Symbolic Representation, Design, and Use of Past Environments.* New York: Cambridge Univ. Press, 1988.
Cotruvo, Joseph. "Smokestack Scrubbers: How They Work and Why They Are Used." *Water Technology,* Oct. 22, 2018, https://www.watertechonline.com/wastewater/article/15550703/smokestack-scrubbers-how-they-work-and-why-they-are-used.
Cusick, Allison. "Ohio Azaleas—Among 'the Handsomest' Flowers." *ONAPA News* 6, no. 2 (Spring 2019): 1–3.
Dass, Pawlock, Benjamin Z Houlton, Yingping Wang, and David Warlind. "Grasslands May Be More Reliable Carbon Sinks Than Forests in California." *Environmental Research Letters* 13 (July 10, 2018), https://iopscience.iop.org/article/10.1088/1748-9326/aacb39.
DeGrandi-Hoffman, Gloria, Fabiana Ahumada, Gene Probasco, and Lloyd Schantz. "The Effects of Beta Acids from Hops (*Humulus lupulus*) on Mortality of Varroa destructor (Acari: Varroidae)." *Experimental and Applied Acarology* 58, no. 4 (2012): 407–21.

Eliot, T[homas]. S[tearns]. *Collected Poems 1909–1962*. London: Faber & Faber, 1963.
Ellington, Edward Kennedy [Duke]. *Music Is My Mistress*. New York: Doubleday, 1973.
Emerson, Ralph Waldo. "Nature." In *Selections from Ralph Waldo Emerson*, edited by Stephen E. Whicher, 23. Cambridge, MA: Riverside, 1960.
Faulkner, Edward H. *Plowman's Folly*. New York: Grosset & Dunlap, 1943.
"'Funeral' for Timbering Held." *Ashland Times Gazette*, Mar. 6, 1995.
Gertner, Jon. "The Lives They Lived." *New York Times*. Dec. 21, 2013.
Goldmark, Sandra. "Built Not to Last." *Sierra* 106 (Fall 2021): 50–53.
Gonzalez, Xochitl. "Why Do Rich People Love Quiet? The Sound of Gentrification Is Silence" *Atlantic Monthly*, Aug. 1, 2022, https://www.theatlantic.com/magazine/archive/2022/09/let-brooklyn-be-loud/670600/.
Guy, Jack. "France Has Passed a Law Protecting the Sounds and Smells of the Countryside." *CNN*. Jan. 22, 2021, https://www.cnn.com/travel/article/france-rural-noise-law-scli-intl/index.html.
Hammer, Monica S., Tracy K. Swinburn, and Richard L. Neitzel. "Environmental Noise Pollution in the United States: Developing an Effective Public Health Response." *Environmental Health Perspectives* 122 (Feb. 2014): 115–19.
Hansen, Michael C. "The Teays River." *GeoFacts* 10. Columbus: Ohio Department of Natural Resources, Division of Geological Survey, Nov. 1995.
———. "The Teays River." *On the Fringe: The Journal of the Ohio Nature Plant Society*. 6 (Sept.–Oct. 1988): 4–10.
Havighurst, Walter. *Ohio: A Bicentennial History*. New York: W. W. Norton, 1976.
Henry, Rachel. "Large-Scale Nest Study Shows That Noise and Light Pollution Alter Bird Reproduction." *News*, School for Environment and Sustainability, Univ. of Michigan, Nov. 30, 2022, https://seas.umich.edu/news/large-scale-nest-study-shows-noise-and-light-pollution-alter-bird-reproduction.
Heyman, Stephen. *The Planter of Modern Life: Louis Bromfield and the Seeds of a Food Revolution*. New York: W. W. Norton, 2020.
Hochman, Nate. "Silence Is Okay, Actually." *National Review* 74 (Aug. 1, 2022), https://www.nationalreview.com/corner/silence-is-okay-actually/.
Howard, Sir Albert. *An Agricultural Testament*. 1st American ed. New York: Oxford Univ. Press, 1943.
———. *Soil and Health: A Study of Organic Agriculture*. New York: Devin-Adair, 1945.
Hughes, Langston. *The Collected Poems of Langston Hughes*. New York: Vintage, 1995.
Igini, Martina. "10 Concerning Fast Fashion Waste Statistics." Earth.org, Aug. 21, 2023, https://earth.org/statistics-about-fast-fashion-waste/.

James, William. *The Principles of Psychology.* New York: Henry Holt, 1890.
Jeffers, Robinson. "Shine, Perishing Republic." *The Collected Poetry of Robinson Jeffers*, edited by Tim Hunt, Vol. 1: 15. Stanford, CA: Stanford Univ. Press, 1988.
Joyce, James. *Ulysses.* 1920. Reprint, New York: Modern Library, 1961.
Kerlin, Kat. "Grasslands More Reliable Carbon Sink Than Trees." College of Agricultural and Environmental Sciences website, Univ. of California, Davis, July 11, 2018, https://caes.ucdavis.edu/news/articles/2018/july/grasslands-more-reliable-carbon-sink-than-trees.
Kinealy, Christine. "Food Exports from Ireland, 1846–47." *History Ireland* 5 (Spring 1997): 32–36.
de Langre, Emmanuel. "Effects of Wind on Plants." *Annual Review of Fluid Mechanics* 40 (Jan. 2008): 141–68.
Leopold, Aldo. *A Sand County Almanac and Sketches Here and There.* 1949. Reprint, New York: Oxford Univ. Press, 1987.
Leturgey, Tracy. "Polo at Ramelton Farm: 1934." *Richland County History* (blog), July 22, 2019, richlandcountyhistory.com/2020/01/18/polo-at-raemelton-farm-1934.
Lewis, Sinclair. "The Boxers of M. Voltaire." *Esquire*, Oct. 1945, 78–79.
Madison, Mike. *Walking the Flatlands: The Rural Landscape of the Lower Sacramento Valley.* Berkeley, CA: Great Valley Books, 2002.
McKee, Timothy. "Mohican: The Long View." Produced by Mohican Advocates, Inc, edited by the Tender Land Co., Vimeo, Apr. 12, 2012. Video, 12 min. 58 sec. https://vimeo.com/40797477.
"National Overview: Facts and Figures on Materials, Wastes, and Recycling." US Environmental Protection Agency website, last updated Nov. 22, 2023, https://www.epa.gov/facts-and-figures-about-materials-waste-and-recycling/national-overview-facts-and-figures-materials.
"Noise and Light Pollution Affect Breeding Habits in Birds." US National Science Foundation website, Nov. 24, 2020, https://new.nsf.gov/news/noise-light-pollution-affect-breeding-habits-birds.
"Noise as a Public Health Hazard." American Public Health Association website, Oct. 26, 2021, https://apha.org/policies-and-advocacy/public-health-policy-statements/policy-database/2022/01/07/noise-as-a-public-health-hazard.
O'Grady, Tom. "Cuyahoga Valley and Summit County Rich in Natural and Cultural History." *Old Barn Post* 11 (Jan. 2012): 4.
———."The Endangered Barn of Ohio's Hill Country." *Old Barn Post* 1 (Jan. 2002): 1.
———. "The 'Hall of Freedom' and the 'Granville Riot' of 1836 in Licking County." *Old Barn Post* 18 (Mar. 2019): 4–7.
———. "Hocking County Bicentennial Barn Demolished." *Old Barn Post* 3 (July 2004): 1.

———. "Ohio Barns: Variations on a Theme." *Old Barn Post* 10 (Nov/ 2011): 3.
———."Seeds of Rebellion Stored in Western Reserve Barn." *Old Barn Post* 12 (July 2013): 1.
O'Leary, Sean. "Appalachia's Natural Gas Counties: Contributing More to the U. S. Economy and Getting Less in Return." Ohio River Valley Institute website, Feb. 10, 2021, https://ohiorivervalleyinstitute.org/fracking-counties-economic-impact-report/.
———. "Fracking Counties Economic Impact Report: Natural Gas Counties' Economies Suffered as Production Boomed." Ohio Valley River Institute website, Feb. 8, 2021, https://ohiorivervalleyinstitute.org/new-report-natural-gas-county-economies-suffered-as-production-boomed/.
Pijanowski, Bryan C. *Principles of Soundscape Ecology: Discovering Our Sonic World*. Chicago: Univ. of Chicago Press, 2024.
Ruskin, John. *The Seven Lamps of Architecture*. New York: Longmans, Green, & Co., 1903.
———. "The Stones of Venice." In *Prose of the Victorian Period*, edited by William E. Buckler, 377. Boston: Houghton Mifflin, 1958.
Schmitz, Oswald J., Magnus Sylvén, Trisha B. Atwood, et al. "Trophic Rewilding Can Expand Natural Climate Solutions." *Nature Climate Change* 13 (Mar. 27, 2023): 324–33.
Seneca. "On Noise." *The Art of the Personal Essay: An Anthology from the Classical Era to the Present*, edited by Phillip Lopate, 5–8. New York: Anchor, 1995.
Shapiro, Michael. "The Sound of Silence." *Sierra* 107 (Sept. 26, 2022): 12–13.
Shelley, Percy Bysshe. *Shelley's Poetry and Prose. A Norton Critical Edition*. 2nd ed. New York: W. W. Norton, 2002.
Silberner, Joanne. "A Healthy Dose of Quiet." *Scientific American* 330 (May 2024): 58.
Smith, Betty. *A Tree Grows in Brooklyn*. New York: Harper & Brothers, 1943.
Stein, Gertrude. *The Autobiography of Alice B. Toklas*. New York: Harcourt, Brace & Company, 1933.
Sullivan, Walter. "A Great Lost River Gets Its Due." *New York Times*, Nov. 29, 1983.
Tagore, Rabindranath. *Gitanjali: A Collection of Prose Translations Made by the Author from the Original Bengali*. New York: Scribner, 1997.
Temple, Sir William. *Upon the Gardens of Epicurus with Other Seventeenth Century Garden Essays*. London: Chatto & Windus, 1908.
Thoreau, Henry David. *Walden and Other Writings*, edited by Brooks Atkinson. New York: Modern Library, 1937.
———. *Walden and Resistance to Civil Government*, edited by William Rossi. 2nd ed. New York: W. W. Norton, 1992.

Tolstoy, Leo. *The Kreutzer Sonata and Other Stories*. 1889. Reprint, New York: Penguin Classics, 2008.
Turner, James. *The Politics of Landscape: Rural Scenery and Society in English Poetry 1630–1660*. New York Oxford Univ. Press, 1979.
Ver Steeg, Karl. "The Teays River." *Ohio Journal of Science* 46 (Nov. 1946): 297–307.
Washington, Booker T. "Atlanta Exposition Address." Sept. 18, 1895. Available at *Teaching American History*, https://teachingamericanhistory.org/document/atlanta-exposition-address-2/.
Wexler, Mark. "Birds Coping with Chronic Clamor: A Growing Body of Research Reveals How Noise Pollution Alters Avian Behavior." *National Wildlife* 55, no. 2 (2017): 40–43.
Wilde, Oscar. *The Complete Works of Oscar Wilde*. Vol. 2, *De Profundis; Epistola: In Carcere et Vinculus*, edited by Ian Small. Oxford: Oxford Univ. Press, 2005.
Wright, James. *Above the River: The Complete Poems of James Wright*. New York: Farrar, Straus & Giroux and Univ. Press of New England, 1990.
Yeats, William Butler. *The Collected Works of William Butler Yeats*. Vol. 1, *The Poems*. New York: Macmillan, 1989.

Works Consulted

"Basic Information about Land Fill Gas." United States Environmental Protection Agency website, last updated Sept. 20, 2024, https://www.epa.gov/lmop/basic-information-about-landfill-gas.
Berry, Wendell. *Bringing It to the Table: On Farming and Food*. Berkeley, CA: Counterpoint. 2009.
———. *The Gift of Good Land: Further Essays Cultural and Agricultural*. San Francisco: North Point, 1981.
———. *The Unsettling of America: Culture and Agriculture*. 3rd ed. New York: Counterpoint, 1996.
———. *The Way of Ignorance and Other Essays*. Emeryville, CA: Shoemaker & Hoard, 2005.
Blomberg, Les. "Noise, Sovereignty, and Civility." Noise Pollution Clearinghouse website, accessed Oct. 10, 2024, https://www.nonoise.org/library/civnsov/civnsov.htm.
Bullard, Robert. *Dumping in Dixie*. Boulder, CO: Westview, 1990.
"Burberry Burns Bags, Clothes, and Perfume Worth Millions." *BBC*, July 19, 2018. https://www.bbc.com/news/business-44885983.
Christian, Rudy. "Floor Framing in Ohio Forebay Barns: 1820–1920." *Old Barn Post* 19 (Oct. 2020): 4–5.
———. "Saving the Barns at Malabar Farm." *Old Barn Post* 12 (Dec. 2013): 1–7.

Christy, Ann D., and Trent A. Bower. "Your Old Barn: Economic Incentives and Preservation Tools." Factsheet 2, *Ohioline*, Ohio State Univ. Extension, Apr. 11, 2011, https://ohioline.osu.edu/factsheet/AEX-642-11.

Claudio, Luz. "Waste Couture: Environmental Impact of the Clothing Industry." *Environmental Health Perspectives* 115 (Sept. 2007): A449-54.

Ehrenhalt, Alan. "The Noise Wars of Urban America." *Governing*, Nov. 4, 2022, https://www.governing.com/assessments/the-noise-wars-of-urban-america.

Goldsmith, Mike. "History of Noise." *Acoustics, Astronomy, Mathematics, Science Writing*, accessed Oct. 10, 2024, https://mikegoldsmith.weebly.com/history-of-noise.html.

Haskell, David George. *Sounds Wild and Broken: Sonic Marvels, Evolution's Creativity, and the Crisis of Sensory Extinction*. New York: Penguin Random House, 2022.

Huber, Greg. "Whirling Swastikas and Heart Travel to Ohio Barn on 1819 Datestone," *Old Barn Post* 22 (Jan. 2023): 6.

Jackson, Wes. *Becoming Native to This Place*. Lexington: Univ. Press of Kentucky, 1994.

Johnson, Nathan. "Harnessing Nature to Fight Climate Change." *Green Watch*, Spring 2021, 6-7.

Karuga, James. "Largest Landfills, Waste Sites, and Trash Dumps in the World." *World Facts*, Mar. 13, 2019, https://www.worldatlas.com/articles/largest-landfills-waste-sites-and-trash-dumps-in-the-world.html.

Larson, Thomas. *The Saddest Music Ever Written: The Story of Samuel Barber's Adagio for Strings*. New York: Pegasus Books, 2010.

Kirk-Hall, Peggy, Evin Bachelor, and Eric Romick. *Farmland Owner's Guide to Solar Leasing*. Columbus: Ohio State Univ. and National Agricultural Law Center, 2019.

Muir, John. *My First Summer in the Sierra*. Boston: Houghton Mifflin, 1911.

Oelschlaeger, Max. *The Idea of Wilderness: From Prehistory to the Age of Ecology*. New Haven: Yale Univ. Press, 1991.

O'Grady, Tom. "Agriculture Was the Engine of Ohio's Early Economy." *Old Barn Post* 20 (Nov. 2021): 3-5.

———. "Ohio's Primeval Forests Still Disappearing." *Old Barn Post* 21 (Dec. 2022): 4-6.

———. "Some of Ohio's Oldest Barns Turn Up along Zane's Trace." *Old Barn Post* 9 (Dec. 2010): 3.

———. "Stars and Barns: Partners in the Landscape." *Old Barn Post* 11 (Dec. 2012): 4-8.

———. "Tired Old I-House." *Old Barn Post* 19 (Oct. 2020): 5.

Tallamy, Douglas. *The Nature of Oaks: The Rich Ecology of Our Most Essential Native Trees*. Portland, OR: Timber Press, 2021.

Strasser, Susan. *Waste and Want: A Social History of Trash*. New York: Holt, 2000.

Index

Page references in *italics* refer to illustrative material.

Abbey, Edward, 123
Abbott, Anneliese, 124
abolitionists, 21
acre, defined, 150
"Adagio for Strings" (Barber), 67
Adena people, 8
Adorno, Theodore, 69
advertising and marketing, 93
Aeneid, 45
aerial applicator aircraft, 73–75
African Americans, 133–34. *See also* racism
Agraria Center for Regenerative Practice, Greene County, 33, 163
An Agricultural Testament (Howard), 129
agrometeorology, 164–65
Aircraft Compare, 73
Aircraft Owners and Pilots Association, 77
airplane noise, 60, 72–75, 77–79
air pollution, 78, 169–70, 172. *See also* carbon emissions
Akron, 5, 32
alcohol, 83
Allegheny Plateau, 101
Allegheny River, 194
Alliance to End Plastic Waste, 94
All Ohio Barn, 34
American Consolidated Natural Resources Incorporated (ACNR), 102, 103
American Electric Power, 165
American Tobacco Company, 116

Amish people, 131, 141, 175
amusia, 70
"Ancestral Houses" (Yeats), 45–46
animal husbandry: Bromfield on, 130–31, 142–43; chickens and ducks, 131, 149, 160, 165–66, 188–89; concentrated animal feeding operations, 146; dairy cows, 148, 153, 154–56, 158; goats, 131; horses, 150–52; lambs, 148; manure and water pollution, 154–55; pigs, 131, 148–49, 157, 159–60
Animals and Other People (Bromfield), 130–31
animals and wildlife: chipmunks, 56; deer, 56, 131, 199–200; groundhogs, 85, 131, 200; mountain lions, 8; raccoons, 57; squirrels, 56, 57. *See also* birds
Apex Regional landfill, Las Vegas, 90
aphids, 114–15
Appalachian Jacob's Ladder (*Polemonium van-bruntiae*), 111
Appalachian range, 2, 3, 13, 33, 101
"Appalachia's Natural Gas Counties" (O'Leary), 180
archaeology, 90
arson, 41–43
Artanna, 147
Artemis, 119
Ashland, 31, 163
Ashland County: Byers Woods Park, 91–92; Commissioners, 179; farm tours in, 154, 157; fracking in, 171–76, 179; Green Township, 23, 31, 71, 176–77 (*see also* Wedding Pines, Green Township); Mohican State

· 209 ·

210 · INDEX

Ashland County (cont.)
  Park, 6–7; organic farm in, 160; Park District, 91; recycling center in, 88; Soil and Water Conservation District, 74–75, 166; Solid Waste District, 94
Ashland County Atlas (Caldwell), 30
Ashland County Barns and Rural Heritage Society, 31
Ashland County Historical Society, 31
Ashland Times-Gazette, 7
Ashland–West Holmes Career Center, 91
Ashtabula County, 21
Association for the Study of Literature and Environment, 161
Athens County, 157
Atlantic Monthly, 63
Atlantic Ocean, 3
Attenborough, David, 117
Awake and Rehearse (Bromfield), 125
Azariah, Ashley, 22
Aziza, Annisa Nurul, 90

Back Porch Swing Band, 156
Baldwin, James, 66
Bancroft, Ashley Azariah, 22
Bancroft, Hubert Howe, 22
Bancroft, Samuel, 22
Bancroft House, Licking County, 22
Bantargebang landfill, Indonesia, 90
Barber, Samuel, 67
Barberton Farm, Belmont County, 32
Barkcamp State Park, 103
Barn Again! program, 31
Barnett Shale, Texas, 174
barns, 15–37; birds living in, 18, 55; decoration of, 19–20; German-style bank barns, 4, 16–18, 17–18, 24–25, 31–32, and heritage of Ohio, 16–17, 20–22, 31–33, 36–37; loss and demolition of, 33–34, 41–42; of Malabar Farm, 141, 143; New England–style flat barns, 16–18, 19, 22, 32; as official historical structure of Ohio, 15; preservation of, 34–37; repurposing of, 32–33; reusing of timbers from, 34; survey in Ashland County, 31–32; Sweitzer barns, 17, 18; types of, 16–19, 17–19; Underground Railroad and abolitionists, 21–22; at Wedding Pines, 17, 23–28
Beck, Frederick, 127, 128
Beebe, Lucius, 125–26
bees, 50, 131, 136, 161, 164
Beethoven, Ludwig van, 67
Bellville Messenger, 9
Belmont County, 32, 97, 100, 179–80, 194
Berger, Beth, 179–80

Berry, Wendell, 92, 121, 123, 144, 199
Berry family, 127, 128
Bexley, 87
Bible verses: Ecclesiastes 1:9, 196; Exodus 3:2–6, 110; Genesis 28:12, 111; 1 Peter 2:6–8, 9; Psalm 118:22, 9
Biden, Joseph R., 96, 103, 181
billboards, 93
birds: barns, living in, 18, 55; birdhouses for, 156; at Byers Woods Park, 91–92; at Doris Duke Woods, 118; at Dysart Woods Laboratory and National Natural Landmark, 104; at Hammond Woods, 112, 114; and hedgerows, 55–56, 131; and insecticides, 130; insects for, 55, 112, 131, 158, 160; migration route over Mississippi River Watershed, 13; at Mohican-Memorial State Forest and Mohican State Park, 10, 12; noise pollution, effects of, 61–62; and nursery logs, 107; at Wedding Pines, 48–50, 53–56, 58
Black, Donald, 40
Black, Franklin "Frank" Blymyer, 38–39, 40, 42, 45, 46–47
Black, Joel, 40
Black, Margaret, 40
Black, Moses, 38, 41, 46
Black Fork River, 4, 176
black lung disease, 103
Bloom, Allan, 68–69
Bloomberg, Les, 76–77
Bloomingdale, 192
Bluebird Farm, Harrison County, 158
bluebirds, 53, 62
Blymyer, Elizabeth, 38
Boise State University, 61
Bordo Ponicente landfill, Mexico City, 90
Borges, Matt, 102
Bosquet, 126
"The Boxers of M. Voltaire" (Lewis), 128
Branson (naturalist), 107, 113
British Columbia, 3
Bromfield, Louis, 121–43; and agricultural sustainability, 132–36, 138, 142–43; on animal husbandry, 130–31, 142–43; on barns, 35–36; career in New York, 125; on farmers, 144–45; grave site, 142; land sale and Doris Duke Woods, 116; living in France, 125–26; at Malabar Farm, 9, 23, 46, 121–24, 127–32, 137–38; on Norway spruces, 31; old-time farmers on, 153; The Rains Came, 128; on water conservation, 132; writings in Farm Quarterly, 188; and WWI, 124. See also Bromfield, Louis, publications

Bromfield, Louis, publications: *Animals and Other People*, 130–31; *Early Autumn*, 125; *The Farm*, 126–27; *A Few Brass Tacks*, 138–41; *From My Experience*, 128, 129, 131, 135, 137–38; *The Green Bay Tree*, 125; "A Hymn to Hawgs," 131; *Malabar Farm*, 125, 128, 132–35, 142; *Pleasant Valley*, 35–36, 126, 127–29, 136–37, 144–45; *Possession*, 125
Bromfield, Mary, 142
Brown, John, 21
Brown, Lancelot "Capability," 118
Brown, Sherrod, 178
Brown University, 63–64
Brubaker, Benjamin, 33
Brubaker, Peter, 33
Buckeye Forest Council (now Buckeye Environmental Network), 6, 99, 171
Buffalo (city), 5
Burberry, 91
burning bush (*Euonymus alatus*), 110–11, 112
Bush, George W., 171
Butler, 3, 178
Butternut Cave trail, Malabar Farm, 118
Byers, Eugene, 91
Byers, Marilyn, 91
Byers Woods Park, Ashland County, 91–92

Cabot Oil & Gas, 175–78
Caldwell, J. A., 30
California Air Resources Board, 78
California Polytechnic State University, 61–62
Camp Mohican, Perrysville, 10
Canada geese, 48–49, 61
Canada lilies, 113–14
canals, 4–5, 20
carbon emissions: carbon contracts for, 166; and carbon sinks, 100, 122, 165, 166–67; from landfills, 91; and soil management, 155
Carey, Michael, 103
Carnegie, Andrew, 46
Carpenter, George, 192
Carpenter, Reid, 39
Carroll County, 179
cars and noise pollution, 60, 72, 78
Carson, Rachel, 130, 199
Carter, Robert A., 30
Carter farm, Ross County, 32
cattle, 148, 153, 154–56, 158
Center for Regenerative Design and Collaboration (CRDC), Costa Rica, 94
Center for the Study of Carbon Dioxide and Global Change, 102
Chalfant, Mrs., 190

Chan, Hanjie, 99
Chapman, John ("Johnny Appleseed"), 8, 192, 195–97
Charles Mill (lake), 11
Chassaignac, Charles, 43
Chernobyl nuclear disaster, Ukraine (1986), 94
Chesapeake Energy Corporation, 11, 12, 175
Chesapeake & Ohio Canal Company, 43
Chillicothe, 1, 2
China, recycling shipped to, 88
Chinese sumac, 108
chinoiserie, 108
chipmunks, 56
Churchman, Jacob, 29
Church of the Nazarene, 162
cigarettes, 76, 83
Civilian Conservation Corps (CCC), 10, 11, 152–53
Clark, Joseph B., 174
Clark, Roger, 6
Clean Power Plan, 102
Clean Water Act (1972), 155
Clear Creek, 106
Clear Fork Creek of the Mohican River, 7, 9, 89
Clearfork Gorge/Clearfork Narrows, 7–8, 14
Clear Fork Gorge State Nature Preserve, 10
Clear Fork River, 3, 4
Cleo Rudd Fisher Museum, Loudonville, 16
Cleveland, 5, 42, 43
Cleveland-Hopkins Airport, 73
climate change, 100, 103, 129, 166–67. *See also* carbon emissions
Climate Trust, 167
Clinton Shale Layer, 176
The Closing of the American Mind (Bloom), 68–69
clothing, 91, 95–96
coal-burning power plants, 12, 169–70
coal mining, 98–105
Coffin, Marian Cruger, 40
Colborne, Theo, 173
College of Wooster, 7
Columbus, 43
Committee for a Constructive Tomorrow, 102
common alumroot, 113
community gardens, 161–63
Competitive Institute, 102
composting, 95
computer chips, 198
concentrated animal feeding operations, 146
consumerism, 91–95
Copus, James, 59
coral reefs, 94

Cordray, Richard, 178
Cotruvo, Joseph, 170
Cotton States and International Exposition, Atlanta (1895), 144, 167–68
cougars, 8
Council of Sybaris, 66
Country Living, 34
COVID-19 pandemic, supply chain issues and, 96
Crandall Canyon Mine, Utah, 101–2
Crestline, 3
Criley, W. W., 9
Crocetti, Dino Paul, 190
Cross Creek, 183
Cullen, Michael C., 30
Cuyahoga County, 87, 158
Cuyahoga River, 5
Cuyahoga Valley National Park, 4–5, 158–59

dairy cows, 148, 153, 154–56, 158
Dass, Pawlok, 167
Daughters of the American Revolution, 10
DDT, 130
deer, 56, 131, 199–200
Delaware County, 165
Delaware people, 8, 59
dendrochronology, 98
Denison University, 1, 22
Department of Natural Resources. *See* Ohio Department of Natural Resources (ODNR)
"De Profundis" (Wilde), 192
derecho storm (2022), 14, 31, 142
Devon Energy Corporation, 175
DeWine, Mike, 12, 77, 117, 178
Dimock Township, Pennsylvania, 175
Dionysus, 119–20
Disabled Riding Association, Great Britain, 44
Donegal Castle, Ireland, 41
dopamine, 68
Doris Duke Foundation, 117
Doris Duke Woods, 116–20
doves, 55
Dow, Lorenzo, 192
Drake, Max, 123, 129
dressage horses, 43–44
ducks, 160
Duke (dog), 183–84, 185
Duke, Doris, 116, 120
Duke, James Buchanan, 116
Dutchman's breeches, 114
Dutch settlers, 20
dynamic obsolescence, 92
Dysart, Margaret, 97

Dysart, Orin B., 97
Dysart Defenders, 99
Dysart Woods Laboratory and National Natural Landmark, 97–100, 103–5

Early Autumn (Bromfield), 125
Earth.org, 91
Eastern Breeder, 188
eastern firefly (*Photinus pyralis*), 52
Ecclesiastes 1:9, 196
ecology, 198
economy, 197–98
"Economy" (Xenophon), 197–98
ecosystems, 199
Edwards, Kim, 179
Eliot, T. S., 182
Elizabeth II (queen), 67
Ellington, Duke, 68
Emerson, Ralph Waldo, 146
Empowerment Alliance, 12
energy: coal-burning power plants, 12, 169–70; coal mining for, 98–105; dependence on, 197; methane from landfills, 90–91; nuclear power plants, 12, 94, 197; oil and gas development, 12, 142, 171–81 (*see also* fracking); powerplant emissions, 102; renewable, 93, 165–66, 179
Energy Policy Act (2005), 171
engine noise, 60–61, 72–75, 77–79
England, nature preservation in, 117–18
The English Garden (Mason), 118
English immigrants, 20
English saddle horseback riding, 185
environmental impact assessments, 170–71
Environmental Integrity Project, 155
Environmental Protection Agency (EPA), 90, 103, 155
Environmental Research Letters, 167
Erie Canal, 5
Erielhonoan people, 8
Erie people, 8
Erigan River, 2
Everett Park, 162
Exodus 3:2–6, 110

factory farming, 146, 189
Fairfield County, 33
fairy flies, 114–15
Fallows, James, 78
The Farm (Bromfield), 126–27
Farmland Owner's Guide to Solar Leasing (Kirk-Hall), 166
Farm Quarterly, 188
farms and farming, 144–68; aerial applicator aircraft for, 73–75; agrometeorology, 164–

65; and crop rotation, 130, 149, 158, 166; experimental, 122, 165–66; factory farming, 146, 189; gender roles, 149, 152, 184; hay, growing, 150–51, 166–67; insecticides for, 52–53, 73, 114, 130, 155, 188; literature on, 121–22, 128–30, 144–45; lost to development, 146, 167, 186; modern adaptations for, 154–60; noise pollution from, 63, 73–75; organic, 155, 156–61, 166; permaculture, 159; pioneer farmer in Knox County, 147–53; public gardens and micro-farms, 161–64; subsidies for, 143; and sustainability, 123, 129–30, 132–36, 138, 142–43, 144–45, 155–57, 166–67; threats to lifestyle of, 145–46, 153, 167–68. See also animal husbandry; barns; soil erosion; soil fertility
Farris, Floyd, 174
fast fashion, 91
Faulkner, Edward H., 129
Federal Aviation Administration, 77
Federal Bureau of Investigation (FBI), 122
Federal Historic Preservation Tax Incentives Program, 34
Federal Trade Commission, 96
Ferguson, William, 127, 128
Ferguson family, 9
fertilizers, 130, 143, 155, 188
feverfew (*Parthenium integrifolium*), 119
A Few Brass Tacks (Bromfield), 138–41
Fiber Arts Guild, Malabar Farm, 128
Firelands, 20
First Energy Solutions, 102
flame azalea (*Rhododendron calendulaceum*), 1, 5
Fleming, Deborah, childhood memories of, 182–94; ancestors' stories, 186–90; Bloomingdale, 192; childhood home, 182–83, 193; horseback riding, 184–85; Ohio River, 193–94; Reeds Mill, 190–92; rural land lost to development, 186
Florida Museum of Natural History, 62
flowers and plants: at Doris Duke Woods, 119; flame azalea, 1, 5; at Hammond Woods, 111, 113–14; at Wedding Pines, 50–52, 57–58. See also invasive species
flycatchers, 55, 62, 114
food waste, 95
Forbes family, 21
Foreman, Dave, 13
forests, 106–20; Doris Duke Woods, 116–20; Dysart Woods Laboratory and National Natural Landmark, 97–100, 103–5; Hammond Woods, 106–16
"For the Love of Farming" (Berry), 123

4-H, 185
Fowke, Gerard, 1
Fox, Josh, 171
foxes, 56
Frack-Free Ohio, 171, 173
fracking, 169–81; in Ashland County, 171–76, 179; dangers of, 171–76; and employment, 175, 180; innovations in, 176; near Malabar Farm, 142; political support for, 12, 174, 178–79; protests against, 176–77; and sacrifice zones, 180–81; in state parks, 12
France, rural noise in, 63
Franklin County, 87
Fredericktown, 3
Frick, Henry Clay, 46
Friends of Ohio Barns, 16, 32
Friends of the Land, 116, 120
From My Experience (Bromfield), 128, 129, 131, 135, 137–38
Fruechte des Feldes, 158
Fugitive Slave Acts (1793–1850), 21

Gadell-Newton, Constance, 178
Galatia Mine, Illinois, 102
Gambier, 147
garage sales, 94–95
Garden of Eden, 119
gardens: design of, 108–11, 117–18; at Kingwood Center and Garden, 39; public, 161–63
garlic mustard (*Alliaria petiolata*), 107–8
Gasland (film), 171
Gaudineer Scenic Area, West Virginia, 101
geese, 48–49, 61
Geib, M. Margaret, 18–19, 28
gender roles, 149, 152, 184
General Motors, 92
Generation Now, 12
Genesis 28:12, 111
geology of Ohio, 1–5, 2
German immigrants, 3, 5, 20
German-style bank barns, 4, 16–18, 17–18, 24–25, 31–32
ghetto palm, 109–10
Giddings, Joshua, 21
Gillet, Louis, 127
Giraud, Joël, 63
Gitanjali (Tagore), 59
glaciers, 2–3, 7
Goldmark, Sandra, 92
Gonzales, Anne, 15
Gonzalez, Xochitl, 63–65
Gorge Overlook of Mohican State Park, 7–8, 89

Granville, 22, 155, 163, 178
Granville Riot (1836), 22
grass farming, 150–51, 166–67
great blue herons, 49–50
Great Depression, 10, 11, 41–42, 95, 188–89
Great Flood (1913), 5, 11, 132
Great Lakes, 3
Great Railroad Strike (1877), 42–43
Greek valerian (*Polemonium reptans*), 111
The Green Bay Tree (Bromfield), 125
Greene County, 32–33, 163
The Green Field Dairy, Wayne County, 158
Greenlawn Cemetery, State Road 39, 29
Greentown, 59
Green Township, Ashland County, 23, 31, 71, 176–77. *See also* Wedding Pines, Green Township
groundhogs, 85, 131, 200
Groveport River, 3
Guernsey County, 179
Guide to the Lakes (Wordsworth), 118
Gulf of Mexico, 3, 137, 143, 194

Habitat for Humanity, 94
Hall, David, 173
"Hall of Freedom" barn, 22
Hamilton, Alexander, 122
Hammond, Matthew, 12
Hammond Woods, 106–16
Harley-Davidson, 79
Harpers Ferry raid (1859), 21
Harris, Bill, 7
Harrison County, 11, 158, 179
Hartel, Liz, 43–44
Harvest, 178
harvester butterflies, 114–15
Havighurst, Walter, 19
hay, 150–51, 166–67
Hazelbaker, Joseph, 6
Heartland Institute, 102
heathens, 196
Hemlock Falls, Richland County, 3
Herald Star (Steubenville), 81
herbicides, 73
Heritage School greenhouse, 163
herons, 49–50
Herring, Clement, 9, 127, 128
Herring, John Frederick, 9
Hesed Agape Ministries, Mansfield, 4
Heyman, Stephen, 123–24, 125, 128, 142
hiking: at Doris Duke Woods, 117–18; at Malabar Farm, 118, 142; at Strasburg Ecological Center, 165; at Zaleski Forest, 75
Hildreth, P., 1
Hippocrates, 43

Hochman, Nate, 64–65
Hocking County, 33
Hocking Valley, 21
Hog Hollow, 8–9
Holmes County, 11, 156
"Home of the Free" (Berry), 92
"Honey" (Wright), 194
Honey Creek, 24, 28, 30, 49, 50–51
Hoover, J. Edgar, 122
Hopewell people, 8
horizontal hydraulic fracturing. *See* fracking
horseback riding, 43–45, 89, 184–85
horsedrawn plows and machines, 150–52
"Horses" (Berry), 144
Houlton, Benjamin Z., 167
Householder, Larry, 102
Howard, Albert, 129
Hudson River, 5
Huffman, Daniel A., 30
Hughes, Langston, 194
humans: intelligence of, 198–99, 201; as invasive species, 200
hummingbirds, 53
"A Hymn to Hawgs" (Bromfield), 131
hyperacusis, 70–71

Iesseau, Corinne, 63
Igini, Martina, 91
I houses, 27, 28, 103
The *Iliad*, 45
Illinois, 2, 27
Indiana, 2, 27
Industrial Revolution, 60, 117, 136, 139–41
Inflation Reduction Act (2022), 181
Ingraffea, Anthony, 173
insects: and agrometeorology, 164; bees, 50, 136, 161, 164; beetles, 164; and birds, 55, 112, 131, 156; and crop rotation, 130, 158, 166; in Hammond Woods, 114–15; insecticides for, 52–53, 73, 114, 130, 155, 188; invasive, 110; and nursery logs, 107
International Climate Science Coalition, 102
Inuit people, 80
invasive species: in Doris Duke Woods, 117; following floods, 51; in Hammond Woods, 107–14; and hedgerows, 131; humans as, 200; and rewilding, 13; tenant farming in National Parks and, 159
Iowa, 27
Irish immigrants, 3, 5, 20, 41–43, 45–46, 110
Irish Potato Famine (1848–1849), 41–42, 110

Jackson, Andrew, 43
Jackson, Wes, 121, 199
Jackson County, 1

Jacob's Ladder (*Polemonium caeruleum*), 111
Jacoby Creek, 163
James, William, 67
Jeffers, Robinson, 92
Jefferson, Thomas, 121, 139, 144
Jefferson County, 179, 193
Jeff Gordon Community Garden, Newark, Ohio, 162
Jeffords, Jim, 34
Jelloway, 173
J. Evans Foundation, 162
Jim Crow laws, 133–34
Johnny Appleseed, 8, 192, 195–97
Johnstown, 163
Joseph, Brett, 178
Joyce, James, 66
Julius Caesar, 66

Kasich, John, 77
Kaskaskia (Osage) people, 97
Kent, William, 118
Kidron, 74
killdeer, 53
King, Charles Kelly, 39, 46
Kingwood Estate (Kingwood Center and Garden), Mansfield, 39
Kingwood Foundation, 39
Kingwood Gardens, 40–41
Kirk-Hall, Peggy, 166
Klein, David, 159
Knox County: farm tours in, 156; fracking in, 173, 175; modern pioneer farm in, 147–53; Muskingum Watershed Conservancy District, 11; organic farm in, 157; parks in, 152–53; schools in, 152; Teays River Valley, 3
Knox Dolomite Shale Layer, 176
Korean War, 11
Kreutzer Sonata (Beethoven), 67
"The Kreutzer Sonata" (Tolstoy), 66–67

lake effect, 164–65
Lake Erie, 4, 21, 143, 165
Lake Michigan, 165
Lake Tight, 2, 5
Lal, Rattan, 167
"The Lamp of Sacrifice" (Ruskin), 35
landfills, 90–92
landscape vistas: Doris Duke Woods, 118; Gorge Overlook of Mohican State Park, 7–8, 89; rivers, 193–94; rural landscape, 33, 93, 146
Leaf Blower Regulation Amendment Act (2018, Washington, DC), 78
Leis, Stephanie, 12

Leopold, Aldo: on ecosystems, 199; literature on farms, 121; "Marshland Elegy," 49; on natural places as human right, 60; *A Sand County Almanac*, 60, 130
Lerner, Steve, 180–81
Letters from an American Farmer (Saint John de Crevecoeur), 121
Lewis, Sinclair, 128
Licking County, 11, 22, 162, 198
Licking County Land Bank, 162
"Life Without Principle" (Thoreau), 135
Lightbody, Mary, 167
littering, 79, 81–86, 88–89
"Little Gidding" (Eliot), 182
Little Miami River watershed, 163
logging: Doris Duke Woods, 116–17, 120; Hammond Woods, 112–13; in Mohican State Park, 6–7, 12, 14; protesting, 6
Loudonville, 10, 16, 31, 173
Lowe's and Tractor Supply Company, 163
Lowey, Nita, 77
Luber, Mick, 158
Luna moths (*Actias luna*), 114
Lycan, Eric, 12
Lyons, Paul, 8
Lyons, Tommy, 8
Lyons Falls, Mohican State Park, 8

Madison, Mike, 79–80
Malabar Coast of India, 128
Malabar Farm: as agricultural experiment, 122; barn fire, 141; Bromfield's purchase and farming of, 121–24, 127–32, 137–38; Butternut Cave trail, 118; current state of, 141–43; Doris Duke Woods, 116–20; historic preservation of, 46; noise pollution at, 75; previously owned by Clement Herring, 9; springhouse at, 23; trail repair at, 89
Malabar Farm (Abbott), 124
Malabar Farm (Bromfield), 125, 128–29, 132–35, 142
Malabar Farm Foundation, 143
Malabar Farm Inn, 128, 142
Malabar Farm State Park, 116–20
Manchester, Susan, 167
Mansfield: barns in, 25, 38–39; Frank Black's funding of building in, 45; in *The Farm*, 126; fracking in, 172, 173; geological uplift near, 3; and Great Depression, 42; Hesed Agape Ministries church in, 4; Raemelton Therapeutic Equestrian Center, 38–40, 43, 47; Weirick family descendants, 25
Mansfield Blockhouse, 59

manure, 130, 146, 151, 154–55
Marcellus shale formation, 173, 176, 180
Marietta, 21
marketing, 93
"Marshland Elegy" (Leopold), 49
Martin, Dean, 190
Martins Ferry, 180, 194
Marx, Karl, 122, 139, 141
Mason, William, 118
Maupin, Gordon T., 11
May Day riots (1894), 42
McCarthy, Brian, 98, 99–100
McCleary, William, 29
McCollough, F. R. & I. L., 9
McGaughy, Gladys Dysart, 97
McKee, Timothy, 12
Mennonites, 131
Merkurialis, 43
methane, 90–91
micro-farms, 163–64
Mid-Ohio Dressage Association, 44
Mid-Ohio Food Bank, 164
Miller, Eric, 106, 107, 111, 112–13, 116, 173
mineral rights, 99–100, 175–77, 184
Mingo Junction, 192
Mingo people, 59
mining, 98–105, 170, 184, 188. *See also* fracking
misophonia, 70
Mississippi River, 2, 3, 132, 194
Mississippi River Watershed, 13
Mitchell, George, 174
mockingbirds (*Mimus polyglottos*), 55–56
Mohican (video), 12
Mohican Gardens, 32
Mohican-Memorial State Forest and Mohican State Park, 6–14; Gorge Overlook, 7–8, 89; history of, 7–12; logging in, 6–7, 12, 14; motorcycle rally at, 72; Muskingum Watershed Conservancy District, 11–13; trash cleanup days in, 88–89
Mohican River, 4, 88. *See also* Clear Fork Creek of the Mohican River
Mohicanville, 32
monarch butterflies, 52
Monongahela River, 194
Monroe County, 179
Moore, Robert D., 102
Morgan County, 11
Morse, Intrepid, 192
motorcycles and noise pollution, 72, 79
mountain lions, 8
Mount Jeez, 128, 143
Mount Logan, 16

Mount Vernon, 147
Muir, John, 123, 196–97, 199
Murray, Robert E., 101–3
Murray Energy Incorporated, 101
music, 66–71
musical anhedonia, 70
Muskingum County, 11
Muskingum River, 11, 21
Muskingum Watershed Conservancy District (MWCD), 11, 12, 132, 176
mycorrhizal networks, 104–5, 129
My First Summer in the Sierra (Muir), 196

National Academy of Sciences, 180
National Business Aviation Association, 77
National Natural Landmark, 97
National Park Service, 34, 158–59
National Quiet Skies Coalition, 77
National Register of Historic Places, 34, 35, 40
National Resources Conservation Service (NRCS), 159, 164
National Review, 64–65
National Transportation Safety Board, 74
National Trust for Historic Preservation, 31
Native Americans, 8, 49, 50, 59, 80, 97, 115
natural gas development, 12, 142, 171–81. *See also* fracking
Nature, 61
"Nature" (Emerson), 146
Nature Conservancy, 97–98, 163, 173
The Nature of Oaks (Tallamy), 112
nature preservation, 130. *See also* forests
"The Negro Speaks of Rivers" (Hughes), 194
Neguse, Joe, 77
neighbors and noise, 71
Newark, 162–63
New Deal program, 138
New England–style flat barns, 16–18, 19, 22, 32
Newfoundland, 3
New Philadelphia, 11
Newville, 9
Newville Iron Bridge, 7
Night Owls (music group), 190
Nissenson, Hugh, 8
Nixon, Richard, 155, 174
Noble County, 11, 179
Noise Control Act (1972), 77
Noise Free America, 77, 78
noise pollution, 60–80; birds, effect on, 61–62; campaigns to reduce, 76–80; engines as, 72–75, 77–79; farming as, 63, 73–75; health implications of, 76–77; and hyperacusis, 70–71; music as, 66–71; and natural places, 60–61; voices as, 63–66

Noise Pollution Clearinghouse, 76
North American Riding for the Handicapped Association, 44
North Carolina, 2
North Central Ohio Land Conservancy (NCOLC), 106, 116, 120
"Notes on the State of Virginia" (Jefferson), 144
nuclear power plants, 12, 94, 197
nursery logs, 107

Obama, Barack, 102, 173–74
Occupy movement, 95
"Ode to Joy" (Beethoven), 67
Odin, 120
Office of Noise Abatement and Control (ONAC), 77
O'Grady, Tom, 16, 21, 36, 37
Ohio: barns as official historical structure of, 15; Current Agricultural Use Value rule, 167; derecho storm of 2022, 14, 31, 142; environmental impact assessment rules in, 170–71; geology of, 1–5, 2; Great Flood of 1913, 5, 11, 132; loss of farmland to development, 146, 167, 186; mining in, 98–105, 170, 184, 188 (see also fracking); old-growth forests in (see forests); plastics, laws on, 87; slavery prohibition in, 21–22; state seal and symbols, 15–16. See also individual places
Ohio (Havighurst), 19
Ohio & Erie Canal, 4–5, 20
Ohio Anti-Slavery Convention, 22
Ohio Brass, 38–39, 47
Ohio Conservancy Law, 11
Ohio Department of Natural Resources (ODNR): Division of Forestry, 14, 107; Division of Mining Resource Management, 99; Division of Oil and Gas, 172–73; Doris Duke Woods, protection of, 116–17, 120; Mohican State Forest, protection of, 6–7, 10, 12
Ohio Ecological Food and Farm Association (OEFFA), 146, 155–56, 157, 167
Ohio Environmental Council, 77
Ohio Federation of Women's Clubs, 10–11
Ohio Historic Preservation Tax Credit Program, 35
Ohio Humanities Council, 16
Ohio Oil and Gas Association, 12
Ohio Oil and Gas Energy Educational Project, 178
Ohio River, 3, 4, 169, 193–94
Ohio River Valley Institute (ORVI), 180
Ohio Seventh District Court of Appeals, 99

Ohio Soil Health Initiative, 155
Ohio State University, 155, 157, 161
Ohio Supreme Court, 176
Ohio University, 98, 99
Ohio Valley Barn Salvage, 34
Ohio Valley Coal Company (OVCC), 98–100, 101–3
Ohio Valley Reclaimed Wood, 34
oil and gas development, 12, 142, 171–81. See also fracking
Old Growth Forest Hall of Fame, 97–98
old-growth forests. See forests
O'Leary, Sean, 180
Olentangy River, 162
"On Noise" (Seneca the Younger), 65–66
"On Popular Music" (Adorno), 69
Ontario (city), 3
orchards, 149, 159–61, 192, 196
organic farming, 155, 156–61, 166
Out of My Life and Thought (Schweitzer), 138
overconsumption, 70, 91–95
owls, 53–54, 61

Pacific Coast, 3
pagans, 196
Panic (1893), 39, 42
Peninsula (town), 160
permaculture, 159
Perry County, 19–20
Perrysville, 10, 23, 175
Persian Gulf War, 11
pesticides, 114, 155, 188. See also insects
1 Peter 2:6–8, 9
phonophobia, 70
Photinus of Sirmium, 52
Picquet, Victor, 126
Pike County, 1
planned obsolescence, 92
The Planter of Modern Life (Heyman), 123–24
plastic bags, 84, 87
plastic waste, 84, 87–88, 90, 94
Pleasant Hill Lake, 11, 132, 141–42
Pleasant Valley (Bromfield), 35–36, 126, 127–29, 136–37, 144–45
Plowman's Folly (Faulkner), 129
pollution: air, 78, 169–70, 172 (see also carbon emissions); littering and trash, 79, 81–86, 88–89, 94; water, 143, 154–55, 171–73, 175–76, 178. See also trash
polo, 40, 45
Portman, Rob, 178
Portsmouth, 2, 5
Possession (Bromfield), 125
power tools, 78
Price, Uvedale, 118

Priest, William, 29
Professional Association of Therapeutic Horsemanship, 44
progress, economy, and preservation, 195–201; economy, 197–98; human intelligence, 198–201; independence and resilience, 197–98; Thoreau's philosophy, 195–97
protests: against fracking, 176–77; against logging, 6; Occupy movement, 95
Psalm 118:22, 9
public gardens, 161–63
Puente Hills landfill, Los Angeles, 90
purple martins, 156

quail, 158
Quiet Skies Congressional Caucus, 77

raccoons, 57
racism: in cities, 140; and Jim Crow laws, 133–34; and noise, 63–65; slavery, 21–22
Raemelton Farm, Mansfield, 38–47; arson at, 41–42; history of, 38–40; on National Register of Historic Places, 40; Raemelton Equestrian Center, 39–43; Raemelton House, 40–41; Raemelton Riding Club, 40; Raemelton Stable, 39–42, 46–47
Raemelton Therapeutic Equestrian Center, Mansfield, 38–40, 43–44, 47
railroads, 5, 42–43, 62, 79, 197
The Rains Came (Bromfield), 128
Ramelton, Ireland (Rae Mealton), 38
Rath Mealtain (Fort Mealtan), 41
Reagan, Ronald, 77
recycling, 83–84, 87–88, 90, 94
Reeda, Rhonda, 178
Reeds Mill, 185, 190–92
Reeds Mill Creek, 190–91
Reeds Mill Inn, 190–91
repairing items, 96
resilience, 198
Resin8, 94
rewilding, 13
Rewilding Institute, 13
Richland County: in *The Farm*, 126; geological uplift in, 3–4; grist mills in, 9, 30; Muskingum Watershed Conservancy District, 11; Raemelton Therapeutic Equestrian Center, 38–40, 43, 47; Shagbark Woods, 106; Teays River Valley, 3. *See also* Malabar Farm; Raemelton Farm, Mansfield
Richland County Source, 40
Robinson, Thomas, 29
Romanchuk, Mark, 117

Romney, Ann, 44
Romney, Mitt, 44
Roosevelt, Franklin D., 152
Ross, Joseph, 192
Ross County, 16, 32
Royer, Jack, 30
Ruhl, Margaret, 179
Ruskin, John, 35
Russia, attack on Ukraine (2022), 197

Sackett v. EPA (2023), 155
sacrifice zones, 180–81
Saint John de Crevecoeur, Hector, 121
Saint Lawrence Seaway, 3
SaintPierre-d'Oléron, 63
Salazar, Ken, 173–74
A Sand County Almanac (Leopold), 60, 130
Sand Ridge Cemetery, Ashland County, 6
Sand Ridge Church, Ashland County, 6, 9–10, 13–14
Sands, Olive, 43
Sandusky River, 4
sapsuckers, 112
Sawyer, Frank, 6
Schaeffer, Eric, 154–55
Schafrath, Richard, 7
Schrack, Charles, 127, 128
Schrack, David, 127, 128
Schweitzer, Albert, 138
Scioto River, 16
Scottish immigrants, 3
scrub jays, 61–62
Seneca the Younger, 65
"The Seven Lamps of Architecture" (Ruskin), 35
Shagbark Woods, 106
Shalter, Annie, 152
Shalter, George, 147–53
Sharawagdi, 108–9
Shawandasse Tula (Shawanwaki/Shawnee) people, 97
Shawnee people, 49, 59
Shelley, Percy Bysshe, 69
"Shine, Republic" (Jeffers), 92
shopping, 70, 87, 91, 92–93
Sierra Club, Akron chapter, 6
Silent Spring (Carson), 130
Slater's Run, 9
slavery, 21–22
Sloan, Alfred P., 92
Smith, Betty, 110
Smith, James, 8
smoking, 76, 83
Soil and Health (Howard), 129
soil erosion: Bromfield on, 129–30, 132–35;

and chemical runoff, 143; and contour rows, 160; and cover crops, 74; dry dams for, 113; and factory farming, 146; hay and prevention of, 149; and invasive species, 108, 111–12; and low tillage, 130; and Ohio Soil Health Initiative, 156; and strip mining, 170; trees and windbreaks, 156, 158
soil fertility: and cover crops, 74, 122, 157, 164; and crop rotation, 149, 158, 166; and fertilizer use, 130, 143, 155, 188; lime for, 149–50; Ohio Soil Health Initiative and, 155; and organic farming, 156–60; and temperature, 166; weed control, 157
solar power, 93, 165–66, 179
"Sonny's Blues" (Baldwin), 66
sound. *See* noise pollution
southern-style beaked barns, 16, 32
sparrows, 61, 158
Split Estate (film), 173
spotted lanternflies, 110
springhouses, 23, 24, 137, 183
squirrels, 56, 57
Stanolind Oil & Gas Company, 174
Stark, George, 177
Stark County, 11
steel mills, 169
Stegner, Wallace, 123
Steubenville, 187
Steubenville Motor Company, Reeds Mill, 190
Stevens, Jack and Pat, 30
Stockton, Robert F., 46
Stowe, 158
Strasburg Ecological Center, 165–66
strip-mining, 170, 184, 188
Successful Farming, 31
Sudokwon landfill, South Korea, 90
Sugar Grove Farm, Fairfield County, 33
Summit County, 11, 158
Summit Lake, 3–4
superstitions, 19–20, 29
Supreme Court, Ohio, 176
Surface Mining Control and Reclamation Act (Ohio, 1977), 170
Sustainable Agricultural Research Education (SARE), 159, 163
swallows, 55, 156
Swedenborgian religion, 196
Sweitzer barns, 17, 18

Taft, Bob, 35
Tagore, Rabindranath, 59
Tallamy, Douglas, 112
Taylor, William, 29
Teays River, 1, 2, 3, 5
Teays River Valley, 1–3, 2

Temple, William, 108–9
Tennessee Valley Authority, 132
Therien, Alek, 200
Thomas, Harry and Betty, 30
Thompson, Robert, 30
Thoreau, Henry David, 181, 195–97, 199. See also *Walden* (Thoreau)
thrushes, 131, 158
Tight, William, 1
TimberFramers Guild, 141
Tissot, 43
"To a Skylark" (Shelley), 69
tobacco use, 76, 83
Together We Grow Gardens, 162
Tolstoy, Leo, 66–67
toxic algae blooms, 143
traffic noise, 60, 72, 78
trash: and garage sales, 94–95; landfills for, 90–92; littering, 79, 81–86, 88–89; at Malabar Farm, 89; and overconsumption, 91–95; plastic waste, 84, 87–88, 90, 94; recycling, 83–84, 87–88, 90, 94; reducing, 87, 95–96; and repairing items, 96; at Wedding Pines, 83–86, 96
A Tree Grows in Brooklyn (Smith), 110
Tree of Heaven (*Ailanthus*), 108–10
The Tree of Life (Nissenson), 8
trees: carbon sequester, 165–67; dendrochronology, 98; etymology, 120; fallen, 14, 107; and mycorrhizal networks, 104–5; pioneer customs of planting, 30–31; sacred, 119–20. *See also* forests; logging; orchards
Trevelyan, Charles Edward, 42
Trump, Donald, 102, 103
Tuffy (cat), 184
Tuscarawas County, 11

Ukraine: Chernobyl nuclear disaster of 1986, 94; Russian attack of 2022, 197
Ulysses (Joyce), 66
Underground Railroad, 21
University of California, Davis, 161
University of Colorado–Boulder, 62
"Upon the Gardens of Epicurus" (Temple), 108–9
US Army Corps of Engineers, 11
US Bureau of Economic Analysis, 180
US Department of Agriculture (USDA), 146, 163, 167
US Department of Energy, 174, 180
US Department of Labor, 102
US Department of Mineral Resources, 99
USS *Kearsarge*, 39
USS *Kentucky*, 39

USS *Oriskany*, 94
Utica shale region, 176, 180

Valley View Spur in Shagbark Woods, 106
Vance, Squire, 10
Veldman, Joseph, 167
Vermillion River, 4
Veterans' Memorial Shrine, 88
VICE Indonesia, 90
Vietnam War, 11
Virginia, 2, 20, 21, 36
voices as noise pollution, 63–66
Vonderheid Act (1913), 11

Wade, Benjamin, 21
Walden (Thoreau): Bromfield's *Malabar Farm* compared, 132–35; on groundhogs, 200; on noise, 62; on overconsumption, 95; on reading, 195; on simplicity, 197; on sustainable farming, 129; on time, 59
Walden Pond State Reservation, Massachusetts, 62–63
Walhonding River, 4
Walking the Flatlands (Madison), 79
Walton Hall Estate, Yorkshire, England, 117
Wang, Yingping, 167
Warlind, David, 167
Warner, Gale, 165
Warner, Louise, 165
War of 1812, 20
Washington, Booker T., 144, 167–68
Washington County, 11
water conservation, 132, 143
water pollution, 143, 154–55, 171–73, 175–76, 178
Water-Powered Mills of Richland County (Carter & Cullen), 30
Water Technology, 170
Waterton, Charles, 117
Wayne County, 11, 157, 158, 175
Wedding Pines, Green Township, 48–59; barn at, 17, 23–28; birds at, 48–50, 53–56, 58; butterflies and insects at, 52–53; flowers and plants at, 50–52, 57–58; history of, 29–31; house at, 26–28, 27; seasonal changes at, 58; trash collection along road, 81, 83–86, 96; wildlife at, 56–57
Weirick, Amanda E., 29
Weirick, G. Elzie and Maud D., 29–30
Weirick, J. Henry and Maude I., 29
Weirick, Joseph, 29, 30
Weirick, Peter, 9
Weirick family descendants, 25–26, 28
West, J. A., 9
Western Reserve, 21
West Virginia, 2, 101, 180
wetlands, 48–50, 132, 155
Wheeler, Andrew, 102
Whistler, Evelyn, 33
Whistler, Susan, 33
white-crowned sparrows, 61
white oak trees, 112–13
Whitmore, William, 7
"Why Do Rich People Love Quiet?" (Gonzalez), 63–65
Wilde, Oscar, 192
Wilhelm, Hubert G. H., 19
Wintersville, 190, 192
Wisconsin glacier, 7
Wood, Mary Appleton, 125
woodpeckers, 112
Woodside Farm, Belmont County, 32
wooly alder aphids (*Prociphilus tessellatus*), 114–15
Wordsworth, William, 118
Works Progress Administration (WPA), 132, 152–53
World War I, 10, 43, 124
World War II, 10–11, 122–23, 147
Wright, James, 194

Xenophon, 109, 197–98

Yeats, W. B., 45–46
yellowbellied sapsuckers, 112
Yellowstone National Park, 13, 75
Yggdrasil, 120

Zaleski Forest, 75, 104
Zane's Trace, 20
Zaporizhzhia Nuclear Power Station, Ukraine, 197